Expository Thoughts on the Gospels

MARK

J. C. Ryle

THE BANNER OF TRUTH TRUST

THE BANNER OF TRUTH TRUST
3 Murrayfield Road, Edinburgh EH 12 6EL
P.O. Box 621, Carlisle, Pennsylvania, 17013, U.S.A.

★

First published 1857
First Banner of Truth Trust edition 1985
ISBN 0 85151 441 3

★

Printed and bound in Great Britain by
Hazell Watson & Viney Limited,
Member of the BPCC Group,
Aylesbury, Bucks

PREFACE.

THE volume now in the reader's hands, is a continuation of a work already commenced by "Expository Thoughts on St. Matthew."

The nature of the work has been so fully explained in the preface to the volume on St. Matthew, that it seems unnecessary to say anything on the subject. It may be sufficient to repeat that the reader must not expect to find in these "Expository Thoughts," a learned, critical commentary on the Gospels. If he expects this he will be disappointed. The work before him makes no pretence to being anything more than a continuous series of short practical Expositions.

The main difference between this volume and the one which has preceded it, will be found to consist in the occasional explanatory foot-notes. The subjects of these notes will generally prove to be difficult passages or expressions in the inspired text. I cannot pretend to say that I have thrown any new light on the difficulties in St. Mark. But I can honestly say that I have endeavoured to put the reader in possession of all that can be said on each difficulty.

In composing these Expositions on St. Mark, I have tried to keep continually before me the three-fold object which I had in view, when I first commenced writing on the

Gospels. I have endeavoured to produce something which may be useful to heads of families in the conduct of family prayers,—something which may assist those who visit the poor and desire to read to them,—and something which may aid all readers of the Bible in the private study of God's Word. In pursuance of this three-fold object, I have adhered steadily to the leading principles with which I began. I have dwelt principally on the things needful to salvation. I have purposely avoided all topics of minor importance. I have spoken plainly on all subjects, and have striven to say nothing which all may not understand.

I cannot expect that the work will satisfy all who want some book to read at family prayers. In fact I know, from communications which I have received, that some think the expositions too long. The views of the heads of families as to the length of their family prayers are so exceedingly various that it would be impossible to please one class without displeasing others. In some households the family prayers are so short and hurried, that I should despair of writing anything suitable to the master's wants. In such households a few verses of Scripture, read slowly and reverently, would probably be more useful than any commentary at all. As for those who find four pages too much to read at one time, and yet desire to read my Expository Thoughts, I can only suggest that they have an easy remedy in their own hands. They have only to leave out one or two divisions in each exposition, and they will find it as short as they please.

In preparing for publication this volume on St. Mark, I have looked through all those Commentaries mentioned in my Preface to the volume on St. Matthew, which throw any light on St. Mark.* After careful examination, I feel obliged to say, that, in my humble judgment, very few commentators, whether ancient or modern, seem to give this Gospel the attention it deserves. It has been too often treated as a mere abridgement of St. Matthew. This view of it I believe to be an entire mistake.

The only large separate Commentary on St. Mark that I have been able to meet with, is a remarkable work consisting of 1666 folio pages, by George Petter, Vicar of Brede, in the county of Sussex, published in the year 1661. It is a work which from its scarcity, price, and size, is much less known than it deserves. The greater part of the impression is said to have perished in the great fire of London. Some account of this book may not be uninteresting to some readers.

Petter's Commentary was originally preached by him in the form of expository lectures to his own congregation. He began to preach on it, June 7th, 1618, and continued preaching on it most Sundays with very little intermission till May 28th, 1643. The dates of each sermon are given on the margin.

The doctrine of this remarkable book is excellent,—Protestant, evangelical, and spiritual. The learning of the author

---

* It is needless to repeat their names.

must also have been not inconsiderable, if we may judge by
the number and variety of his quotations. His faults of style
and composition are the faults of the day in which he lived,
and must therefore be charitably judged. But for laborious
investigation of the meaning of every word, for patient discussion of every question bearing on the text, for fulness of
matter, for real thoughtfulness, and for continual practical
application, there is no work on St. Mark which, in my
opinion, bears comparison with Petter's.   Like Goliah's
sword, "there is none like it."

I now send forth these "Expository Thoughts on St. Mark"
with an earnest prayer that it may please God to use the
volume for His glory. It has been written under the pressure
of many public duties, and amidst many interruptions.   No
one is more conscious of its defects than myself. But I can
honestly say, that my chief desire, if I know anything of my
heart, in this and all my writings, is to lead my readers to
Christ and faith in Him, to repentance and holiness, to the
Bible and to prayer.

If these are the results of this volume in any one case,
the labour I have bestowed upon it will be more than repaid.

Helmingham Rectory,
   Sep., 1857.

TABLE OF CONTENTS.

TABLE OF CONTENTS OF FOOT NOTES.

EXPOSITORY THOUGHTS

ON THE GOSPELS.

MARK I. 1—8.

1 THE beginning of the Gospel of Jesus Christ, the Son of God;

2 As it is written in the prophets, Behold, I send my messenger before thy face, which shall prepare thy way before thee.

3 The voice of one crying in the wilderness, Prepare ye the way of the Lord, make his paths straight.

4 John did baptize in the wilderness, and preach the baptism of repentance for the remission of sins.

5 And there went out unto him all the land of Judæa, and they of Jerusalem, and were all baptized of him in the river of Jordan, confessing their sins.

6 And John was clothed with camel's hair, and with a girdle of a skin about his loins; and he did eat locusts and wild honey;

7 And preached, saying, There cometh one mightier than I after me, the latchet of whose shoes I am not worthy to stoop down and unloose.

8 I indeed have baptized you with water: but he shall baptize you with the Holy Ghost.

THE Gospel of St. Mark, which we now begin, is in some respects unlike the other three Gospels. It tells us nothing about the birth and early life of our Lord Jesus Christ. It contains comparatively few of His sayings and discourses. Of all the four inspired histories of our Lord's earthly ministry, this is by far the shortest.

But we must not allow these peculiarities to make us undervalue St. Mark's Gospel. It is a Gospel singularly full of precious facts about the Lord Jesus, narrated in a simple, terse, pithy, and condensed style. If it tells us few of our Lord's sayings, it is eminently rich in its catalogue of His doings. It often contains minute historical details of deep interest, which are wholly omitted in Matthew, Luke, and John. In short, it is no mere abridged copy of St. Matthew, as some have rashly asserted, but the independent narrative of an independent witness, who was inspired to write a history of our Lord's *works*, rather than of His *words*. Let us read it with holy reverence. Like all the rest of Scripture, every word of St. Mark is "given by inspiration of God," and every word is "profitable." *

Let us observe, in these verses, *what a full declaration we have of the dignity of our Lord Jesus Christ's person*. The very first sentence speaks of Him as "the Son of God."

These words, "the Son of God," conveyed far more to Jewish minds than they do to ours. They were nothing less than an assertion of our Lord's divinity. They were a declaration that Jesus was Himself very God, and "equal with God." (John v. 18.)

There is a beautiful fitness in placing this truth in the very beginning of a Gospel. The divinity of Christ is the citadel and keep of Christianity. Here lies the infinite value of the satisfaction He made upon the cross. Here lies the peculiar merit of His atoning death for sinners. That death was not the death of a mere man,

---

* "St. Mark has the special gift of terse brevity, and of graphic painting in wonderful combination. While on every occasion he compresses the discourses, works, and history into the simplest possible kernel, he on the other hand, unfolds the scenes more clearly than St. Matthew does, who excels in the discourses. Not only do single incidents become in his hands complete pictures, but even when he is very brief, he often gives, with one pencil stroke, something new and peculiarly his own."—*Stier's Words of the Lord Jesus.*

like ourselves, but of one who is "over all, God blessed
for ever." (Rom. ix. 3.) We need not wonder that the
sufferings of one person were a sufficient propitiation for
the sin of a world, when we remember that He who
suffered was "the Son of God."

Let believers cling to this doctrine with jealous watchfulness. With it, they stand upon a rock. Without it,
they have nothing solid beneath their feet. Our hearts
are weak. Our sins are many. We need a Redeemer
who is able to save to the uttermost, and deliver from the
wrath to come. We have such a Redeemer in Jesus
Christ. He is "the mighty God." (Isaiah ix. 6.)

Let us observe, in the second place, *how the beginning
of the Gospel was a fulfilment of Scripture.* John the
Baptist began his ministry, "as it is written in the
prophets."

There was nothing unforeseen and suddenly contrived in
the coming of Jesus Christ into the world. In the very
beginning of Genesis we find it predicted that "the seed of
the woman should bruise the serpent's head." (Gen. iii.
15.) All through the Old Testament we find the same
event foretold with constantly increasing clearness. It
was a promise often renewed to patriarchs, and repeated
by prophets, that a Deliverer and Redeemer should one
day come. His birth, His character, His life, His death,
His resurrection, His forerunner, were all prophecied of,
long before He came. Redemption was worked out and
accomplished in every step, just "as it was written."

We should always read the Old Testament with a desire
to find something in it about Jesus Christ. We study this
portion of the Bible with little profit, if we can see in it

nothing but Moses, and David, and Samuel, and the prophets. Let us search the books of the Old Testament more closely. It was said by Him whose words can never pass away, "these are they which testify of me." (John v. 40.)

Let us observe, in the third place, *how great were the effects which the ministry of John the Baptist produced for a time on the Jewish nation.* We are told that "there went out to him all the land of Judæa, and they of Jerusalem, and were all baptized of him in the river of Jordan."

The fact here recorded is one that is much overlooked. We are apt to lose sight of him who went before the face of our Lord, and to see nothing but the Lord Himself. We forget the morning star in the full blaze of the Sun. And yet it is clear that John's preaching arrested the attention of the whole Jewish people, and created an excitement all over Palestine. It aroused the nation from its slumbers, and prepared it for the ministry of our Lord, when He appeared. Jesus Himself says, "He was a burning and a shining light :—ye were willing to rejoice for a season in his light." (John v. 35.)

We ought to remark here how little dependence is to be placed on what is called "popularity." If ever there was one who was a popular minister for a season, John the Baptist was that man. Yet of all the crowds who came to his baptism, and heard his preaching, how few, it may be feared, were converted! Some, we may hope, like Andrew, were guided by John to Christ. But the vast majority, in all probability, died in their sins. Let us remember this whenever we see a crowded church.

A great congregation no doubt is a pleasing sight. But the thought should often come across our minds, "How many of these people will reach heaven at last?" It is not enough to hear and admire popular preachers. It is no proof of our conversion that we always worship in a place where there is a crowd. Let us take care that we hear the voice of Christ Himself, and follow Him.

Let us observe, in the last place, *what clear doctrine characterized John the Baptist's preaching.* He exalted Christ: "There cometh one mightier than I after me." He spoke plainly of the Holy Ghost: "He shall baptize you with the Holy Ghost."

These truths had never been so plainly proclaimed before by mortal man. More important truths than these are not to be found in the whole system of Christianity at this day. The principal work of every faithful minister of the Gospel, is to set the Lord Jesus fully before His people, and to show them His fulness and His power to save.—The next great work he has to do, is to set before them the work of the Holy Ghost, and the need of being born again, and inwardly baptized by His grace.—These two mighty truths appear to have been frequently on the lips of John the Baptist. It would be well for the church and the world, if there were more ministers like him.

Let us ask ourselves, as we leave the passage, "How much we know by practical experience of the truths which John preached?" What think we of Christ? Have we felt our need of Him, and fled to Him for peace? Is He king over our hearts, and all things to our souls?—What think we of the Holy Ghost? Has

He wrought any work in our hearts? Has He renewed, and changed them? Has He made us partakers of the divine nature? Life or death depend on our answer to these questions. "If any man have not the Spirit of Christ he is none of his." (Rom. viii. 9.)

MARK I. 9—20.

9 And it came to pass in those days, that Jesus came from Nazareth of Galilee, and was baptized of John in Jordan.

10 And straightway coming up out of the water, he saw the heavens opened, and the Spirit like a dove descending upon him:

11 And there came a voice from heaven, *saying,* Thou art my beloved Son, in whom I am well pleased.

12 And immediately the spirit driveth him into the wilderness.

13 And he was there in the wilderness forty days, tempted of Satan; and was with the wild beasts; and the angels ministered unto him.

14 Now after that John was put in prison, Jesus came into Galilee, preaching the Gospel of the kingdom of God,

15 And saying, The time is fulfilled, and the kingdom of God is at hand: repent ye, and believe the Gospel.

16 Now as he walked by the sea of Galilee, he saw Simon and Andrew his brother casting a net into the sea: for they were fishers.

17 And Jesus said unto them, Come ye after me, and I will make you to become fishers of men.

18 And straightway they forsook their nets, and followed him.

19 And when he had gone a little farther thence, he saw James the *son* of Zebedee, and John his brother, who also were in the ship mending their nets.

20 And straightway he called them: and they left their father Zebedee in the ship with the hired servants, and went after him.

THIS passage is singularly full of matter. It is a striking instance of that brevity of style, which is the peculiar characteristic of St. Mark's Gospel. The baptism of our Lord, His temptation in the wilderness, the commencement of His preaching, and the calling of His first disciples, are all related here in eleven verses.

Let us notice, in the first place, *the voice from heaven which was heard at our Lord's baptism.* We read, "There came a voice from heaven, saying, Thou art my beloved Son, in whom I am well pleased."

That voice was the voice of God the Father. It

declared the wondrous and ineffable love which has existed between the Father and the Son from all eternity. "The Father loveth the Son, and hath given all things into His hand." (John iii. 35.) It proclaimed the Father's full and complete approbation of Christ's mission to seek and save the lost. It announced the Father's acceptance of the Son as the Mediator, Substitute, and Surety of the new covenant.

There is a rich mine of comfort in these words, for all Christ's believing members. In themselves, and in their own doings, they see nothing to please God. They are daily sensible of weakness, shortcoming, and imperfection in all their ways. But let them recollect that the Father regards them as members of His beloved Son Jesus Christ. He sees no spot in them. (Cant. iv. 7.) He beholds them as " in Christ," clothed in His righteousness, and invested with His merit. They are " accepted in the Beloved," and when the holy eye of God looks at them, He is " well pleased."

Let us notice, in the second place, *the nature of Christ's preaching*. We read that He came saying, "Repent ye, and believe the Gospel."

This is that old sermon which all the faithful witnesses of God have continually preached, from the very beginning of the world. From Noah down to the present day the burden of their address has been always the same,—"Repent and believe."

The apostle Paul told the Ephesian elders, when he left them for the last time, that the substance of his teaching among them had been "repentance towards God, and faith towards our Lord Jesus Christ." (Acts xx. 21.)

He had the best of precedents for such teaching. The Great Head of the Church had given him a pattern. Repentance and faith were the foundation stones of Christ's ministry.—Repentance and faith must always be the main subjects of every faithful minister's instruction.

We need not wonder at this, if we consider the necessities of human nature. All of us are by nature born in sin and children of wrath, and all need to repent, be converted, and born again, if we would see the kingdom of God.—All of us are by nature guilty and condemned before God, and all must flee to the hope set before us in the Gospel, and believe in it, if we would be saved. All of us, once penitent, need daily stirring up to deeper repentance. All of us, though believing, need constant exhortation to increased faith.

Let us ask ourselves what we know of this repentance and faith. Have we felt our sins, and forsaken them? Have we laid hold on Christ, and believed? We may reach heaven without learning, or riches, or health, or worldly greatness. But we shall never reach heaven, if we die impenitent and unbelieving. A new heart, and a lively faith in a Redeemer are absolutely needful to salvation. May we never rest till we know them by experience, and can call them our own! With them all true Christianity begins in the soul. In the exercise of them consists the life of religion. It is only through the possession of them, that men have peace at the last. Churchmembership and priestly absolution alone save no one. They only die in the Lord who "repent and believe."

Let us notice, in the third place, *the occupation of those who were first called to be Christ's disciples.* We read that our Lord called Simon and Andrew, when they were " casting a net into the sea," and James and John while they were " mending their nets."

It is clear from these words, that the first followers of our Lord were not the great of this world. They were men who had neither riches, nor rank, nor power. But the kingdom of Christ is not dependent on such things as these. His cause advances in the world, "not by might, nor by power, but by my Spirit, saith the Lord of hosts." (Zech. iv. 6.) The words of St. Paul will always be found true : "Not many wise men after the flesh, not many mighty, not many noble are called. But God hath chosen the foolish things of the world to confound the wise, and God hath chosen the weak things of the world to confound the things which are mighty." (1 Cor. i. 26, 27.) The church which began with a few fishermen, and yet overspread half the world, must have been founded by God.

We must beware of giving way to the common notion, that there is anything disgraceful in being poor, and in working with our own hands. The Bible contains many instances of special privileges conferred on working men. Moses was keeping sheep, when God appeared to him in the burning bush. Gideon was thrashing wheat, when the angel brought him a message from heaven. Elisha was ploughing, when Elijah called him to be prophet in his stead. The apostles were fishing, when Jesus called them to follow Him. It is disgraceful to be covetous, or proud, or a cheat, or a gambler, or a drunkard, or a glutton, or unclean. But it is no disgrace to be poor. The labourer

who serves Christ faithfully is far more honourable in
God's eyes, than the nobleman who serves sin.

Let us notice, in the last place, *the office to which our
Lord called his first disciples.* We read that He said,
"Come ye after me, and I will make you to become
fishers of men."

The meaning of this expression is clear and unmistakeable. The disciples were to become fishers for souls.
They were to labour to draw men out of darkness into
light, and from the power of Satan to God. They were
to strive to bring men into the net of Christ's church,
that so they might be saved alive, and not perish ever-
lastingly.

We ought to mark this expression well. It is full of
instruction. It is the oldest name by which the ministerial office is described in the New Testament. It lies
deeper down than the name of bishop, elder, or deacon.
It is the first idea which should be before a minister's
mind. He is not to be a mere reader of forms, or
administrator of ordinances. He is to be a "fisher" of
souls. The minister who does not strive to live up to
this name, has mistaken his calling.

Does the fisherman strive to catch fish ? Does he use
all means, and grieve if unsuccessful ? The minister
ought to do the same.—Does the fisherman have patience?
Does he toil on day after day, and wait, and work on in
hope ? Let the minister do the same.—Happy is that
man, in whom the fisher's skill, and diligence, and
patience, are all combined !

Let us resolve to pray much for ministers. Their office
is no light one, if they do their duty. They need the

help of many intercessions from all praying people. They have not only their own souls to care for, but the souls of others. No wonder that St. Paul cries, "Who is sufficient for these things?" (2 Cor. ii. 16.) If we never prayed for ministers before, let us begin to do it this day.

MARK I. 21—34.

21 And they went into Capernaum; and straightway on the sabbath day he entered into the synagogue, and taught.

22 And they were astonished at his doctrine: for he taught them as one that had authority, and not as the Scribes.

23 And there was in their synagogue a man with an unclean spirit; and he cried out,

24 Saying, Let *us* alone; what have we to do with thee, thou Jesus of Nazareth? art thou come to destroy us? I know thee who thou art, the Holy One of God.

25 And Jesus rebuked him, saying, Hold thy peace, and come out of him.

26 And when the unclean spirit had torn him, and cried with a loud voice, he came out of him.

27 And they were all amazed, insomuch that they questioned among themselves, saying, What thing is this? what new doctrine is this? for with authority commandeth he even the unclean spirits, and they do obey him.

28 And immediately his fame spread abroad throughout all the region round about Galilee.

29 And forthwith, when they were come out of the synagogue, they entered into the house of Simon and Andrew, with James and John.

30 But Simon's wife's mother lay sick of a fever, and anon they tell him of her.

31 And he came and took her by the hand, and lifted her up; and immediately the fever left her, and she ministered unto them.

32 And at even, when the sun did set, they brought unto him all that were diseased, and them that were possessed with devils.

33 And all the city was gathered together at the door.

34 And he healed many that were sick of divers diseases, and cast out many devils; and suffered not the devils to speak, because they knew him.

THESE verses begin the long list of miracles which St. Mark's Gospel contains. They tell us how our Lord cast out devils in Capernaum, and healed Peter's wife's mother of a fever.

We learn, in the first place, from these verses, the *uselessness of a mere intellectual knowledge of religion.* Twice we are specially told that the unclean spirits knew our

Lord. In one place it says, "they knew Him." In another, the devil cries out, "I know thee who thou art, the Holy one of God." They knew Christ, when Scribes were ignorant of Him, and Pharisees would not acknowledge Him. And yet their knowledge was not unto salvation!

The mere belief of the facts and doctrines of Christianity will never save our souls. Such belief is no better than the belief of devils. They all believe and know that Jesus is the Christ. They believe that He will one day judge the world, and cast them down to endless torment in hell. It is a solemn and sorrowful thought, that on these points some professing Christians have even less faith than the devil. There are some who doubt the reality of hell and the eternity of punishment. Such doubts as these find no place except in the hearts of self-willed men and women. There is no infidelity among devils. "They believe and tremble." (James ii. 19.)

Let us take heed that our faith be a faith of the heart as well as of the head. Let us see that our knowledge has a sanctifying influence on our affections and our lives. Let us not only know Christ but love Him, from a sense of actual benefit received from Him. Let us not only believe that He is the Son of God and the Saviour of the world, but rejoice in Him, and cleave to Him with purpose of heart. Let us not only be acquainted with Him by the hearing of the ear, but by daily personal application to Him for mercy and grace. "The life of Christianity," says Luther, "consists in possessive pronouns." It is one thing to say "Christ is a Saviour." It is quite another to say "He is my Saviour and my

Lord." The devil can say the first. The true Christian alone can say the second.*

We learn, in the second place, *to what remedy a Christian ought to resort first, in time of trouble.* He ought to follow the example of the friends of Simon's wife's mother. We read that when she "lay sick of a fever," they " told Jesus of her."

There is no remedy like this. Means are to be used diligently, without question, in any time of need. Doctors are to be sent for, in sickness. Lawyers are to be consulted, when property or character needs defence. The help of friends is to be sought. But still after all, the first thing to be done, is to cry to the Lord Jesus Christ for help. None can relieve us so effectually as He can. None is so compassionate, and so willing to relieve. When Jacob was in trouble he turned to his God first— ; " Deliver me, I pray thee, from the hand of Esau." (Gen. xxxii. 11.) When Hezekiah was in trouble, he first spread Sennacherib's letter before the Lord ;—" I beseech thee, save thou us out of his hand." (2 Kings xix. 19.) When Lazarus fell sick, his sisters sent immediately to Jesus ; —" Lord," they said, " he whom thou lovest is sick." (John xi. 2.) Now let us do likewise. " Cast thy burden upon the Lord, and He shall sustain thee." " Casting all your care upon Him." " In everything by prayer

* " Rest not in an historical knowledge or faith. If thou do, it will not save thee; for if it would it would save the devils : for they have their literal knowledge and general belief of the word. Dost thou think it enough to know and believe that Christ lived and died for sinners ? The devil and his angels know and believe as much. Labour then to outstrip them, and to get a better faith than is in them."—*Petter on Mark.* 1661.

and supplication with thanksgiving, let your requests be
made known to God." (Psa. lv. 22 ; 1 Pet. v. 7 ;
Phil. iv. 6.)

Let us not only remember this rule, but practise it too.
We live in a world of sin and sorrow. The days of
darkness in a man's life are many. It needs no prophet's
eye to foresee that we shall all shed many a tear, and
feel many a heart-wrench, before we die. Let us be
armed with a receipt against despair, before our troubles
come. Let us know what to do, when sickness, or bereave-
ment, or cross, or loss, or disappointment breaks in upon
us like an armed man. Let us do as they did in Simon's
house at Capernaum. Let us at once " tell Jesus."

We learn, in the last place, from these verses, *what a
complete and perfect cure the Lord Jesus makes, when He
heals.* He takes the sick woman by the hand, and lifts
her up, and " immediately the fever left her." But this
was not all. A greater miracle remained behind. At
once we are told " she ministered unto them." That
weakness and prostration of strength which, as a general
rule, a fever leaves behind it, in her case was entirely
removed. The fevered woman was not only made well
in a moment, but in the same moment made strong and
able to work.*

---

* Let us not fail to observe here, that Peter, one of our Lord's
principal apostles had a wife. Yet he was called to be a disciple,
and afterwards chosen to be an apostle. More than this, we find
St. Paul speaking of him as a married man, in his Epistle to the
Corinthians, many years after this. (1 Cor. ix. 5.)

How this fact can be reconciled with the compulsory celibacy
of the clergy, which the Church of Rome enforces and requires, it
is for the friends and advocates of the Roman Catholic Church to
explain. To a plain reader, it seems a plain proof that it is not

We may see in this case a lively emblem of Christ's dealing with sin-sick souls. That blessed Saviour not only gives mercy and forgiveness;—He gives renewing grace besides. To as many as receive Him as their Physician, He gives power to become the sons of God. He cleanses them by His Spirit, when He washes them in His precious blood. Those whom He justifies, He also sanctifies. When He bestows an absolution, He also bestows a new heart. When He grants free forgiveness for the past, He also grants strength to "minister" to Him for the time to come. The sin-sick soul is not merely cured, and then left to itself. It is also supplied with a new heart and a right spirit, and enabled so to live as to please God.

There is comfort in this thought for all who feel a desire to serve Christ, but at present are afraid to begin. There are many in this state of mind. They fear that if they come forward boldly, and take up the cross, they shall by and bye fall away. They fear that they shall not be able to persevere, and shall bring discredit on their profession. Let them fear no longer. Let them know that Jesus is an Almighty Saviour, who never forsakes those who once commit themselves to Him. Once raised by His mighty hand from the death of sin, and washed in His precious blood, they shall go on "ministering to Him" to their life's end. They shall have power to overcome the world, and crucify the flesh, and resist

wrong for ministers to be married men. And when we add to this striking fact, that St. Paul, when writing to Timothy, says, that "a bishop should be the husband of one wife," (1 Tim. iii. 2,) it is clear that the whole Romish doctrine of clerical celibacy is utterly opposed to holy Scripture.

the devil. Only let them begin, and they shall go on.
Jesus knows nothing of half-cured cases and half-finished
work. Let them trust in Jesus and go forward. The
pardoned soul shall always be enabled to serve Christ.

There is comfort here for all who are really serving
Christ, and are yet cast down by a sense of their own
infirmity. There are many in such case. They are
oppressed by doubts and anxieties. They sometimes
think they shall never reach heaven after all, but be cast
away in the wilderness. Let them fear no longer. Their
strength shall be according to their day. The difficulties
they now fear shall vanish out of their path. The lion
in the way which they now dread, shall prove to be
chained. The same gracious hand which first touched
and healed, shall uphold, strengthen, and lead them to
the last. The Lord Jesus will never lose one of His
sheep. Those whom He loves and pardons, He loves
unto the end. Though sometimes cast down, they shall
never be cast away. The healed soul shall always go on
" ministering to the Lord." Grace shall always lead to
glory.

MARK I. 35—39.

35 And in the morning, rising up a great while before day, he went out and departed into a solitary place, and there prayed.

36 And Simon and they that were with him followed after him.

37 And when they had found him, they said unto him, All *men* seek for thee.

38 And he said unto them, Let us go into the next towns, that I may preach there also : for therefore came I forth.

39 And he preached in their synagogues throughout all Galilee, and cast out devils.

EVERY fact in our Lord's life on earth, and every word
which fell from His lips, ought to be deeply interesting

to a true Christian. We see a fact and a saying in the passage we have just read, which deserve close attention.

We see, for one thing, *an example of our Lord Jesus Christ's habits about private prayer.* We are told, that "in the morning, rising up a great while before day, He went out, and departed into a solitary place, and there prayed."

We shall find the same thing often recorded of our Lord in the Gospel history. When He was baptized, we are told that He was "praying." (Luke iii. 21.) When he was transfigured, we are told, that "as He prayed, the fashion of His face was altered." (Luke ix. 29.) Before He chose the twelve apostles, we are told that "He continued all night in prayer to God." (Luke vi. 12.) When all men spoke well of Him, and would fain have made Him a King, we are told that "He went up into a mountain apart to pray." (Mark xiv. 23.) When tempted in the garden of Gethsemane, He said, "Sit ye here, while I shall pray." (Mark xiv. 34.) In short, our Lord prayed always, and did not faint. Sinless as He was, He set us an example of diligent communion with His Father. His Godhead did not render Him independent of the use of all means as a man. His very perfection was a perfection kept up through the exercise of prayer.

We ought to see in all this the immense importance of private devotion. If He who was "holy, harmless, undefiled, and separate from sinners," thus prayed continually, how much more ought we who are compassed with infirmity? If He found it needful to offer up supplications with strong crying and tears, how much more needful is it for us, who in many things offend daily ?

What shall we say to those who never pray at all, in the face of such a passage as this ? There are many such, it may be feared, in the list of baptized people,—many who rise up in the morning without prayer, and without prayer lie down at night,—many who never speak one word to God. Are they Christians ? It is impossible to say so. A praying Master, like Jesus, can have no prayerless servants. The Spirit of adoption will always make a man call upon God. To be prayerless is to be Christless, Godless, and in the high road to destruction.

What shall we say to those who pray, yet give but little time to their prayers ? We are obliged to say that they show at present very little of the mind of Christ. Asking little, they must expect to have little. Seeking little, they cannot be surprised if they possess little. It will always be found that when prayers are few, grace, strength, peace, and hope are small.*

We shall do well to watch our habits of prayer with a holy watchfulness. Here is the pulse of our Christianity. Here is the true test of our state before God. Here true religion begins in the soul, when it does begin. Here it decays and goes backward, when a man backslides from

* " Ministers must pray much, if they would be successful. The apostles spent their time this way. (Acts vi. 3.) Yea, our Lord Jesus preached all day, and continued all night alone in prayer to God. Ministers should be much in prayer. They use to reckon how many hours they spend in reading and study. It were far better both for ourselves and the Church of God, if more time was spent in prayer. Luther's spending three hours daily in secret prayer, and Bradford's studying on his knees, and other instances of men in our time, are talked of rather than imitated."—*Traill.* 1696.

God. Let us walk in the steps of our blessed Master in this respect as well as in every other. Like Him, let us be diligent in our private devotion. Let us know what it is to " depart into solitary places and pray."

We see, for another thing, in this passage, *a remarkable saying of our Lord as to the purpose for which He came into the world.* We find Him saying, " let us go into the next towns, that I may preach there also: for therefore came I forth."

The meaning of these words is plain and unmistakeable. Our Lord declares that He came on earth to be a preacher and a teacher. He came to fulfil the prophetical office, to be the " prophet greater than Moses," who had been so long foretold. (Deut. xviii. 15.) He left the glory which He had from all eternity with the Father, to do the work of an evangelist. He came down to earth to show to man the way of peace, to proclaim deliverance to the captives, and recovering of sight to the blind. One principal part of his work on earth, was to go up and down and publish glad tidings, to offer healing to the broken-hearted, light to them that sat in darkness, and pardon to the chief of sinners, " Therefore," He says, " came I forth."

We ought to observe here, what infinite honour the Lord Jesus puts on the office of the preacher. It is an office which the eternal Son of God Himself undertook. He might have spent His earthly ministry in instituting and keeping up ceremonies, like Aaron. He might have ruled and reigned as a king, like David. But He chose a different calling. Until the time when He died as a sacrifice for our sins, His daily, and almost hourly work was to preach. " Therefore," He says, " came I forth."

Let us never be moved by those who cry down the preacher's office, and tell us that sacraments and other ordinances are of more importance than sermons. Let us give to every part of God's public worship its proper place and honour, but let us beware of placing any part of it above preaching. By preaching, the Church of Christ was first gathered together and founded, and by preaching, it has ever been maintained in health and prosperity. By preaching, sinners are awakened. By preaching, inquirers are led on. By preaching, saints are built up. By preaching, Christianity is being carried to the heathen world.—There are many now who sneer at missionaries, and mock at those who go out into the high-ways of our own land, to preach to crowds in the open air. But such persons would do well to pause, and consider calmly what they are doing. The very work which they ridicule is the work which turned the world upside down, and cast heathenism to the ground. Above all, it is the very work which Christ Himself undertook. The King of kings and Lord of lords Himself was once a preacher. For three long years He went to and fro proclaiming the Gospel. Sometimes we see Him in a house, sometimes on the mountain side, sometimes in a Jewish synagogue, sometimes in a boat on the sea. But the great work He took up was always one and the same. He came always preaching and teaching. "Therefore," He says, " came I forth."

Let us leave the passage with a solemn resolution never to " despise prophesying." (1 Thess. v. 20.) The minister we hear may not be highly gifted. The sermons that we listen to may be weak and poor. But after all, preaching is God's grand ordinance for converting and saving souls. The faithful preacher of the Gospel is handling the very weapon which the Son of God was not ashamed to employ. This is the work of which Christ has said, "Therefore came I forth."

MARK. I. 40—45.

40 And there came a leper to him, beseeching him, and kneeling down to him, and saying unto him, If thou wilt, thou canst make me clean.

41 And Jesus, moved with compassion, put forth *his* hand, and touched him, and saith unto him, I will; be thou clean.

42 And as soon as he had spoken, immediately the leprosy departed from him, and he was cleansed.

43 And he straitly charged him, and forthwith sent him away;

44 And he saith unto him, See thou say nothing to any man: but go thy way, shew thyself to the Priest, and offer for thy cleansing those things which Moses commanded, for a testimony unto them.

45 But he went out, and began to publish *it* much, and to blaze abroad the matter, insomuch that Jesus could no more openly enter into the city, but was without in desert places: and they came to him from every quarter.

We read in these verses, how our Lord Jesus Christ healed a leper. Of all our Lord's miracles of healing none were probably more marvellous than those performed on leprous people. Two cases only have been fully described in the gospel history. Of these two, the case before us is one.

Let us try to realize, in the first place, *the dreadful nature of the disease which Jesus cured.*

Leprosy is a complaint of which we know little or nothing in our northern climate. In Bible lands it is far more common. It is a disease which is utterly incurable. It is no mere skin affection, as some ignorantly suppose. It is a radical disease of the whole man. It attacks, not merely the skin, but the blood, the flesh, and the bones, until the unhappy patient begins to lose his extremities, and to rot by inches.—Let us remember beside this, that, amongst the Jews, the leper was reckoned unclean, and was cut off from the congregation of Israel and the ordinances of religion. He was obliged to dwell in a separate house. None might touch him or minister to him. Let us remember all this, and then we may have some idea of the remarkable wretchedness of a leprous person. To use the words of Aaron, when he interceded for Miriam, he was "as one dead, of whom the flesh is half consumed." (Numbers xii. 12.)

But is there nothing like leprosy among ourselves? Yes! indeed there is. There is a foul soul-disease which is engrained into our very nature, and cleaves to our bones and marrow with deadly force. That disease is the plague of sin. Like leprosy, it is a deep-seated disease, infecting every part of our nature, heart, will, conscience, understanding, memory, and affections. Like leprosy, it makes us loathsome and abominable, unfit for the company of God, and unmeet for the glory of heaven. Like leprosy, it is incurable by any earthly physician, and is slowly but surely dragging us down to the second death. And worst of all, far worse than leprosy, it is a disease from which no mortal man is exempt. "We are all," in God's sight, "as an unclean thing." (Isaiah. lxiv. 6.)

Do we know these things? Have we found them out? Have we discovered our own sinfulness, guilt, and corruption? Happy indeed is that person who has been really taught to feel that he is a "miserable sinner," and that there is "no health in him!" Blessed indeed is he who has learned that he is a spiritual leper, and a bad, wicked, sinful creature! To know our disease is one step towards a cure. It is the misery and the ruin of many souls that they never yet saw their sins and their need.

Let us learn, in the second place, from these verses, *the wondrous and almighty power of the Lord Jesus Christ.*

We are told that the unhappy leper came to our Lord, "beseeching Him, and kneeling down," and saying, "If thou wilt, thou canst make me clean." We are told that "Jesus, moved with compassion, put forth his hand and touched him, and said to him, I will, be thou clean." At once the cure was effected. That very instant the deadly plague departed from the poor sufferer, and he was healed. It is but a word, and a touch, and there stands before our Lord, not a leper, but a sound and healthy man.

Who can conceive the greatness of the change in the feelings of this leper, when he found himself healed? The morning sun rose upon him, a miserable being, more dead than alive, his whole frame a mass of sores and corruption, his very existence a burden. The evening sun saw him full of hope and joy, free from pain, and fit for the society of his fellow-men. Surely the change must have been like life from the dead.

Let us bless God that the Saviour with whom we have to do is almighty. It is a cheering and comfortable thought that with Christ nothing is impossible. No heart-disease is so deep-seated but He is able to cure it. No plague of soul is so virulent but our Great Physician can heal it. Let us never despair of any one's salvation, so long as he lives. The worst of spiritual lepers may yet be cleansed. No cases of spiritual leprosy could be worse than those of Manasseh, Saul, and Zacchæus, yet they were all cured;—Jesus Christ made them whole. The chief of sinners may yet be brought nigh to God by the blood and Spirit of Christ. Men are not lost, because they are too bad to be saved, but because they will not come to Christ that He may save them.

Let us learn, in the last place, from these verses, that *there is a time to be silent about the work of Christ, as well as a time to speak.*

This is a truth which is taught us in a remarkable way. We find our Lord strictly charging this man to tell no one of his cure, to "say nothing to any man." We find this man in the warmth of his zeal disobeying this injunction, and publishing and "blazing abroad" his cure in every quarter. And we are told that the result was that Jesus "could no more enter into the city, but was without in desert places."

There is a lesson in all this of deep importance, however difficult it may be to use it rightly. It is clear that there are times when our Lord would have us work for Him quietly and silently, rather than attract public attention by a noisy zeal. There is a zeal which is "not according to knowledge," as well as a zeal which is righteous and praiseworthy. Everything is beautiful in its season. Our Master's cause may on some occasions be more advanced by quietness and patience, than in any other way. We are not to "give that which is holy to dogs," nor "cast pearls before swine." By forgetfulness of this we may even do more harm than good, and retard the very cause we want to assist.

The subject is a delicate and difficult one, without doubt. Unquestionably the majority of Christians are far

more inclined to be silent about their glorious Master
than to confess Him before men,—and do not need the
bridle so much as the spur.   But still it is undeniable
that there is a time for all things ; and to know the time
should be one great aim of a Christian.   There are good
men who have more zeal than discretion, and even help
the enemy of truth by unseasonable acts and words.*

Let us all pray for the Spirit of wisdom and of a sound
mind.   Let us seek daily to know the path of duty, and
ask daily for discretion and good sense.   Let us be bold
as a lion in confessing Christ, and not be afraid to " speak
of Him before princes," if need be.   But let us never forget that " Wisdom is profitable to direct," (Eccles. x. 11.)
and let us beware of doing harm by an ill-directed zeal.

* It would not be wise for a speaker at an English public meeting to proclaim the names of the families in Italy where the Bible
is read, and to point out the streets and houses where these families
resided.   Such a speaker might be well-meaning, and full of zeal.
He might really desire to glorify Christ, and publish the triumphs
of His grace.   But he would be guilty of a sad indiscretion, and show
great ignorance of the very lesson which the verses before us contain.
The words of an old commentator on this subject deserve notice :

" In that our Saviour forbids this leper to publish this miracle
at this unseasonable time, we learn that all truths are not fit to be
professed or uttered at all times.   Though we must never deny
any truth, being demanded of it, or lawfully enjoined to profess it,
yet there is a wise concealment of the truth, which is sometimes to
be used.   (Eccles. iii. 7.)

When are we to conceal the truth ?   1.   When the case stands
so, that the uttering of it may bring hurt to the truth itself, as here,
the publishing of this miracle was like to stop Christ's ministry.
2.   When we are in the company of such persons as are more
likely to cavil and scoff at the truth, than to make any good use
of it.   3.   When we are in the company of malicious enemies of
the truth."   (Matt. vii. 6.)—*Petter on Mark.*   1661.

MARK II. 1—12.

1 And again he entered into Capernaum after *some* days; and it was noised that he was in the house.

2 And straightway many were gathered together, insomuch that there was no room to receive *them*, no, not so much as about the door: and he preached the word unto them.

3 And they come unto him, bringing one sick of the palsy, which was borne of four.

4 And when they could not come nigh unto him for the press, they uncovered the roof where he was: and when they had broken *it* up, they let down the bed wherein the sick of the palsy lay.

5 When Jesus saw their faith, he said unto the sick of the palsy, Son, thy sins be forgiven thee.

6 But there were certain of the Scribes sitting there, and reasoning in their hearts,

7 Why doth this *man* thus speak blasphemies? who can forgive sins but God only?

8 And immediately when Jesus perceived in his spirit that they so reasoned within themselves, he said unto them, Why reason ye these things in your hearts?

9 Whether is it easier to say to the sick of the palsy, *Thy* sins be forgiven thee; or to say, Arise, and take up thy bed, and walk?

10 But that ye may know that the Son of man hath power on earth to forgive sins, (he saith to the sick of the palsy,)

11 I say unto thee, Arise, and take up thy bed, and go thy way into thine house.

12 And immediately he arose, took up the bed, and went forth before them all; insomuch that they were all amazed, and glorified God, saying, We never saw it on this fashion.

THIS passage shows us our Lord once more at Capernaum. Once more we find Him doing His accustomed work, preaching the word, and healing those that were sick.

We see, in these verses, *what great spiritual privileges some persons enjoy, and yet make no use of them.*

This is a truth which is strikingly illustrated by the history of Capernaum. No city in Palestine appears to have enjoyed so much of our Lord's presence, during His earthly ministry, as did this city. It was the place where He dwelt, after He left Nazareth. (Matt. iv. 13.) It was the place where many of His miracles were worked, and many of His sermons delivered. But nothing that Jesus said or did seems to have had any effect on the hearts of the inhabitants. They crowded to hear Him, as we read in this passage, "till there was no room about the door." They were amazed. They were astonished. They were filled with wonder at His mighty works. But they were not converted. They lived in the full noon-tide blaze of the Sun of Righteousness, and yet their hearts remained hard. And they drew from our Lord the heaviest condemnation that He ever pronounced against any place, except Jerusalem: "Thou, Capernaum, which art exalted unto heaven, shalt be brought down to hell: for if the mighty works, which have been done in thee, had been done in Sodom, it would have remained until this day. But I say unto you, That it shall be more tolerable for the land of Sodom in the day of judgment, than for thee." (Matt. xi. 23, 24.)

It is good for us all to mark well this case of Capernaum. We are all too apt to suppose that it needs nothing but the powerful preaching of the Gospel to convert people's souls, and that if the Gospel is only brought into a place everybody *must* believe. We forget the amazing power of unbelief, and the depth of man's enmity against God. We forget that the Capernaites heard the most faultless preaching, and saw it confirmed by the most surprising miracles, and yet remained dead in trespasses and sins. We need reminding that the same Gospel which is the savour of life to some, is the savour of death to others, and that the same fire which softens the wax will also harden the clay. Nothing, in fact, seems to harden man's heart so much, as to hear the Gospel regularly, and yet deliberately prefer the service of sin and the world. Never was there a people so highly favoured as the people of Capernaum, and never was there a people who appear to have become so hard.

Let us beware of walking in their steps. We ought often to use the prayer of the Litany, "From hardness of heart, Good Lord, deliver us."

We see, in the second place, from these verses, *how great a blessing affliction may prove to a man's soul.*

We are told that one sick of the palsy was brought to our Lord, at Capernaum, in order to be healed. Helpless and impotent, he was carried in his bed by four kind friends, and let down into the midst of the place where Jesus was preaching. At once the object of the man's desire was gained. The great Physician of soul and body saw him, and gave him speedy relief. He restored him to health and strength. He granted him the far greater blessing of forgiveness of sins. In short the man who had been carried from his house that morning weak, dependent, and bowed down both in body and soul, returned to his own house rejoicing.

Who can doubt that to the end of his days this man would thank God for this palsy? Without it he might probably have lived and died in ignorance, and never seen Christ at all. Without it, he might have kept his sheep on the green hills of Galilee all his life long, and never been brought to Christ, and never heard these blessed words "thy sins be forgiven thee." That palsy was indeed a blessing. Who can tell but it was the beginning of eternal life to his soul?

How many in every age can testify that this palsied man's experience has been their own! They have learned wisdom by affliction. Bereavements have proved mercies. Losses have proved real gains. Sicknesses have led them to the great Physician of souls, sent them to the Bible, shut out the world, shown them their own foolishness, taught them to pray. Thousands can say like David, " It is good for me that I was afflicted, that I might learn thy statutes." (Psal. cxix. 71.)

Let us beware of murmuring under affliction. We may be sure there is a needs-be for every cross, and a wise reason for every trial. Every sickness and sorrow is a gracious message from God, and is meant to call us nearer to Him. Let us pray that we may learn the lesson that each affliction is appointed to convey. Let us see that we " refuse not Him that speaketh."

We see, in the last place, in these verses, *the priestly power of forgiving sins, which is possessed by our Lord Jesus Christ.*

We read that our Lord said to the sick of the palsy, " Son, thy sins be forgiven thee." He said these words with a meaning. He knew the hearts of the Scribes by whom He was surrounded. He intended to shew them that He laid claim to be the true High Priest, and to have the power of absolving sinners, though at present the claim was seldom put forward. But that He had the power He told them expressly. He says, " The Son of man hath power on earth to forgive sins." In saying " thy sins be forgiven thee," He had only exercised His rightful office.

Let us consider how great must be the authority of Him, who has the power to forgive sins ! This is the thing that none can do but God. No angel in heaven, no man upon earth, no church in council, no minister of any denomination, can take away from the sinner's conscience the load of guilt, and give him

peace with God. They may point to the fountain open
for all sin. They may declare with authority whose sins
God is willing to forgive. But they cannot absolve by
their own authority. They cannot put away transgressions.
This is the peculiar prerogative of God, and a prerogative
which He has put in the hands of His Son Jesus Christ.

Let us think for a moment how great a blessing it is,
that Jesus is our great High Priest, and that we know
where to go for absolution! We must have a Priest and
a sacrifice between ourselves and God. Conscience demands an atonement for our many sins. God's holiness
makes it absolutely needful. Without an atoning Priest
there can be no peace of soul. Jesus Christ is the very
Priest that we need, mighty to forgive and pardon,
tender-hearted and willing to save.

And now let us ask ourselves whether we have yet
known the Lord Jesus as our High Priest? Have we
applied to Him? Have we sought absolution? If not,
we are yet in our sins. May we never rest till the Spirit
witnesses with our spirit that we have sat at the feet of
Jesus and heard his voice, saying, "Son, thy sins be forgiven thee."

MARK II. 13—22.

13 And he went forth again by the sea side; and all the multitude resorted unto him, and he taught them.

14 And as he passed by, he saw Levi the *son* of Alphæus sitting at the receipt of custom, and said unto him, Follow me. And he arose and followed him.

15 And it came to pass, that, as Jesus sat at meat in his house, many Publicans and sinners sat also together with Jesus and his disciples: for there were many, and they followed him.

16 And when the Scribes and Pharisees saw him eat with Publicans and sinners, they said unto his disciples, How is it that he eateth and drinketh with Publicans and sinners?

17 When Jesus heard *it*, he saith unto them, They that are whole have no need of the physician, but they that are sick: I came not to call the

righteous, but sinners to repentance.

18 And the disciples of John and of the Pharisees used to fast: and they come and say unto him, Why do the disciples of John and of the Pharisees fast, but thy disciples fast not?

19 And Jesus said unto them, Can the children of the bridechamber fast, while the bridegroom is with them? as long as they have the bridegroom with them, they cannot fast.

20 But the days will come, when the bridegroom shall be taken away from them, and then shall they fast in those days.

21 No man also seweth a piece of new cloth on an old garment: else the new piece that filled it up taketh away from the old, and the rent is made worse.

22 And no man putteth new wine into old bottles: else the new wine doth burst the bottles, and the wine is spilled, and the bottles will be marred: but new wine must be put into new bottles.

THE person who is called Levi, at the beginning of this passage, is the same person who is called Matthew in the first of the four Gospels. Let us not forget this. It is no less than an apostle and an evangelist, whose early history is now before our eyes.

We learn from these verses, *the power of Christ to call men out from the world, and make them His disciples.* We read that he said to Levi, when "sitting at the receipt of custom, Follow me." And at once "he arose and followed him." From a publican he became an apostle, and a writer of the first book in that New Testament, which is now known all over the world.

This is a truth of deep importance. Without a divine call no one can be saved. We are all so sunk in sin, and so wedded to the world, that we should never turn to God and seek salvation, unless He first called us by His grace. God must speak to our hearts by His Spirit, before we shall ever speak to Him. Those who are sons of God, says the 17th Article, are "called according to God's purpose by His Spirit working in due season." Now how blessed is the thought that this calling of sinners is committed to so gracious a Saviour as Christ!

When the Lord Jesus calls a sinner to be His servant,

He acts as a Sovereign; but He acts with infinite mercy. He often chooses those who seem most unlikely to do His will, and furthest off from His kingdom. He draws them to Himself with almighty power, breaks the chains of old habits and customs, and makes them new creatures. As the loadstone attracts the iron, and the southwind softens the frozen ground, so does Christ's calling draw sinners out from the world, and melt the hardest heart. "The voice of the Lord is mighty in operation." Blessed are they, who, when they hear it, harden not their hearts!

We ought never to despair entirely of any one's salvation, when we read this passage of Scripture. He who called Levi, still lives and still works. The age of miracles is not yet past. The love of money is a powerful principle, but the call of Christ is more powerful. Let us not despair even about those who "sit at the receipt of custom," and enjoy abundance of this world's good things. The voice which said to Levi, "Follow me," may yet reach their hearts. We may yet see them arise, and take up the cross, and follow Christ. Let us hope continually, and pray for others. Who can tell what God may be going to do for any one around us? No one is too bad for Christ to call. Let us pray for all.

We learn, for another thing, from these verses, that *one of Christ's principal offices is that of a Physician.* The Scribes and Pharisees found fault with Him for eating and drinking with publicans and sinners. But "when Jesus heard it, He saith unto them, they that are whole have no need of the physician, but they that are sick."

The Lord Jesus did not come into the world, as some suppose, to be nothing more than a law-giver, a king, a teacher, and an example. Had this been all the purpose of His coming, there would have been small comfort for man. Diet-tables and rules of living are all very well for the convalescent, but not suitable to the man labouring under a mortal disease. A teacher and an example might be sufficient for an unfallen being like Adam in the garden of Eden. But fallen sinners like ourselves want healing first, before we can value rules.

The Lord Jesus came into the world to be a physician as well as a teacher. He knew the necessities of human nature. He saw us all sick of a mortal disease, stricken with the plague of sin, and dying daily. He pitied us, and came down to bring divine medicine for our relief. He came to give health and cure to the dying, to heal the broken hearted, and to offer strength to the weak. No sin-sick soul is too far gone for Him. It is His glory to heal and restore to life the most desperate cases. For unfailing skill, for unwearied tenderness, for long experience of man's spiritual ailments, the great Physician of souls stands alone. There is none like Him.

But what do we know ourselves of this special office of Christ? Have we ever felt our spiritual sickness and applied to Him for relief? We are never right in the sight of God until we do. We know nothing aright in religion, if we think the sense of sin should keep us back from Christ. To feel our sins, and know our sickness is the beginning of real Christianity. To be sensible of our corruption and abhor our own transgressions, is the first symptom of spiritual health. Happy indeed are they who have found out their soul's disease ! Let them know that Christ is the very Physician they require, and let them apply to Him witnout delay.

We learn, in the last place, from these verses, that *in religion it is worse than useless to attempt to mix things which essentially differ.* " No man," He tells the Pharisees, " seweth a piece of new cloth on an old garment." " No man putteth new wine into old bottles."

These words, we must of course see, were a parable. They were spoken with a special reference to the question which the Pharisees had just raised : " Why do the disciples of John fast, but thy disciples fast not ? " Our Lord's reply evidently means, that to enforce fasting among His disciples would be inexpedient and unseasonable. His little flock was as yet young in grace, and weak in faith, knowledge, and experience. They must be led on softly, and not burdened at this early stage with requirements which they were not able to bear. Fasting, moreover, might be suitable to the disciples of Him who was only the Bridegroom's friend, who lived in the wilderness, preached the baptism of repentance, was clothed in camel's hair, and ate locusts and wild honey. But fasting was not equally suitable to the disciples of Him, who was the Bridegroom Himself, brought glad tidings to sinners, and came living like other men. In short, to require fasting of His disciples at present, would be putting " new wine into old bottles." It would be trying to mingle and amalgamate things that essentially differed.

The principle laid down in these little parables is one of great importance. It is a kind of proverbial saying, and admits of a wide application. Forgetfulness of it has frequently done great harm in the Church. The evils that have arisen from trying to sew the new patch on the old garment, and put the new wine into old bottles, have neither been few nor small.

How was it with the Galatian Church ? It is recorded in St. Paul's epistle. Men wished in that Church to reconcile Judaism with Christianity, and to circumcise as well as baptize. They endeavoured to keep alive the law of ceremonies and ordinances, and to place it side by side with the Gospel of Christ. In fact they would fain have put the "new wine into old bottles." And in so doing they greatly erred.

How was it with the early Christian Church, after the apostles were dead ? We have it recorded in the pages of Church history. Some tried to make the Gospel more acceptable by mingling it with Platonic philosophy. Some laboured to recommend it to the heathen by borrowing forms, processions, and vestments from the temples of heathen gods. In short, they "sewed the new patch on the old garment." And in so doing they scattered broadcast the seeds of enormous evil. They paved the way for the whole Romish apostasy.

How is it with many professing Christians in the present day ? We have only to look around us and see. There are thousands who are trying to reconcile the service of Christ and the service of the world, to have the name of Christian and yet live the life of the ungodly, —to keep in with the servants of pleasure and sin, and yet be the followers of the crucified Jesus at the same time. In a word, they are trying to enjoy the "new wine," and yet to cling to the " old bottles." They will find one day that they have attempted that which cannot be done.

Let us leave the passage in a spirit of serious self-inquiry. It is one that ought to raise great searchings of heart in the present day. Have we never read what the Scripture says? "No man can serve two masters." "Ye cannot serve God and mammon." Let us place side by side with these texts the concluding words of our Lord in this passage, "New wine must be put into new bottles." *

MARK II. 23—28.

23 And it came to pass, that he went through the corn fields on the sabbath day ; and his disciples began, as they went, to pluck the ears of corn.

24 And the Pharisees said unto him, Behold, why do they on the sabbath day that which is not lawful?

25 And he said unto them, Have ye never read what David did, when he had need, and was an hungered, he, and they that were with him?

26 How he went into the house of God in the days of Abiathar the High Priest, and did eat the shewbread, which is not lawful to eat but for the Priests, and gave also to them which were with him?

27 And he said unto them, The sabbath was made for man, and not man for the sabbath :

28 Therefore the Son of man is Lord also of the sabbath.

THESE verses set before us a remarkable scene in our Lord Jesus Christ's earthly ministry. We see our blessed Master and His disciples going " through the corn fields on the Sabbath day." We are told that His disciples, " as they went, began to pluck the ears of corn." At once we hear the Pharisees accusing them to our Lord, as if they had committed some great moral offence.

* It must always be remembered that the " bottle " here spoken of was not a bottle of glass or of earthenware, but of leather. Unless this is kept in view, the parable is unintelligible to an English mind. A similar remark applies to David's words, " I am become like a bottle in the smoke." (Psal. cxix. 83.)

" Why do they on the sabbath day that which is not lawful?" They received an answer full of deep wisdom, which all should study well, who desire to understand the subject of Sabbath observance.

We see from these verses, *what extravagant importance is attached to trifles by those who are mere formalists in religion.*

The Pharisees were mere formalists, if there ever were any in the world. They seem to have thought exclusively of the outward part, the husk, the shell, and the ceremonial of religion. They even added to these externals by traditions of their own. Their godliness was made up of washings, and fastings, and peculiarities in dress, and will-worship, while repentance, and faith, and holiness were comparatively overlooked.

The Pharisees would probably have found no fault, if the disciples had been guilty of some offence against the moral law. They would have winked at covetousness, or perjury, or extortions, or excess, because they were sins to which they themselves were inclined. But no sooner did they see an infringement of their man-made traditions about the right way of keeping the Sabbath, than they raised an outcry, and found fault.

Let us watch and pray, lest we fall into the error of the Pharisees. There are never wanting Christians who walk in their steps. There are thousands at the present day who plainly think more of the mere outward ceremonial of religion than of its doctrines. They make more ado about keeping saints' days, and turning to the east in the creed, and bowing at the name of Jesus, than about repentance, or faith, or separation from the

world. Against this spirit let us ever be on our guard.
It can neither comfort, satisfy, nor save.

It ought to be a settled principle in our minds, that a
man's soul is in a bad state, when he begins to regard
man-made rites and ceremonies, as things of superior importance, and exalts them above the preaching of the
Gospel. It is a symptom of spiritual disease. There is
mischief within. It is too often the resource of an
uneasy conscience. The first steps of apostasy from
Protestantism to Romanism have often been in this
direction. No wonder that St. Paul said to the Gala-
tians, "Ye observe days, and months, and times, and
years. I am afraid of you, lest I have bestowed on you
labour in vain." (Gal. iv. 10, 11.)

We see, in the second place, from these verses, *the
value of a knowledge of Holy Scripture.*

Our Lord replies to the accusation of the Pharisees by
a reference to Holy Scripture. He reminds His enemies
of the conduct of David, when "he had need and was
an hungred." "Have ye never read what David did?"
They could not deny that the writer of the book of
Psalms, and the man after God's own heart, was not
likely to set a bad example. They knew in fact that he
had not turned aside from God's commandment, all the
days of his life, "save only in the matter of Uriah the
Hittite." (1 Kings xv. 5.) Yet what had David done?
He had gone into the house of God, when pressed by
hunger, and eaten "the shewbread, which is not lawful
to eat but for the priests.*" He had thus shown that

* There is some difficulty in this passage in the mention of
Abiathar as "the High Priest." In the book of Samuel it appears

some requirements of God's laws might be relaxed in case of necessity. To this Scripture example our Lord refers His adversaries. They found nothing to reply to

that Abimelech was the High Priest, when the circumstance here referred to took place. (1 Sam. xxi. 6.)

The explanations of this difficulty are various. They are as follows.—

1. Beza says that both Abiathar and Abimelech had each two names, and that Abiathar was frequently called Abimelech, and Abimelech Abiathar. (See in proof of this, 2 Sam. viii. 17: 1 Chron. viii. 16, and xxiv. 3.)

2. Lightfoot would translate the words, " in the days of Abiathar, the son of the High Priest," and says he is named rather than his father because he brought the Ephod to David, and by him inquiry was made by Urim and Thummim. He also says, that the Jews by "Abiathar" understood the Urim and Thummim, and to say that the thing was done " under Abiathar" would show that it was done by divine direction.

3. Whitby thinks that by " the High Priest" here, we are not to understand him who was strictly so called, but only one who was an eminent man of the order. He quotes as examples, Matt. ii. 4: xxvi. 3: xxvii. 62: John xi. 47: Mark xiv. 10, 43.

4. Some think that both Abimelech and Abiathar officiated as High Priests at the same time. That there was nothing altogether unusual in there being two Chief Priests at once, is shown by 1 Sam. viii. 17, where two names are given as " the Priests."

5. Some think that there has been a mistake made in transcribing the original words of St. Mark in this place, and some words have been inserted, or wrongly written. Beza's manuscript omits the words translated, " in the time of Abiathar the High Priest," altogether. The St. Gall manuscript and the Gothic version have the word " Priest" simply, and not " High Priest." The Persian version has "Abimelech" instead of "Abiathar." However, it is only fair to say that the evidence of the great majority of manuscripts and versions is in favour of the text as it stands.

Some of these solutions of the difficulty are evidently more probable than others. But any one of them is far more reasonable and deserving of belief than to suppose, as some have asserted, that St. Mark made a blunder! Such a theory destroys the whole principle of the inspiration of Scripture. Transcribers of the Bible have possibly made occasional mistakes. The original writers were inspired in the writing of every word, and therefore could not err.

it. The sword of the Spirit was a weapon which they could not resist. They were silenced, and put to shame.

Now the conduct of our Lord on this occasion ought to be a pattern to all His people. Our grand reason for our faith, and practice, should always be, "Thus it is written in the Bible." "What saith the Scripture?" We should endeavour to have the word of God on our side in all debateable questions. We should seek to be able to give a scriptural answer for our behaviour in all matters of dispute. We should refer our enemies to the Bible as our rule of conduct. We shall always find a plain text the most powerful argument we can use. In a world like this we must expect our opinions to be attacked, if we serve Christ, and we may be sure that nothing silences adversaries so soon as a quotation from Scripture.

Let us however remember, that if we are to use the Bible as our Lord did, we must know it well, and be acquainted with its contents. We must read it diligently, humbly, perseveringly, prayerfully, or we shall never find its texts coming to our aid in the time of need. To use the sword of the Spirit effectually, we must be familiar with it, and have it often in our hands. There is no royal road to the knowledge of the Bible. It does not come to man by intuition. The book must be studied, pondered, prayed over, searched into, and not left always lying on a shelf, or carelessly looked at now and then. It is the students of the Bible, and they only, who will find it a weapon ready to hand in the day of battle.

We see, in the last place, from these verses, the *true principle by which all questions about the observance of the Sabbath ought to be decided.* "The Sabbath," says our

Lord, "was made for man, and not man for the Sabbath."

There is a mine of deep wisdom in those words. They deserve close attention, and the more so because they are not recorded in any Gospel but that of St. Mark. Let us see what they contain.

"The Sabbath was made for man." God made it for Adam in Paradise, and renewed it to Israel on Mount Sinai. It was made for all mankind, not for the Jew only, but for the whole family of Adam. It was made for man's benefit and happiness. It was for the good of his body, the good of his mind, and the good of his soul. It was given to him as a boon and a blessing, and not as a burden. This was the original institution.

But "man was not made for the Sabbath." The observance of the day of God was never meant to be so enforced as to be an injury to his health, or to interfere with his necessary wants. The original command to "keep holy the Sabbath Day," was not intended to be so interpreted as to do harm to his body, or prevent acts of mercy to his fellow-creatures. This was the point that the Pharisees had forgotten, or buried under their traditions.

There is nothing in all this to warrant the rash assertion of some, that our Lord has done away with the fourth commandment. On the contrary, He manifestly speaks of the Sabbath Day as a privilege and a gift, and only regulates the extent to which its observance should be enforced. He shows that works of necessity and mercy may be done on the Sabbath Day; but He says not a word to justify the notion that Christians need not "remember the day to keep it holy."

Let us be jealous over our own conduct in the matter of observing the Sabbath. There is little danger of the day being kept too strictly in the present age. There is far more danger of its being profaned and forgotten entirely. Let us contend earnestly for its preservation among us in all its integrity. We may rest assured that national prosperity and personal growth in grace, are intimately bound up in the maintenance of a holy Sabbath.*

* The concluding words of the passage now expounded are remarkable. "The Son of man is Lord also of the Sabbath." They have received some rather strange interpretations, which it may be well to notice,

1. Chrysostom, Grotius, Calovius, and others, think that the "son of man" in this place means "any man," any one naturally born of the family of Adam, and not Christ Himself. To say nothing of the objections that might be brought against the doctrines involved in such a sense, it is an unanswerable objection that the expression "son of man" is never used in this way in the New Testament. Whitby says that it occurs eighty-eight times, and always applies to Christ.

2. Others say that our Lord's meaning is, to assert His own right to dispense with the observance of the fourth commandment. This however seems a very unsatisfactory interpretation. Our Lord declares plainly in one place, that He came "not to destroy the law but to fulfil." He challenges the Jews in another place to convict Him of any breach of the law: "which of you convinceth me of sin?" His enemies, when they brought Him at last before Caiaphas, did not charge Him with breaking the fourth commandment. No doubt they would have done so, had He given them occasion, either by His teaching or practice.

The true meaning appears to be, that our Lord claims the right to dispense with all the traditional rules, and man-made laws about the Sabbath, with which the Pharisees had overloaded the day of rest. As Son of man, who came not to destroy but to save, He asserts His power to set free the blessed Sabbath from the false and superstitious notions with which the Rabbins had clogged and poisoned it, and to restore it to its proper meaning and use. He declares that the Sabbath is His day,—His by creation and institution, since He first gave it in Paradise and at Sinai,—and proclaims His determination to defend and purify His day from

MARK III. 1—12.

1 And he entered again into the synagogue; and there was a man there which had a withered hand.

2 And they watched him, whether he would heal him on the sabbath day; that they might accuse him.

3 And he saith unto the man which had the withered hand, Stand forth.

4 And he saith unto them, Is it lawful to do good on the sabbath days, or to do evil? to save life or to kill? But they held their peace.

5 And when he had looked round about on them with anger, being grieved for the hardness of their hearts, he saith unto the man, Stretch forth thine hand. And he stretched *it* out: and his hand was restored whole as the other.

6 And the Pharisees went forth, and straightway took counsel with the Herodians against him, how they might destroy him.

7 But Jesus withdrew himself with his disciples to the sea: and a great multitude from Galilee followed him, and from Judæa,

8 And from Jerusalem, and from Idumæa, and *from* beyond Jordan; and they about Tyre and Sidon, a great multitude, when they had heard what great things he did, came unto him.

9 And he spake to his disciples, that a small ship should wait on him because of the multitude, lest they should throng him.

10 For he had healed many; insomuch that they pressed upon him for to touch him, as many as had plagues.

11 And unclean spirits, when they saw him, fell down before him, and cried, saying, Thou art the Son of God.

12 And he straitly charged them that they should not make him known.

THESE verses show us our Lord again working a miracle. He heals a man in the synagogue, " which had a withered hand." Always about His Father's business,—always doing good,—doing it in the sight of enemies as well as

Jewish imposition, and to give it to His disciples as a day of blessing, comfort, and benefit, according to its original intention.

Two things are implied in our Lord's words. One is His own divinity. The " Lord of the Sabbath day " could be no less than God Himself. It is like the expression, " In this place is one greater than the temple." (Matt. xii. 6.) The other is His intention of altering the day of rest from the seventh day of the week to the first. At the time that He spoke, neither of these things doubtless were apparent to the Jews, and probably not to His disciples. After His ascension they " would remember his words."

A passage in Mayer's Commentary is worth reading. " It is certain that Christ being a perfect pattern of doctrine in all things, did not transgress, or maintain any transgression against any law of God. Wherefore it is to be held that all His speech here tendeth to nothing else but to convince the Pharisees of blindness and ignorance, touching the right keeping of the Sabbath according to the commandment, it being never required to rest so strictly as they thought."—*Mayer's Commentary.* 1631.

of friends,—such was the daily tenor of our Lord's earthly ministry. And He "left us an example that we should follow His steps." (1 Peter ii. 21.) Blessed indeed are those Christians who strive, however feebly, to imitate their Master!

Let us observe in these verses, *how our Lord Jesus Christ was watched by His enemies.* We read that "they watched Him, whether He would heal him on the Sabbath Day, that they might accuse Him."

What a melancholy proof we have here of the wickedness of human nature! It was the Sabbath Day, when these things happened. It was in the synagogue, where men were assembled to hear the word and worship God. Yet even on the day of God, and at the time of worshipping God, these wretched formalists were plotting mischief against our Lord. The very men who pretended to such strictness and sanctity in little things, were full of malicious and angry thoughts in the midst of the congregation. (Prov. v. 14.)

Christ's people must not expect to fare better than their master. They are always watched by an ill-natured and spiteful world. Their conduct is scanned with a keen and jealous eye. Their ways are noted and diligently observed. They are marked men. They can do nothing without the world noticing it. Their dress, their expenditure, their employment of time, their conduct in all the relations of life, are all rigidly and closely remarked. Their adversaries wait for their halting, and if at any time they fall into an error, the ungodly rejoice.

It is good for all Christians to keep this before their minds. Wherever we go, and whatever we do, let us remember that, like our Master, we are " watched." The thought should make us exercise a holy jealousy over all our conduct, that we may do nothing to cause the enemy to blaspheme. It should make us diligent to avoid even the "appearance of evil." Above all, it should make us pray much, to be kept in our tempers, tongues, and daily public demeanour. That Saviour who was "watched" Himself, knows how to sympathize with His people, and to supply grace to help in time of need.

Let us observe, in the second place, *the great principle that our Lord lays down about Sabbath observance.* He teaches that it is lawful " to do good " on the Sabbath.

This principle is taught by a remarkable question. He asks those around Him, whether it was "lawful to do good or evil on the Sabbath days, to save life, or to kill ? " Was it better to heal this poor sufferer before Him with the withered hand, or to leave him alone ? Was it more sinful to restore a person to health on the Sabbath, than to plot murder, and nourish hatred against an innocent person, as they were doing at that moment against Himself? Was He to be blamed for saving a life on the Sabbath ? Were they blameless who were desirous to kill? No wonder that before such a question as this, our Lord's enemies "held their peace."

It is plain from these words of our Lord, that no Christian need ever hesitate to do a really good work on the Sunday. A real work of mercy, such as ministering to the sick, or relieving pain, may always be done without scruple. The holiness with which the fourth commandment invests the Sabbath Day, is not in the least degree invaded by anything of this kind.

But we must take care that the principle here laid down by our Lord, is not abused and turned to bad account. We must not allow ourselves to suppose that the permission to "do good," implied that every one might find his own pleasure on the Sabbath. The permission to "do good," was never meant to open the door to amusements, worldly festivities, travelling, journeying, and sensual gratification. It was never intended to license the Sunday railway train, or the Sunday steam-boat, or the Sunday Exhibition. These things do good to none, and do certain harm to many. They rob many a servant of his seventh day's rest. They turn the Sunday of thousands into a day of hard toil. Let us beware of perverting our Lord's words from their proper meaning. Let us remember what kind of "doing good" on the Sabbath His blessed example sanctioned. Let us ask ourselves whether there is the slightest likeness between our Lord's works on the Sabbath, and those ways of spending the Sabbath for which many contend, who yet dare to appeal to our Lord's example. Let us fall back on the plain meaning of our Lord's words, and take our stand on them. He gives us a liberty to "do good" on Sunday, but for feasting, sight-seeing, party-giving, and excursions, He gives no liberty at all.

Let us observe, in the last place, *the feelings which the conduct of our Lord's enemies called forth in His heart.* We are told that "He looked round about on them with anger, being grieved for the hardness of their hearts."

This expression is very remarkable, and demands special attention. It is meant to remind us that our Lord Jesus Christ was a man like ourselves in all things, sin only excepted. Whatever sinless feelings belong to the constitution of man, our Lord partook of, and knew by experience. We read that He "marvelled," that He "rejoiced," that He "wept," that He "loved," and here we read that He felt "anger."

It is plain from these words that there is an "anger" which is lawful, right, and not sinful. There is an indignation which is justifiable, and on some occasions may be properly manifested. The words of Solomon and St. Paul both seem to teach the same lesson. "The north wind driveth away rain, so doth an angry countenance a backbiting tongue." "Be ye angry and sin not." (Prov. xxv. 23. Ephes. iv. 26.)

Yet it must be confessed that the subject is full of difficulty. Of all the feelings that man's heart experiences, there is none perhaps which so soon runs into sin as the feeling of anger. There is none which once excited seems less under control. There is none which leads on to so much evil. The length to which ill-temper, irritability, and passion, will carry even godly men, all must know. The history of "the contention" of Paul and Barnabas at Antioch, and the story of Moses being provoked till he "spake unadvisedly with his lips," are familiar to every Bible reader. The awful fact that passionate words are a breach of the sixth commandment, is plainly taught in the Sermon on the Mount. And yet here we see that there is an anger which is lawful.

Let us leave this subject with an earnest prayer, that we may all be enabled to take heed to our spirit in the matter of anger. We may rest assured that there is no human feeling which needs so much cautious guarding

as this. A sinless wrath is a very rare thing. The
wrath of man is seldom for the glory of God. In every
case a righteous indignation should be mingled with
grief and sorrow for those who cause it, even as it
was in the case of our Lord. And this, at all events, we
may be sure of,—it is better never to be angry, than to
be angry and sin.*

MARK III. 13—21.

13 And he goeth up into a mountain, and calleth *unto him* whom he
would: and they came unto him.

14 And he ordained twelve, that
they should be with him, and that he
might send them forth to preach,

15 And to have power to heal sicknesses, and to cast out devils:

16 And Simon he surnamed Peter;

17 And James the *son* of Zebedee,
and John the brother of James; and
he surnamed them Boanerges, which
is, The sons of thunder:

18 And Andrew, and Philip, and
Bartholomew, and Matthew, and
Thomas, and James the *son* of Alphæus, and Thaddæus, and Simon the
Canaanite,

19 And Judas Iscariot, which also
betrayed him: and they went into an
house.

20 And the multitude cometh together again, so that they could not
so much as eat bread.

21 And when his friends heard *of
it*, they went out to lay hold on him:
for they said, He is beside himself.

The beginning of this passage describes the appointment of the twelve apostles. It is an event in our Lord's
earthly ministry, which should always be read with deep
interest. What a vast amount of benefit these few men
have confered on the world! The names of a few Jewish
fishermen are known and loved by millions all over the

* In connection with this subject, Bishop Butler's Sermon on
Resentment deserves perusal. He says at the conclusion' of it:
"That passion, from whence men take occasion to run into the dreadful sins of malice and revenge, even that passion, as implanted in
our nature by God, is not only innocent but a generous movement
of mind. It is in itself, and in its original, no more than indignation against injury and wickedness,—that which is the only deformity in the creation, and the only reasonable object of abhorrence
and dislike."—*Bishop Butler.*

globe, while the names of many kings and rich men are lost and forgotten. It is they who do good to souls who are had "in everlasting remembrance." (Psalm cxii. 6.)

Let us notice in these verses, *how many of the twelve who are here named, had been called to be disciples before they were ordained apostles.*

There are six, at least, out of the number, whose first call to follow Christ is specially recorded. These six are Peter and Andrew, James and John, Philip and Matthew. In short there can be little doubt that eleven of our Lord's apostles, were converted before they were ordained.

It ought to be the same with all ministers of the Gospel. They ought to be men who have been first called by the Spirit, before they are set apart for the great work of teaching others. The rule should be the same with them as with the apostles,—"first converted, then ordained."

It is impossible to overrate the importance of this to the interests of true religion. Bishops and presbyteries can never be too strict and particular in the enquiries they make about the spiritual character of candidates for orders. An unconverted minister is utterly unfit for his office. How can he speak experimentally of that grace which he has never tasted himself? How can he commend that Saviour to his people whom he himself only knows by name? How can he urge on souls the need of that conversion and new birth, which he himself has not experienced? Miserably mistaken are those parents, who persuade their sons to become clergymen, in order to obtain a good living, or follow a respectable

profession! What is it but persuading them to say what
is not true, and to take the Lord's name in vain?
None do such injury to the cause of Christianity, as
unconverted, worldly ministers. They are a support to
the infidel, a joy to the devil, and an offence to
God.

Let us notice, in the second place, *the nature of the
office to which the apostles were ordained.* They were to
"be with Christ." They were to be "sent forth to
preach." They were to have "power to heal sicknesses."
They were to "cast out devils."

These four points deserve attention. They contain
much instruction. Our Lord's twelve apostles, beyond
doubt, were a distinct order of men. They had no
successors when they died. Strictly and literally speaking, there is no such thing as apostolical succession. No
man can be really called a "successor of the apostles,"
unless he can work miracles, and teach infallibly, as they
did. But still, in saying this, we must not forget, that
in many things the apostles were intended to be patterns
and models for all ministers of the Gospel. Bearing this
in mind, we may draw most useful lessons from this
passage, as to the duties of a faithful minister.

Like the apostles, the faithful minister ought to keep
up close communion with Christ. He should be much
"with Him." His fellowship should be "with the Son."
(1 John i. 3.) He should abide in Him. He should be
separate from the world, and daily sit, like Mary, at
Jesus' feet, and hear His word. He should study Him,
copy Him, drink into His Spirit, and walk in His steps.
He should strive to be able to say, when he enters the

pulpit, "that which we have seen and heard, declare we unto you." (1 John i. 3.)

Like the apostles, the faithful minister ought to be a preacher. This must ever be his principal work, and receive the greatest part of his thoughts. He must place it above the administration of the sacraments. (1 Cor. i. 17.) He must exalt it above the reading of forms. An unpreaching minister is of little use to the church of Christ. He is a lampless light-house, a silent trumpeter, a sleeping watchman, a painted fire.

Like the apostles, the faithful minister must labour to do good in every way. Though he cannot heal the sick, he must seek to alleviate sorrow, and to increase happiness among all with whom he has to do. He must strive to be known as the comforter, the counsellor, the peacemaker, the helper, and the friend of all. Men should know him, not as one who rules and domineers, but as one who is "their servant for Jesus' sake." (2 Cor. iv. 5.)

Like the apostles, the faithful minister must oppose every work of the devil. Though not called now to cast out evil spirits from the body, he must be ever ready to resist the devil's devices, and to denounce his snares for the soul. He must expose the tendency of races, theatres, balls, gambling, drunkenness, Sabbath-profanation, and sensual gratifications. Every age has its own peculiar temptations. Many are the devices of Satan. But whatever be the direction in which the devil is most busy, there ought the minister to be, ready to confront and withstand him.

How great is the responsibility of ministers! How heavy their work, if they do their duty! How much they need the prayers of all praying people, in order to support and strengthen their hands! No wonder that St. Paul says so often to the churches, "Pray for us."

Let us notice, in the last place, how *our Lord Jesus Christ's zeal was misunderstood by His enemies.* We are told that they "went out to lay hold of him, for they said, he is beside himself."

There is nothing in this fact that need surprise us. The prophet who came to anoint Jehu was called a "mad fellow." (2 Kings ix. 11.) Festus told Paul that he was "mad." Few things show the corruption of human nature more clearly, than man's inability to understand zeal in religion. Zeal about money, or science, or war, or commerce, or business, is intelligible to the world. But zeal about religion is too often reckoned foolishness, fanaticism, and the sign of a weak mind. If a man injures his health by study, or excessive attention to business, no fault is found:—"He is a diligent man."—But if he wears himself out with preaching, or spends his whole time in doing good to souls, the cry is raised, "He is an enthusiast and righteous over-much." The world is not altered. The "things of the Spirit" are always "foolishness to the natural man." (1 Cor. ii. 14.)

Let it not shake our faith, if we have to drink of the same cup as our blessed Lord. Hard as it may be to flesh and blood to be misunderstood by our relations, we must recollect it is no new thing. Let us call to mind our Lord's words, "He that loveth father and mother more than me is not worthy of me." Jesus knows the bitterness of our trials. Jesus feels for us. Jesus will give us help.

Let us bear patiently the unreasonableness of unconverted men, even as our Lord did. Let us pity their blindness and want of knowledge, and not love them one whit the less. Above all, let us pray that God would change their hearts. Who can tell but the very persons who now try to turn us away from Christ, may one day become new creatures, see all things differently, and follow Christ themselves?

MARK III. 22—30.

22 And the Scribes which came down from Jerusalem said, He hath Beelzebub, and by the prince of the devils casteth he out devils.

23 And he called them *unto him*, and said unto them in parables, How can Satan cast out Satan?

24 And if a kingdom be divided against itself, that kingdom cannot stand.

25 And if a house be divided against itself, that house cannot stand.

26 And if Satan rise up against himself, and be divided, he cannot stand, but hath an end.

27 No man can enter into a strong man's house, and spoil his goods, except he will first bind the strong man; and then he will spoil his house.

28 Verily I say unto you, All sins shall be forgiven unto the sons of men, and blasphemies wherewith soever they shall blaspheme:

29 But he that shall blaspheme against the Holy Ghost hath never forgiveness, but is in danger of eternal damnation:

30 Because they said, He hath an unclean spirit.

WE all know how painful it is to have our conduct misunderstood and misrepresented, when we are doing right. It is a trial which our Lord Jesus Christ had to endure continually, all through His earthly ministry. We have an instance in the passage before us. The "Scribes which came down from Jerusalem" saw the miracles which He worked. They could not deny their reality. What then did they do? They accused our blessed Saviour of being in league and union with the devil. They said, "He hath Beelzebub, and by the prince of the devils casteth he out devils."

In our Lord's solemn answer to this wicked accusation, there are expressions which deserve special attention. Let us see what lessons they contain for our use.

We ought to notice, in the first place, *how great is the evil of dissensions and divisions.*

This is a lesson which is strongly brought out in the beginning of our Lord's reply to the scribes. He shows the absurdity of supposing that Satan would " cast out Satan," and so help to destroy his own power. He appeals to the notorious fact, which even his enemies must allow, that there can be no strength where there is division. " If a kingdom be divided against itself, that kingdom cannot stand."

This truth is one which does not receive sufficient consideration. On no point has the abuse of the right of private judgment produced so much evil. The divisions of Christians are one great cause of the weakness of the visible church. They often absorb energy, time, and power, which might have been well bestowed on better things. They furnish the infidel with a prime argument against the truth of Christianity. They help the devil. Satan indeed is the chief promoter of religious divisions. If he cannot extinguish Christianity, he labours to make Christians quarrel with one another, and to set every man's hand against his neighbour. None knows better than the devil, that " to divide is to conquer."

Let us resolve, so far as in us lies, to avoid all differences, dissensions, and disputes in religion. Let us loathe and abhor them as the plague of the churches. We cannot be too jealous about all saving truths. But it is easy to mistake morbid scrupulosity for conscientiousness, and zeal about mere trifles for zeal about the truth. Nothing justifies separation from a church but the separation of that church from the gospel. Let us be ready to concede much, and make many sacrifices for the sake of unity and peace.

We ought to notice, in the second place, *what a glorious declaration our Lord makes in these verses about the forgiveness of sins.* He says, " all sins shall be forgiven to the sons of men, and blasphemies wherewith soever they shall blaspheme."

These words fall lightly on the ears of many persons. They see no particular beauty in them. But to the man who is alive to his own sinfulness and deeply sensible of his need of mercy, these words are sweet and precious. " All sins shall be forgiven." The sins of youth and age,—the sins of head, and hand, and tongue, and imagination,— the sins against all God's commandments,—the sins of persecutors, like Saul,—the sins of idolaters, like Manasseh,—the sins of open enemies of Christ, like the Jews who crucified Him,—the sins of backsliders from Christ, like Peter,—all, all may be forgiven. The blood of Christ can cleanse all away. The righteousness of Christ can cover all, and hide all from God's eyes.

The doctrine here laid down is the crown and glory of the gospel. The very first thing it proposes to man is free pardon, full forgiveness, complete remission, without money and without price. " Through this man is preached unto you the forgiveness of sins ; and by Him all that believe are justified from all things." (Acts xiii. 39.)

Let us lay hold on this doctrine without delay, if we never received it before. It is for us, as well as for others.

We too, this very day, if we come to Christ, may be completely forgiven. "Though our sins have been as scarlet, they shall be white as snow." (Isaiah i. 18.)

Let us cleave firmly to this doctrine, if we have received it already. We may sometimes feel faint, and unworthy, and cast down. But if we have really come to Jesus by faith, our sins are clean forgiven. They are cast behind God's back,—blotted out of the book of His remembrance,—sunk into the depths of the sea. Let us believe and not be afraid.

We ought to notice, in the last place, that *it is possible for a man's soul to be lost for ever in hell.* The words of our Lord are distinct and express. He speaks of one who "hath never forgiveness, but is in danger of eternal damnation."

This is an awful truth, beyond doubt. But it is a truth, and we must not shut our eyes against it. We find it asserted over and over again in Scripture. Figures of all kinds are multiplied, and language of every sort is employed, in order to make it plain and unmistakeable. In short, if there is no such thing as "eternal damnation," we may throw the Bible aside, and say that words have no meaning at all.

We have great need to keep this awful truth steadily in view in these latter days. Teachers have risen up, who are openly attacking the doctrine of the eternity of punishment, or labouring hard to explain it away. Men's ears are being tickled with plausible sayings about "the love of God," and the impossibility of a loving God permitting an everlasting hell. The eternity of punishment is spoken of as a mere "speculative question," about which men may believe anything they please.—In the midst of all this flood of false doctrine, let us hold firmly the old truths. Let us not be ashamed to believe that there is an eternal God,—an eternal heaven,—and an eternal hell. Let us recollect that sin is an infinite evil. It needed an atonement of infinite value to deliver the believer from its consequences,—and it entails an infinite loss on the unbeliever who rejects the remedy provided for it. Above all, let us fall back on plain Scriptural statements, like that before us this day. One plain text is worth a thousand abstruse arguments.

Finally, if it be true that there is an "eternal damnation," let us give diligence that we ourselves do not fall into it. Let us escape for our lives and not linger. (Gen. xix. 16, 17.) Let us flee for refuge to the hope set before us in the Gospel, and never rest till we know and feel that we are safe. And never, never let us be ashamed of seeking safety. Of sin, worldliness, and the love of pleasure, we may well be ashamed. But we never need be ashamed of seeking to be delivered from an eternal hell.*

* There is an expression in the passage now expounded, which appears to demand special notice. It is confessedly one of the hard things of Scripture, and has often troubled the hearts of Bible-readers. I refer to the saying of our Lord, " He that blasphemeth against the Holy Ghost hath never forgiveness." It seems that there is such a thing as an *unpardonable sin.*

Some interpreters have endeavoured to cut the knot of the difficulty, by maintaining that the sin here referred to was entirely confined to the time when our Lord was on earth. They say that when the Scribes and Pharisees saw the evidence of our Lord's miracles, and yet refused to believe in Him as the Messiah, they committed the unpardonable sin. Their assertion that our Lord worked miracles through Beelzebub, was blasphemy against the Holy Ghost.

There might be something in this view, if the passage under consideration stood entirely alone,—though even then he would be

MARK III. 31—35.

31 There came then his brethren and his mother, and, standing without, sent unto him, calling him.

32 And the multitude sat about him, and they said unto him, Behold, thy mother and thy brethren without seek for thee.

33 And he answered them, saying,

Who is my mother, or my brethren?

34 And he looked round about on them which sat about him, and said, Behold my mother and my brethren!

35 For whosoever shall do the will of God, the same is my brother, and my sister, and mother.

In the verses which immediately precede this passage, we see our blessed Lord accused by the Scribes of being in league with the devil. They said, "he hath Beelzebub, and by the prince of the devils casteth he out devils."

In the verses we have now read, we find that this absurd charge of the Scribes was not all that Jesus had

a bold man who would assert that there were no hardened Scribes and Pharisees among the 3000 converted and forgiven on the day of Pentecost. But, unfortunately for this theory, the doctrine here laid down is to be found in other places of Scripture beside this. I allude of course to the well-known passages, Heb. vi. 4—6. Heb. x. 26., and 1 John v. 17. In all these places there seems a reference to a sin which is not forgiven.

What then is the unpardonable sin? It must be frankly confessed that its precise nature is nowhere defined in Holy Scripture. The most probable view is, that it is a combination of clear intellectual knowledge of the Gospel, with deliberate rejection of it, and wilful choice of sin. It is an union of light in the head, and hatred in the heart. Such was the case of Judas Iscariot. We must not flatter ourselves that none have walked in his steps. In the absence of any definition in Scripture, we shall probably not get much nearer to the mark than this. Yet even this view must be carefully handled. The limits which knowledge combined with unbelief must pass, in order to become the unpardonable sin, are graciously withheld from us. It is mercifully ordered of God, that man can never decide positively of any brother, that he has committed a sin which cannot be forgiven.

But although it is difficult to define what the unpardonable sin is, it is far less difficult to point out what it is not. A few words on this point may possibly help to relieve tender consciences.

We may lay it down as nearly certain, that those who are troubled with fears that they have sinned the unpardonable sin,

to endure at this time. We are told that "his brethren
and his mother came, and, standing without, sent unto
him, calling him." They could not yet understand the
beauty and usefulness of the life that our Lord was living.
Though they doubtless loved Him well, they would fain
have persuaded him to cease from His work, and "spare
himself." Little did they know what they were doing!
Little had they observed or understood our Lord's words
when He was only twelve years old, "wist ye not that I
must be about my Father's business?"* (Luke ii. 49.)

are the very people who have not sinned it. The very fact that
they are afraid and anxious about it, is the strongest possible
evidence in their favour. A troubled conscience,—an anxiety
about salvation, and a dread of being cast away,—a concern
about the next world, and a desire to escape from the wrath
of God,—will probably never be found in the heart of that
person, who has sinned the sin for which there is no forgiveness.
It is far more probable that the general marks of such a person
will be utter hardness of conscience,—a seared heart,—an absence
of any feeling,—a thorough insensibility to spiritual concern. The
subject may safely be left here. There is such a thing as a sin
which is never forgiven. But those who are troubled about it,
are most unlikely to have committed it.

The following quotation from Thomas Fuller deserves attention :
"The sin against the Holy Ghost is ever attended with these
two symptoms,—absence of all contrition, and of all desire of forgiveness. Now, if thou canst truly say that thy sins are a burden
to thee,—that thou dost desire forgiveness, and wouldst give anything to attain it, be of good comfort; thou hast not yet, and, by
God's grace, never shall commit that unpardonable offence. I
will not define how near thou hast been unto it. As David said to
Jonathan, 'there is but a step between me and death,'—so, may
be, thou hast missed it very narrowly; but assure thyself thou art
not as yet guilty thereof."—*Fuller's Cause and Cure of a Wounded
Conscience.*

* The remarks of Scott on the conduct of our Lord's mother on
this occasion, are worth quoting: " It is plain that many of these
intimations were suited, and doubtless prophetically intended, to
be a Scriptural protest against the idolatrous honour, to this day,
by vast multitudes, rendered to Mary the mother of Jesus. She

It is interesting to remark the quiet, firm perseverance of our Lord, in the face of all discouragements. None of these things moved Him. The slanderous suggestions of enemies, and the well-meant remonstrances of ignorant friends, were alike powerless to turn Him from His course. He had set His face as a flint towards the cross and the crown. He knew the work He had come into the world to do. He had a baptism to be baptized, and was straitened till it was accomplished. (Luke xii. 50.)

So let it be with all true servants of Christ. Let nothing turn them for a moment out of the narrow way, or make them stop and look back. Let them not heed the ill-natured remarks of enemies. Let them not give way to the well-intentioned but mistaken entreaties of unconverted relations and friends. Let them reply in the words of Nehemiah, "I am doing a great work and I cannot come down." (Neh. vi. 3.) Let them say, "I have taken up the cross, and I will not cast it away."

was, no doubt, an excellent and honourable character, but evidently not perfect. She is entitled to great estimation, and high veneration, but surely not to religious confidence and worship."

It is difficult to mention any doctrine more completely destitute of Scriptural foundation, than the Romish doctrine of the efficacy of the Virgin Mary's intercession, or the utility of addressing our prayers to her. As to the doctrine of the immaculate conception of the Virgin Mary, which has been lately accredited by the Romish Church, it is a mere man-made figment, without a single word of Scripture to support it. Holy and full of grace as the Virgin Mary was, it is plain that she regarded herself as one "born in sin," and needing a Saviour. We have her own remarkable words in evidence of this last point: "My spirit hath rejoiced in God my Saviour." (Luke i. 47.)

As to the opinion of the Fathers on the conduct of the mother of our Lord in this place, Whitby has collected some curious expressions:— "Theophylact taxes her with vain-glory and guilt, in endeavouring to draw Jesus from teaching the word. Tertullian pronounceth her guilty of incredulity,—Chrysostom of vain-glory, infirmity and madness, for this very thing."

We learn from these verses one mighty lesson. We learn, *who they are that are reckoned the relations of Jesus Christ.* They are they who are His disciples, and " do the will of God." Of such the great Head of the Church says, "the same is my brother, and sister, and mother."

How much there is in this single expression ! What a rich mine of consolation it opens to all true believers ! Who can conceive the depth of our Lord's love towards Mary the mother that bare Him, and on whose bosom He had been nursed ? Who can imagine the breadth of His love towards His brethren according to the flesh, with whom the tender years of His childhood had been spent ? Doubtless no heart ever had within it such deep well-springs of affection as the heart of Christ. Yet even He says, of all who " do the will of God," that each " is his brother, and sister, and mother."

Let all true Christians drink comfort out of these words. Let them know that there is One at least, who knows them, loves them, cares for them, and reckons them as His own family. What though they be poor in this world ? They have no cause to be ashamed, when they remember that they are the brethren and sisters of the Son of God.—What though they be persecuted and ill-treated in their own homes because of their religion ? They may remember the words of David, and apply them to their own case, " When my father and mother forsake me, then the Lord will take me up." (Psal. xxvii. 10.)

Finally, let all who persecute and ridicule others

because of their religion, take warning by these words,
and repent? Whom are they persecuting and ridiculing?
The relations of Jesus the Son of God! The family of
the King of kings and Lord of lords!—Surely they
would do wisely to hold their peace, and consider well
what they are doing. Those whom they persecute have
a mighty Friend: "Their redeemer is mighty; he shall
plead their cause." (Prov. xxiii. 11.)

MARK IV. 1—20.

1 And he began again to teach by the sea side: and there was gathered unto him a great multitude, so that he entered into a ship, and sat in the sea; and the whole multitude was by the sea on the land.

2 And he taught them many things by parables, and said unto them in his doctrine,

3 Hearken; Behold, there went out a sower to sow:

4 And it came to pass, as he sowed, some fell by the way side, and the fowls of the air came and devoured it up.

5 And some fell on stony ground, where it had not much earth; and immediately it sprang up, because it had no depth of earth:

6 But when the sun was up, it was scorched; and because it had no root, it withered away.

7 And some fell among thorns, and the thorns grew up, and choked it, and it yielded no fruit.

8 And other fell on good ground, and did yield fruit that sprang up and increased; and brought forth, some thirty, and some sixty, and some an hundred.

9 And he said unto them, He that hath ears to hear, let him hear.

10 And when he was alone, they that were about him with the twelve asked of him the parable.

11 And he said unto them, Unto you it is given to know the mystery of the kingdom of God: but unto them that are without, all *these* things are done in parables:

12 That seeing they may see, and not perceive; and hearing they may hear, and not understand; lest at any time they should be converted, and *their* sins should be forgiven them.

13 And he said unto them, Know ye not this parable? and how then will ye know all parables?

14 The sower soweth the word.

15 And these are they by the way side, where the word is sown; but when they have heard, Satan cometh immediately, and taketh away the word that was sown in their hearts.

16 And these are they likewise which are sown on stony ground; who, when they have heard the word, immediately receive it with gladness;

17 And have no root in themselves, and so endure but for a time: afterward, when affliction or persecution ariseth for the word's sake, immediately they are offended.

18 And these are they which are sown among thorns; such as hear the word,

19 And the cares of this world, and the deceitfulness of riches, and the lusts of other things entering in, choke the word, and it becometh unfruitful.

20 And these are they which are sown on good ground; such as hear the word, and receive *it*, and bring forth fruit, some thirty-fold, some sixty, and some an hundred.

THESE verses contain the parable of the sower. Of all the parables spoken by our Lord, none is probably so well-known as this. There is none which is so easily understood by all, from the gracious familiarity of the figures which it contains.* There is none which is of such universal and perpetual application. So long as there is a Church of Christ and a congregation of Christians, so long there will be employment for this parable.

The language of the parable requires no explanation. To use the words of an ancient writer, "it needs application, not exposition." Let us now see what it teaches.

We are taught, in the first place, *that there are some hearers of the Gospel, whose hearts are like the way-side in a field.*

These are they who hear sermons, but pay no attention to them. They go to a place of worship, for form, or fashion, or to appear respectable before men. But they take no interest whatever in the preaching. It seems to them a mere matter of words, and names, and unintelligible talk. It is neither money, nor meat, nor

* "Our Saviour borroweth his comparisons from easy and familiar things, such as the sower, the seed, the ground, the growth, the withering, the answering or failing of the sower's expectations, all of them things well known, and by all these would teach us some spiritual instruction. For there is no earthly thing, which is not fitted to put us in mind of some heavenly. Christ cannot look upon the sun, the wind, fire, water, a hen, a little grain of mustard seed,—nor upon ordinary occasions, as the penny given for the day's work, the wedding garment and ceremonies of the Jews about it, nor the waiting of servants at their master's table, or children asking bread and fish at their father's table, but he applies all to some special use of edification in grace.

Earthly things must remind us of heavenly. We must translate the book of nature into the book of grace."—*Thomas Taylor on the Parable of the Sower.* 1634.

drink, nor clothes, nor company;—and as they sit under
the sound if it, they are taken up with thinking of other
things. It matters nothing whether it is law or Gospel.
It produces no more effect on them than water on a
stone. And at the end they go away, knowing no more
than when they came in.

There are myriads of professing Christians in this state
of soul. There is hardly a church or chapel, where
scores of them are not to be found. Sunday after Sunday they allow the devil to catch away the good seed
that is sown on the face of their hearts. Week after
week they live on, without faith, or fear, or knowledge,
or grace,—feeling nothing, caring nothing, taking no more
interest in religion, than if Christ had never died on the
cross at all. And in this state they often die and are
buried, and are lost for ever in hell. This is a mournful
picture, but only too true.

We are taught, in the second place, *that there are
some hearers of the Gospel, whose hearts are like the stony
ground in a field.*

These are they on whom preaching produces temporary impressions, but no deep, lasting, and abiding
effect. They take pleasure in hearing sermons in which
the truth is faithfully set forth. They can speak with
apparent joy and enthusiasm about the sweetness of the
Gospel, and the happiness which they experience in listening to it. They can be moved to tears by the appeals of
preachers, and talk with apparent earnestness of their
own inward conflicts, hopes, struggles, desires, and fears.
But unhappily there is no stability about their religion.
" They have no root in themselves, and so endure but for

a time." There is no real work of the Holy Ghost within their hearts. Their impressions are like Jonah's gourd, which came up in a night and perished in a night. They fade as rapidly as they grow. No sooner does " affliction and persecution arise for the word's sake," than they fall away. Their goodness proves as " the morning cloud, and the early dew." (Hosea vi. 4.) Their religion has no more life in it than the cut flower. It has no root, and soon withers away.

There are many in every congregation which hears the Gospel, who are just in this state of soul. They are not careless and inattentive hearers, like many around them, and are therefore tempted to think well of their own condition. They feel a pleasure in the preaching to which they listen, and therefore flatter themselves they must have grace in their hearts. And yet they are thoroughly deceived. Old things have not yet passed away. There is no real work of conversion in their inward man. With all their feelings, affections, joys, hopes, and desires, they are actually on the high road to destruction.*

We are taught, in the third place, *that there are some hearers of the Gospel, whose hearts are like the thorny ground in a field.*

These are they who attend to the preaching of Christ's truth, and to a certain extent obey it. Their understanding assents to it. Their judgment approves of it.

* All who wish to understand the character of the " Stony-ground hearers," should study the treatise of Jonathan Edwards, on the Religious Affections. Few Christians, who have not looked into the subject, have any idea of the lengths to which a person may go in religious feelings, while he is at the same time utterly destitute of the grace of God.

Their conscience is affected by it. Their affections are in favour of it. They acknowledge that it is all right, and good, and worthy of all reception. They even abstain from many things which the Gospel condemns, and adopt many habits which the Gospel requires. But here unhappily they stop short. Something appears to chain them fast, and they never get beyond a certain point in their religion. And the grand secret of their condition is the world. "The cares of the world, and the deceitfulness of riches, and the lusts of other things," prevent the word having its full effect on their souls. With everything apparently that is promising and favourable in their spiritual state, they stand still. They never come up to the full standard of New Testament Christianity. They bring no fruit to perfection.

There are few faithful ministers of Christ who could not point to cases like these. Of all cases they are the most melancholy. To go so far and yet go no further,—to see so much and yet not see all,—to approve so much and yet not give Christ the heart, this is indeed most deplorable! And there is but one verdict that can be given about such people. Without a decided change they will never enter the kingdom of heaven. Christ will have all our hearts. "If any man will be a friend of the world, he is the enemy of God." (James iv. 4.)

We are taught in the last place, *that there are some hearers of the Gospel, whose hearts are like the good ground in a field.*

These are they who really receive Christ's truth into the bottom of their hearts, believe it implicitly, and obey it thoroughly. In these the fruits of that truth will be seen,—uniform, plain, and unmistakeable results in heart and life. Sin will be truly hated, mourned over, resisted, and renounced. Christ will be truly loved, trusted in, followed, loved, and obeyed. Holiness will show itself in all their conversation, in humility, spiritual-mindedness, patience, meekness, and charity. There will be something that can be seen. The true work of the Holy Ghost cannot be hid.

There will always be some persons in this state of soul, where the Gospel is faithfully preached. Their numbers may very likely be few, compared to the worldly around them. Their experience and degree of spiritual attainment may differ widely, some bringing forth thirty, some sixty, and some a hundred-fold. But the fruit of the seed falling into good ground will always be of the same kind. There will always be visible repentance, visible faith in Christ, and visible holiness of life. Without these things, there is no saving religion.

And now let us ask ourselves, What are we? Under which class of hearers ought we to be ranked? With what kind of hearts do we hear the word?—Never, never may we forget, that there are three ways of hearing without profit, and only one way of hearing aright! Never, never may we forget that there is only one infallible mark of being a right-hearted hearer! That mark is to bear fruit. To be without fruit, is to be in the way to hell.

MARK. IV. 21—25.

21 And he said unto them, Is a candle brought to be put under a | bushel, or under a bed? and not to be set on a candlestick?

22 For there is nothing hid, which shall not be manifested; neither was any thing kept secret, but that it should come abroad.

23 If any man have ears to hear, let him hear.

24 And he saith unto them, Take heed what ye hear: with what measure ye mete, it shall be measured to you: and unto you that hear shall more be given.

25 For he that hath, to him shall be given: and he that hath not, from him shall be taken even that which he hath.

THESE verses seem intended to enforce the parable of the sower on the attention of those who heard it. They are remarkable for the succession of short, pithy, proverbial sayings which they contain. Such sayings are eminently calculated to arrest an ignorant hearer. They often strike, and stick in the memory, when the main subject of the sermon is forgotten.*

We learn from these verses, *that we ought not only to receive knowledge, but to impart it to others.*

A candle is not lighted in order to be hidden and concealed, but to be set on a candlestick and used. Religious light is not given to a man for himself alone, but for the benefit of others. We are to try to spread and diffuse our knowledge. We are to display to others the precious treasure that we have found, and persuade them to seek it for themselves. We are to tell them of the

* The passage now under consideration is one among many proofs, that our Lord used the same words and the same ideas on many different occasions. The proverbial saying about the "candlestick under a bushel," will be found in the Sermon on the Mount. So also the saying, "there is nothing hid that shall not be manifested,"—and the saying, "with what measure ye mete, it shall be measured to you again,"—are both to be found in the Gospel of St. Matthew, but in both cases in an entirely different connexion from the passage in St. Mark now before us. (Matt. x. 26, and Matt. vii. 2.)

The subject is one that deserves attention. The needless difficulties that have been created by attempting to harmonize the Gospels, and to make out that our Lord never said the same thing more than once, are neither few nor small.

good news that we have heard, and endeavour to make them believe it and value it themselves.

We shall all have to give account of our use of knowledge one day. The books of God in the day of judgment will show what we have done. If we have buried our talent in the earth,—if we have been content with a lazy, idle, do-nothing Christianity, and cared nothing what happened to others, so long as we went to heaven ourselves,—there will be a fearful exposure at last : " There is nothing hid, which shall not be manifested."

It becomes all Christians to lay these things to heart. It is high time that the old tradition, that the clergy alone ought to teach and spread religious knowledge, should be exploded and cast aside for ever. To do good and diffuse light is a duty for which all members of Christ's Church are responsible, whether ministers or laymen. Neighbours ought to tell neighbours, if they have found an unfailing remedy in time of plague. Christians ought to tell others that they have found medicine for their souls, if they see them ignorant, and dying for want of it. What saith the apostle Peter ? " As every man hath received the gift, even so minister the same one to another." (1 Peter iv. 10.) They will be happy days for the Church when that text is obeyed.

We learn, in the second place, from these verses, *the importance of hearing, and of considering well what we hear.*

This is a point to which our Lord evidently attaches great weight. We have seen it already brought out in the parable of the sower. We see it here enforced in two remarkable expressions. "If any man have an ear to hear, let him hear." "Take heed what ye hear."

Hearing the truth is one principal avenue through which grace is conveyed to the soul of man. "Faith cometh by hearing." (Rom. x. 17.) One of the first steps towards conversion is to receive from the Spirit a hearing ear. Seldom are men brought to repentance and faith in Christ without "hearing." The general rule is that of which St. Paul reminds the Ephesians, " ye also trusted, after that ye heard the word of truth." (Eph. i. 13.)

Let us bear this in mind when we hear preaching decried as a means of grace. There are never wanting men who seek to cast it down from the high place which the Bible gives it. There are many who proclaim loudly that it is of far more importance to the soul to hear liturgical forms read, and to receive the Lord's Supper, than to hear God's word expounded. Of all such notions let us beware. Let it be a settled principle with us that "hearing the word," is one of the foremost means of grace that God has given to man. Let us give to every other means and ordinance its proper value and proportion. But never let us forget the words of St. Paul, " despise not prophecyings," and his dying charge to Timothy, " Preach the word." * (1 Thess. v. 20. 2 Tim. iv. 2.)

* " Public and continual preaching of God's word is the ordinary means and instrument of the salvation of mankind. St. Paul calleth it the ministry of reconciliation of man unto God. By preaching of God's word, the glory of God is enlarged, faith is nourished, and charity increased. By it the ignorant is instructed, the negligent exhorted and invited, the stubborn rebuked, the weak conscience comforted, and to all those that sin of malicious wickedness, the wrath of God is threatened. By preaching, due obedience to Christian princes and magistrates is planted in the hearts of subjects : for obedience proceedeth of conscience, conscience is grounded upon the word of God, the word of God

We learn, in the last place, from these verses, *the importance of a diligent use of religious privileges.* What says our Lord? " Unto you that hear shall more be given. He that hath, to him shall be given : and he that hath not, from him shall be taken even that which he hath."

This is a principle which we find continually brought forward in Scripture. All that believers have is undoubtedly of grace. Their repentance, faith, and holiness, are all the gift of God. But the degree to which a believer attains in grace, is ever set before us as closely connected with his own diligence in the use of means, and his own faithfulness in living fully up to the light and knowledge which he possesses. Indolence and laziness are always discouraged in God's word. Labour and pains in hearing, reading, and prayer, are always represented as bringing their own reward. " The soul of the diligent shall be made fat." (Prov. xiii. 4.) " An idle soul shall suffer hunger." (Prov. xix. 15.)

Attention to this great principle is the main secret of spiritual prosperity. The man who makes rapid progress in spiritual attainments,—who grows visibly in grace, and knowledge, and strength, and usefulness,—will always be found to be a diligent man. He leaves no stone unturned to promote his soul's well-doing. He is diligent over his Bible, diligent in his private devotions, diligent as a hearer of sermons, diligent in his attendance at the Lord's table. And he reaps according as he sows. Just

worketh his effect by preaching. So as generally when preaching wanteth obedience faileth."—*Archbishop Grindal's Letter to Queen Elizabeth.*

as the muscles of the body are strengthened by regular exercise, so are the graces of the soul increased by diligence in using them.

Do we wish to grow in grace? Do we desire to have stronger faith, brighter hope, and clearer knowledge? Beyond doubt we do, if we are true Christians. Then let us live fully up to our light, and improve every opportunity. Let us never forget our Lord's words in this passage. "With what measure we mete" to our souls, "it shall be measured to us again." The more we do for our souls, the more shall we find God does for them.

MARK IV. 26—29.

26 And he said, So is the kingdom of God, as if a man should cast seed into the ground;
27 And should sleep, and rise night and day, and the seed should spring and grow up, he knoweth not how.
28 For the earth bringeth forth fruit of herself; first the blade, then the ear, after that the full corn in the ear.
29 But when the fruit is brought forth, immediately he putteth in the sickle, because the harvest is come.

THE parable contained in these verses is short, and only recorded in St. Mark's Gospel. But it is one that ought to be deeply interesting to all who have reason to hope that they are true Christians. It sets before us the history of the work of grace in an individual soul. It summons us to an examination of our own experience in divine things.

There are some expressions in the parable which we must not press too far. Such are the "sleeping and rising" of the husband-man, and the "night and day." In this, as in many of our Lord's parables, we must carefully keep in view the main scope and object of the whole story, and not lay too much stress on lesser points. In the case before us the main thing taught is the close resemblance between some familiar operations in the culture of corn, and the work of grace in the heart. To this let us rigidly confine our attention.

We are taught firstly, that, as in the growth of corn, so in the work of grace, *there must be a sower*.

The earth, as we all know, never brings forth corn of itself. It is a mother of weeds, but not of wheat. The hand of man must plough it, and scatter the seed, or else there would never be a harvest.

The heart of man, in like manner, will never of itself turn to God, repent, believe, and obey. It is utterly barren of grace. It is entirely dead towards God, and unable to give itself spiritual life. The Son of man must break it up by His Spirit, and give it a new nature. He must scatter over it by the hand of His labouring ministers the good seed of the word.

Let us mark this truth well. Grace in the heart of man is an exotic. It is a new principle from without, sent down from heaven and implanted in his soul. Left to himself no man living would ever seek God. And yet in communicating grace, God ordinarily works by means. To despise the instrumentality of teachers and preachers, is to expect corn where no seed has been sown.

We are taught, secondly, that, as in the growth of corn, so in the work of grace, *there is much that is beyond man's comprehension and control*.

The wisest farmer on earth can never explain all that takes place in a grain of wheat, when he has sown it. He knows the broad fact that unless he puts it into the land, and covers it up, there will not be an ear of corn in time of harvest. But he cannot command the prosperity of each grain. He cannot explain why some grains come up and others die. He cannot specify the hour or the minute when life shall begin to show itself. He cannot define what that life is. These are matters he must leave alone. He sows his seed, and leaves the growth to God. "God giveth the increase."* (1 Cor. iii. 7.)

The workings of grace in the heart in like manner, are utterly mysterious and unsearchable. We cannot explain why the word produces effects on one person in a congregation, and not upon another. We cannot explain why, in some cases,—with every possible advantage, and in spite of every entreaty,—people reject the word, and continue dead in trespasses and sins. We cannot explain why in other cases,—with every possible difficulty, and with no encouragement,—people are born again, and become decided Christians. We cannot define the manner in which the Spirit of God conveys life to a soul, and the exact process by which a believer receives a new nature. All these are hidden things to us. We see certain results, but we can go no further. "The

* "A grain of corn, committed to the ground by the hand of man, will sprout and shoot ; the shoot will disclose the stem, the stem the ear, and the ear the fruit : and were the most illiterate and unphilosophical person to be asked why all this should necessarily follow from the mere act of burying a seed in the earth, he might be disposed to laugh at the apparent simplicity of the question. Yet no human wisdom was ever able to return the answer to this question,—no human sagacity ever yet could penetrate into the true causes of this effect ; and no human knowledge, upon such subjects, has ever gone further than the mere discovery, by a regular and constant experience, that such and such consequences will uniformly follow from such and such previous acts."—*Greswell on the Parables. Vol.* 2 ; *p.* 132.

wind bloweth where it listeth, and thou hearest the
sound thereof, but canst not tell whence it cometh, and
whither it goeth : so is every one that is born of the
Spirit." (John iii. 10.)

Let us mark this truth also, for it is deeply instructive.
It is humbling no doubt to ministers, and teachers of
others. The highest abilities, the most powerful preaching, the most diligent working, cannot command success.
God alone can give life. But it is a truth at the same
time, which supplies an admirable antidote to over-
carefulness and despondency. Our principal work is to
sow the seed. That done, we may wait with faith and
patience for the result. "We may sleep, and rise night
and day," and leave our work with the Lord. He alone
can, and, if He thinks fit, He will give success.

We are taught, thirdly, that, as in the growth of corn,
so in the work of grace, *life manifests itself gradually*.

There is a true proverb which says, "Nature does
nothing at a bound." The ripe ear of wheat does not
appear at once, as soon as the seed bursts forth into life.
The plant goes through many stages, before it arrives at
perfection,—"first the blade, then the ear, then the full
corn in the ear." But in all these stages one great thing
is true about it,—even at its weakest, it is a living plant.

The work of grace, in like manner, goes on in the heart
by degrees. The children of God are not born perfect
in faith, or hope, or knowledge, or experience. Their beginning is generally a "day of small things." They see
in part their own sinfulness, and Christ's fulness, and the
beauty of holiness. But for all that, the weakest child
in God's family is a true child of God. With all his

weakness and infirmity he is alive. The seed of grace has really come up in his heart, though at present it be only in the blade. He is " alive from the dead." And the wise man says, " a living dog is better than a dead lion." (Eccles. ix. 4.)

Let us mark this truth also, for it is full of consolation. Let us not despise grace, because it is weak, or think people are not converted, because they are not yet as strong in the faith as St. Paul. Let us remember that grace, like everything else, must have a beginning. The mightiest oak was once an acorn. The strongest man was once a babe. Better a thousand times have grace in the blade than no grace at all.

We are taught, lastly, that, as in the growth of corn, so in the work of grace, *there is no harvest till the seed is ripe.*

No farmer thinks of cutting his wheat when it is green. He waits till the sun, and rain, and heat, and cold, have done their appointed work, and the golden ears hang down. Then, and not till then, he puts in the sickle, and gathers the wheat into his barn.

God deals with His work of grace exactly in the same way. He never removes His people from this world till they are ripe and ready. He never takes them away till their work is done. They never die at the wrong time, however mysterious their deaths appear sometimes to man. Josiah, and James the brother of John were both cut off in the midst of usefulness. Our own King Edward the Sixth was not allowed to reach man's estate. But we shall see in the resurrection morning that there was a needs-be. All was done well about their deaths, as well as about their births. The Great Husbandman never cuts His corn till it is ripe.

Let us leave the parable with this truth on our minds, and take comfort about the death of every believer. Let us rest satisfied, that there is no chance, no accident, no mistake about the decease of any of God's children. They are all " God's husbandry," and God knows best when they are ready for the harvest.

MARK IV. 30—34.

30 And he said, Whereunto shall we liken the kingdom of God? or with what comparison shall we compare it?

31 *It is* like a grain of mustard seed, which, when it is sown in the earth, is less than all the seeds that be in the earth:

32 But when it is sown, it groweth up, and becometh greater than all herbs, and shooteth out great branch-es; so that the fowls of the air may lodge under the shadow of it.

33 And with many such parables spake he the word unto them, as they were able to hear *it*.

34 But without a parable spake he not unto them: and when they were alone, he expounded all things to his disciples.

THE parable of the mustard seed is one of those parables which partake of the character both of history and prophecy. It seems intended to illustrate the history of Christ's visible church on earth, from the time of the first advent down to the judgment day. The seed cast into the earth, in the preceding parable, showed us the work of grace in a heart. The mustard seed shows us the progress of professing Christianity in the world.

We learn, in the first place, that, like the grain of mustard seed, *Christ's visible church was to be small and weak in its beginnings.*

A grain of mustard seed was a proverbial expression among the Jews for something very small and insignificant. Our Lord calls it "less than all the seeds that be in the earth." Twice in the Gospels we find our Lord using the figure as a word of comparison, when speaking of a weak faith. (Matt. xvii. 20. Luke xvii. 6.) The idea was doubtless familiar to a Jewish mind, however strange it may sound to us. Here, as in other places, the Son of God shows us the wisdom of using language familiar to the minds of those whom we address.

It would be difficult to find an emblem which more faithfully represents the history of the visible church of Christ, than this grain of mustard seed.

Weakness and apparent insignificance were undoubtedly the characteristics of its beginning. How did its Head and King come into the world? He came as a feeble infant, born in a manger at Bethlehem, without riches, or armies, or attendants, or power.—Who were the men that the Head of the Church gathered round Himself, and appointed His apostles? They were poor and unlearned persons,—fishermen, publicans, and men of like occupations, to all appearance the most unlikely people to shake the world.—What was the last public act of the earthly ministry of the great Head of the Church? He was crucified, like a malefactor, between two thieves, after having been forsaken by nearly all His disciples, betrayed by one, and denied by another.—What was the doctrine which the first builders of the Church went forth from the upper chamber in Jerusalem to preach to mankind? It was a doctrine which to the Jews was a stumbling-block, and to the Greeks foolishness. It was a proclamation that the great Head of their new religion had been put to death on a cross, and that notwithstanding this, they offered life through His death to the world!—In all this the mind of man can perceive nothing but weakness and feebleness. Truly the emblem of the grain of mustard seed was verified and fulfilled to the very letter. To the eyes of man the beginning of the visible church was contemptible, insignificant, powerless, and small.

We learn, in the second place, that, like the mustard seed, *the visible church, once planted, was to grow and greatly increase.*

"The grain of mustard seed," says our Lord, "when it is sown, groweth up and becometh greater than all herbs." These words may sound startling to an English ear. We are not accustomed to such a growth in our cold northern climate. But to those who know eastern countries, there is nothing surprising in it. The testimony of well-informed and experienced travellers is distinct, that such an increase is both possible and probable.*

No figure could be chosen more strikingly applicable to the growth and increase of Christ's visible church in the world. It began to grow from the day of Pentecost, and grew with a rapidity, which nothing can account for but the finger of God. It grew wonderfully when three

* To show the size to which the mustard plant will grow in Eastern Countries, Lightfoot quotes the following passage from Rabbinical writers. "There was a stalk of mustard in Sichim, from which sprang out three boughs, one of which was broken off, and covered the tent of a potter, and produced three cabs of mustard." Rabbi Simeon Ben Chalaphta said, "a stalk of mustard seed was in my field, into which I was wont to climb, as men are wont to climb into a fig-tree."

The enormous size to which the rhododendron, the heath, and the fern will grow, in some climates which suit them, better than ours, should be remembered by an English reader of this parable.

thousand souls were converted at once, and five thousand
more in a few days afterwards. It grew wonderfully,
when at Antioch, and Ephesus, and Philippi, and Corinth,
and Rome, congregations were gathered together, and
Christianity firmly established. It grew wonderfully,
when at last the despised religion of Christ overspread
the greater part of Europe, and Asia Minor, and North
Africa, and, in spite of fierce persecution and opposition,
supplanted heathen idolatry, and became the professed
creed of the whole Roman empire. Such growth must
have been marvellous in the eyes of many. But it was
only what our Lord foretold in the parable before us.
"The kingdom of God is like a grain of mustard seed."

The visible church of Christ has not yet done growing.
Notwithstanding the melancholy apostasy of some of its
branches, and the deplorable weakness of others, it is still
extending and expanding over the world. New branches
have continually been springing up in America, in India,
in Australia, in Africa, in China, in the Islands of the
South Seas, during the last fifty years. Evils undoubtedly there are many. False profession and corruption abound. But still, on the whole, heathenism is
waning, wearing out, and melting away. In spite of all
the predictions of Voltaire and Payne, in spite of foes
without and treachery within, the visible church pro-
gresses,—the mustard plant still grows.

And the prophecy, we may rest assured, is not yet
exhausted. A day shall yet come, when the great Head
of the church shall take to Himself His power, and
reign, and put down every enemy under His feet. The
earth shall yet be filled with the knowledge of God, as

the waters cover the sea. (Isai. ii. 2.) Satan shall yet be bound. The heathen shall yet be our Lord's inheritance, and the utmost parts of the earth His possession. And then this parable shall receive its full accomplishment. The little seed shall become " a great tree," and fill the whole earth. (Dan. iii. 35.)

Let us leave the parable with a resolution never to despise any movement or instrumentality in the church of Christ, because at first it is weak and small. Let us remember the manger of Bethlehem, and learn wisdom. The name of Him who lay there, a helpless infant, is now known all over the globe. The little seed which was planted in the day when Jesus was born, has become a great tree, and we ourselves are rejoicing under its shadow. Let it be a settled principle in our religion, never to " despise the day of small things." (Zech. iv. 10.) One child may be the beginning of a flourishing school, —one conversion the beginning of a mighty church,— one word the beginning of some blessed christian enterprise,—one seed the beginning of a rich harvest of saved souls.*

* It is fair to say that the view which I have adopted of the meaning of this parable, is not the view which is held by some interpreters.

Some think that the parable is intended to show the progress of the work of grace in the heart of an individual believer. I am not prepared to say that this may not have been in our Lord's mind, in speaking the parable. I think it quite possible that the parable admits of a double interpretation; for the experience of a believer and the experience of the whole church, are much the same. My principal objection to this view is, that it does not appear to suit the language of the parable so well as that which I have maintained.

Some few interpreters think that the mustard seed signifies the principle of evil and corruption, and that the main object of the

MARK IV. 35—41.

35 And the same day, when the even was come, he saith unto them, Let us pass over unto the other side.

36 And when they had sent away the multitude, they took him even as he was in the ship. And there were also with him other little ships.

37 And there arose a great storm of wind, and the waves beat into the ship, so that it was now full.

38 And he was in the hinder part of the ship, asleep on a pillow: and they awake him, and say unto him,

Master, carest thou not that we perish?

39 And he arose, and rebuked the wind, and said unto the sea, Peace, be still. And the wind ceased, and there was a great calm.

40 And he said unto them, Why are ye so fearful? how is it that ye have no faith?

41 And they feared exceedingly, and said one to another, What manner of man is this, that even the wind and the sea obey him?

THESE verses describe a storm on the sea of Galilee, when our Lord and His disciples were crossing it, and a miracle performed by our Lord in calming the storm in a moment. Few miracles recorded in the Gospel were so likely to strike the minds of the disciples as this. Four of them at least were fishermen. Peter, Andrew, James, and John, had probably known the sea of Galilee, and its storms, from their youth. Few events in our Lord's

parable is to show how insidiously apostasy would begin in the church, and how completely it would at last overgrow and fill the whole body. I own that I cannot for a moment see the soundness of this interpretation. To say nothing of other reasons, there seems an excessive harshness in this sense, when we consider the opening words of the parable, "Wherewith shall we liken the kingdom of God?" One would rather expect the question to have been "wherewith shall we liken the kingdom of the devil?" if the whole parable is occupied with describing the progress of evil.

I confess that I think the meaning of "the fowls of the air," is a point which admits of some question. Many think that it signifies the number of converts to Christianity, who as the church increased, joined themselves to it, and came " as doves to the windows." (Isaiah lx. 8.) Some think that it signifies the number of worldly and false professors who joined the church from mere carnal motives, when it began to be great and prosperous, as in the days of Constantine. When we remember that the "fowls of the air," in the parable of the sower, (Mark. iv. 4—15.) are declared by our Lord Himself to mean "Satan," we must admit that there is considerable force in this interpretation.

journeyings to and fro upon earth, contain more rich instruction than the one related in this passage.

Let us learn, in the first place, *that Christ's service does not exempt His servants from storms.* Here were the twelve disciples in the path of duty. They were obediently following Jesus, wherever He went. They were daily attending on His ministry, and hearkening to His word. They were daily testifying to the world, that, whatever Scribes and Pharisees might think, they believed on Jesus, loved Jesus, and were not ashamed to give up all for His sake. Yet here we see these men in trouble, tossed up and down by a tempest, and in danger of being drowned.

Let us mark well this lesson. If we are true Christians, we must not expect everything smooth in our journey to heaven. We must count it no strange thing, if we have to endure sicknesses, losses, bereavements, and disappointments, just like other men. Free pardon and full forgiveness, grace by the way and glory at the end,—all this our Saviour has promised to give. But He has never promised that we shall have no afflictions. He loves us too well to promise that. By affliction He teaches us many precious lessons, which without it we should never learn. By affliction He shows us our emptiness and weakness, draws us to the throne of grace, purifies our affections, weans us from the world, makes us long for heaven. In the resurrection morning we shall all say, "it is good for me that I was afflicted." We shall thank God for every storm.

Let us learn, in the second place, *that our Lord Jesus Christ was really and truly man.* We are told in these verses, that when the storm began, and the waves beat over the ship, he was in the hinder part "asleep." He had a body exactly like our own,—a body that could hunger, and thirst, and feel pain, and be weary, and need rest. No wonder that His body needed repose at this time. He had been diligent in His Father's business all the day. He had been preaching to a great multitude in the open air. No wonder that " when the even was come," and His work finished, he fell "asleep."

Let us mark this lesson also attentively. The Saviour in whom we are bid to trust, is as really man as He is God. He knows the trials of a man, for He has experienced them. He knows the bodily infirmities of a man, for He has felt them. He can well understand what we mean, when we cry to Him for help in this world of need. He is just the very Saviour that men and women, with weary frames and aching heads, in a weary world, require for their comfort every morning and night. "We have not an high priest which cannot be touched with the feeling of our infirmities." (Heb. iv. 15.)

Let us learn, in the third place, *that our Lord Jesus Christ, as God, has almighty power.* We see Him in these verses doing that which is proverbially impossible. He speaks to the winds, and they obey Him. He speaks to the waves, and they submit to His command. He turns the raging storm into a calm with a few words,— "Peace, be still." Those words were the words of Him who first created all things. The elements knew the voice of their Master, and, like obedient servants, were quiet at once.

Let us mark this lesson also, and lay it up in our minds. With the Lord Jesus Christ nothing is impossible. No stormy passions are so strong but He can tame them. No temper is so rough and violent but He can change it. No conscience is so disquieted, but He can speak peace to it, and make it calm. No man ever need despair, if He will only bow down his pride, and come as a humbled sinner to Christ. Christ can do miracles upon his heart.—No man ever need despair of reaching his journey's end, if he has once committed his soul to Christ's keeping. Christ will carry him through every danger. Christ will make him conqueror over every foe.—What though our relations oppose us? What though our neighbours laugh us to scorn? What though our place be hard? What though our temptations be great? It is all nothing, if Christ is on our side, and we are in the ship with Him. Greater is He that is for us, than all they that are against us.

Finally, we learn from this passage, *that our Lord Jesus Christ is exceedingly patient and pitiful in dealing with His own people.* We see the disciples on this occasion showing great want of faith, and giving way to most unseemly fears. They forgot their Master's miracles and care for them in days gone by. They thought of nothing but their present peril. They awoke our Lord hastily, and cried, " carest thou not that we perish? " We see our Lord dealing most gently and tenderly with them. He gives them no sharp reproof. He makes no threat of casting them off, because of their unbelief. He.

simply asks the touching question, " Why are ye so fearful ? How is it that ye have no faith ? "

Let us mark well this lesson. The Lord Jesus is
very pitiful and of tender mercy. " As a father pitieth
his children, even so the Lord pitieth them that fear
Him." (Psalm ciii. 13.) He does not deal with believers according to their sins, nor reward them according to their iniquities. He sees their weakness. He
is aware of their short-comings. He knows all the
defects of their faith, and hope, and love, and courage.
And yet He will not cast them off. He bears with them
continually. He loves them even to the end. He raises
them when they fall. He restores them when they err.
His patience, like His love, is a patience that passeth
knowledge. When He sees a heart right, it is His
glory to pass over many a short-coming.

Let us leave these verses with the comfortable recollection that Jesus is not changed. His heart is still
the same that it was when He crossed the sea of Galilee
and stilled the storm. High in heaven at the right hand
of God, Jesus is still sympathizing,—still almighty,—still
pitiful and patient towards His people.—Let us be more
charitable and patient towards our brethren in the faith.
They may err in many things, but if Jesus has received
them and can bear with them, surely we may bear with
them too.—Let us be more hopeful about ourselves.
We may be very weak, and frail, and unstable ; but if
we can truly say that we do come to Christ and believe
on Him, we may take comfort. The question for conscience to answer is not, "Are we like the angels ? are

we perfect as we shall be in heaven?" The question is, "Are we real and true in our approaches to Christ? Do we truly repent and believe?"*

MARK V. 1—17.

1 And they came over unto the other side of the sea, into the country of the Gadarenes.

2 And when he was come out of the ship, immediately there met him out of the tombs a man with an unclean spirit,

3 Who had *his* dwelling among the tombs; and no man could bind him, no, not with chains:

4 Because that he had been often bound with fetters and chains, and the chains had been plucked asunder by him, and the fetters broken in pieces: neither could any *man* tame him.

5 And always, night and day, he was in the mountains, and in the tombs, crying, and cutting himself with stones.

6 But when he saw Jesus afar off, he ran and worshipped him,

7 And cried with a loud voice, and said, What have I to do with thee, Jesus, *thou* Son of the most high God? I adjure thee by God, that thou torment me not.

8 For he said unto him, Come out of the man, *thou* unclean spirit.

9 And he asked him, What *is* thy name? And he answered, saying, My name *is* legion: for we are many.

10 And he besought him much that he would not send them away out of the country.

11 Now there was there nigh unto the mountains a great herd of swine feeding.

12 And all the devils besought him, saying, Send us into the swine, that we may enter into them.

13 And forthwith Jesus gave them leave. And the unclean spirits went out, and entered into the swine: and the herd ran violently down a steep place into the sea, (they were about two thousand;) and were choked in the sea.

14 And they that fed the swine fled, and told *it* in the city, and in the country. And they went out to see what it was that was done.

15 And they come to Jesus, and see him that was possessed with the devil, and had the legion, sitting, and clothed, and in his right mind: and they were afraid.

16 And they that saw *it* told them how it befel to him that was possessed with the devil, and *also* concerning the swine.

17 And they began to pray him to depart out of their coasts.

THESE verses describe one of those mysterious miracles which the gospels frequently record,—the casting out of a devil. Of all the cases of this kind in the New Testa-

---

* The sea of Galilee, or Tiberias, on which the circumstances recorded in this passage, took place, is an inland lake, through which the river Jordan flows, about fifteen miles long and six broad. It lies in a deep valley, much depressed below the level of the sea,—its surface being 652 feet below that of the Mediterranean,—and is surrounded on most sides by steep

ment, none is so fully described as this one. Of all the three evangelists who relate the history, none gives it so fully and minutely as St. Mark.

We see, in the first place, in these verses, *that the possession of a man's body by the devil, was a real and true thing in the time of our Lord's earthly ministry.*

It is a painful fact, that there are never wanting professing Christians who try to explain away our Lord's miracles. They endeavour to account for them by natural causes, and to show that they were not worked by any extraordinary power. Of all miracles, there are none which they assault so strenuously as the casting out of devils. They do not scruple to deny Satanic possession entirely. They tell us that it was nothing more than lunacy, or frenzy, or epilepsy, and that the idea of the devil inhabiting a man's body is absurd.

The best and simplest answer to such sceptical ob-

hills.   Owing to these last circumstances, sudden squalls or storms are reported by all travellers to be very common on the lake.

The sea of Galilee and the country surrounding it, were favoured with more of our blessed Lord's presence, during His earthly ministry, than any other part of Palestine.   Capernaum, Tiberias, Bethsaida, and the country of the Gergesenes were all on its shores, or in the immediate neighbourhood of this lake.   It was on the sea of Galilee that our Lord walked.   It was on its shore that He appeared to His disciples after His resurrection.   Sitting in a boat on its waters and in a house hard by, He delivered the seven parables recorded in the 13th chapter of St. Matthew.   On its banks, He called Peter, and Andrew, James and John.   From it, He commanded His disciples to draw the miraculous draught of fishes.   Within sight of it, He twice fed the multitude with a few loaves and fishes.   On its shore, He healed the man possessed with devils; and into it the two thousand swine plunged headlong after that miracle had been wrought.

Few localities in the Holy Land were so immediately connected with our Lord's ministry as the sea of Galilee and the country round it.

jections, is a reference to the plain narratives of the Gospels, and especially to the one before us at this moment. The facts here detailed are utterly inexplicable, if we do not believe Satanic possession. It is notorious that lunacy, and frenzy, and epilepsy are not infectious complaints, and at any rate cannot be communicated to a herd of swine! And yet men ask us to believe, that as soon as this man was healed, two thousand swine ran violently down a steep place into the sea, from a sudden impulse, without any apparent cause to account for their so doing! Such reasoning is the height of credulity. When men can satisfy themselves with such explanations, they are in a pitiable state of mind.

Let us beware of a sceptical and incredulous spirit in all matters relating to the devil. No doubt there is much in the subject of Satanic possession which we do not understand, and cannot explain. But let us not therefore refuse to believe it. The Eastern king who would not believe in the possibility of ice, because he lived in a hot country, and had never seen it, was not more foolish than the man who refuses to believe in Satanic possession, because he never saw a case himself, and cannot understand it. We may be sure, that upon the subject of the devil and his power, we are far more likely to believe too little than too much. Unbelief about the existence and personality of Satan, has often proved the first step to unbelief about God.

We see, in the second place, in these verses, *what an awfully cruel, powerful, and malicious being Satan is.* On all these three points, the passage before us is full of instruction.

The *cruelty* of Satan appears in the miserable condition of the unhappy man, of whose body he had possession. We read that he dwelt "among the tombs," that "no man could bind him, no, not with chains,"—that no man could tame him,—and that he was "always night and day in the mountains, and in the tombs, crying, and cutting himself with stones," naked, and without clothing. Such is the state to which the devil would bring us all, if he only had the power. He would rejoice to inflict upon us the utmost misery, both of body and mind. Cases like this are faint types of the miseries of hell.

The *power* of Satan appears in the awful words which the unclean spirit used, when our Lord asked, "What is thy name?" He answered, saying, "My name is Legion : for we are many." We probably have not the faintest idea of the number, subtlety, and activity of Satan's agents. We forget that he is king over an enormous host of subordinate spirits who do his will. We should probably find, if our eyes were opened to see spirits, that they are about our path, and about our bed, and observing all our ways, to an extent of which we have no conception. In private and in public, in church and in the world, there are busy enemies ever near us, of whose presence we are not aware.

The *malice* of Satan appears in the strange petition, "send us into the swine." Cast forth from the man, whose body they had so long inhabited and possessed, they still thirsted to do mischief. Unable to injure any more an immortal soul, they desired leave to injure the dumb beasts which were feeding near. Such is the true character of Satan. It is the bent of his nature to do harm, to kill, and to destroy. No wonder that he is called Apollyon, the destroyer.

Let us beware of giving way to the senseless habit of jesting about the devil. It is a habit which furnishes awful evidence of the blindness and corruption of human nature, and one which is far too common. When it is seemly in the condemned criminal to jest about his executioner, then, and not till then, it will be seemly for mortal man to talk lightly about Satan. Well would it be for us all, if we strove more to realize the power and presence of our great spiritual enemy, and prayed more to be delivered from him. It was a true saying of an eminent Christian, now gone to rest, "No prayer is complete which does not contain a petition to be kept from the devil."

We see, in the last place, from these verses, *how complete is our Lord's power and authority over the devil.* We see it in the cry of the unclean spirit, "I adjure thee by God, that thou torment me not." We see it in the command, "Come out of the man, thou unclean spirit," and the immediate obedience that followed. We see it in the blessed change that at once took place in him that was possessed: he was found "sitting, and clothed, and in his right mind." We see it in the petition of all the devils,—"send us into the swine," confessing their consciousness that they could do nothing without leave. All these things show that one mightier than Satan was there. Strong as the great enemy of man was, he was in the presence of One stronger than he. Numerous as his hosts were, he was confronted with One who could command more than twelve legions of angels. "Where the word of the king is, there is power." (Eccles. viii. 4.)

The truth here taught is full of strong consolation for all true Christians. We live in a world full of difficulties and snares. We are ourselves weak and compassed with infirmity. The awful thought that we have a mighty spiritual enemy ever near us, subtle, powerful, and malicious as Satan is, might well disquiet us, and cast us down. But, thanks be unto God, we have in Jesus an almighty Friend, who is "able to save us to the uttermost." He has already triumphed over Satan on the cross. He will ever triumph over him in the hearts of all believers, and intercede for them that their faith fail not. And He will finally triumph over Satan completely, when He shall come forth at the second advent, and bind him in the bottomless pit.

And now, Are we ourselves delivered from Satan's power? This after all is the grand question that concerns our souls.—He still reigns and rules in the hearts of all who are children of disobedience. (Ephes. ii. 3.) He is still a king over the ungodly. Have we, by grace, broken his bonds, and escaped his hand? Have we really renounced him and all his works? Do we daily resist him and make him flee? Do we put on the whole armour of God and stand against his wiles? May we never rest till we can give satisfactory answers to these questions.*

* The whole subject of the demoniacs, or cases of Satanic possession recorded in the New Testament, is unquestionably full of deep mystery. The miserable sufferings of the unhappy people possessed,—their clear knowledge that our Lord was the Son of God, — their double consciousness, sometimes the spirit speaking, sometimes the man,—all these are deep mysteries. And it can hardly be otherwise. We know little of beings that we cannot see and touch. We know nothing of the manner in which a spirit

MARK V. 18—20.

18 And when he was come into the ship, he that had been possessed with the devil prayed him that he might be with him.

19 Howbeit Jesus suffered him not, but saith unto him, Go home to thy friends, and tell them how great things the Lord hath done for thee, and hath had compassion on thee.

20 And he departed, and began to publish in Decapolis how great things Jesus had done for him : and all *men* did marvel.

THE after-conduct of those whom our Lord Jesus Christ healed and cured when upon earth, is a thing which is not often related in the Gospels. The story often describes the miraculous cure, and then leaves the after history of the person cured in obscurity, and passes on to other things.

But there are some deeply interesting cases, in which the after-conduct of persons cured is described ; and the

operates on the mind of a creature with flesh and bones like ourselves. We can see plainly that there were many persons possessed with devils during our Lord's earthly ministry. We can see plainly that bodily possession was something distinct from possession of heart and soul. We can conjecture the reason of their permitted possession,—to make it plain that our Lord came to destroy the works of the devil. But we must stop here. We can go no further.

Let us, however, beware of supposing that Satanic possession was entirely confined to our Lord's time, and that there is no such thing in our own days. This would be a rash and unwarrantable conclusion. Awful as the thought is, there are sometimes cases in asylums for the insane, which, if they are not cases of Satanic possession, approach as nearly to it as possible.—In short I believe the opinion of not a few eminent physicians is clear and decided that Satanic possession still continues, though cases are exceedingly rare.

Of course it would be presumption to handle so fearful a doctrine lightly, and to pronounce positively of any particular person that "he had a devil." But if such things have been,—and the New Testament puts this beyond question,—no good reason can be assigned why they should not be again. Human nature is not changed since our Lord was on earth. Satan is not yet bound. Satanic possession is therefore neither impossible nor improbable, though limits may be set to the frequency of it, through the mercy of God.

man from whom the devil was cast out in the country of the Gadarenes is one. The verses before us tell the story. Few as they are, they are full of precious instruction.

We learn from these verses, that *the Lord Jesus knows better than His people, what is the right position for them to be in.* We are told that when our Lord was on the point of leaving the country of the Gadarenes, the man " that had been possessed with the devil, prayed him that he might be with him." We can well understand that request. He felt grateful for the blessed change that had taken place in himself. He felt full of love towards his Deliverer. He thought he could not do better than follow our Lord, and go with Him as His companion and disciple. He was ready to give up home and country, and go after Christ. And yet, strange as it appears at first sight, the request was refused. "Jesus suffered him not." Our Lord had other work for him to do. Our Lord saw better than he did in what way he could glorify God most. " Go home to thy friends," He says, "and tell them how great things the Lord hath done for thee, and hath had compassion on thee."

There are lessons of profound wisdom in these words. The place that Christians wish to be in, is not always the place which is best for their souls. The position that they would choose, if they could have their own way, is not always that which Jesus would have them occupy.

There are none who need this lesson so much as believers newly converted to God. Such persons are often very poor judges of what is really for their good. Full of the new views which they have been graciously taught, excited with the novelty of their present position, seeing everything around them in a new light, knowing little yet of the depths of Satan and the weakness of their own hearts,—knowing only that a little time ago they were blind, and now, through mercy, they see,—of all people they are in the greatest danger of making mistakes. With the best intentions, they are apt to fall into mistakes about their plans in life, their choices, their moves, their professions. They forget that what we like best is not always best for our souls, and that the seed of grace needs winter as well as summer, cold as well as heat, to ripen it for glory.

Let us pray that God would guide us in all our ways after conversion, and not allow us to err in our choices, or to make hasty decisions. That place and position is most healthful for us in which we are kept most humble,—most taught our own sinfulness,—drawn most to the Bible and prayer,—led most to live by faith and not by sight. It may not be quite what we like. But if Christ by His providence has placed us in it, let us not be in a hurry to leave it. Let us therein abide with God. The great thing is to have no will of our own, and to be where Jesus would have us be.*

* I cannot help remarking, in connection with our Lord's words in this passage, that it admits of question, whether men do not *sometimes* act unadvisedly in giving up a secular calling, in order to enter the ministry of the Gospel. In plain words, I doubt whether men, who have been suddenly converted to God in the army, the navy, the law, or the merchant's office, do not *sometimes* forsake their professions with undue precipitation, in order to become clergymen.

It seems to be forgotten that conversion alone is no proof that we are called and qualified to become teachers of others. God may be glorified as really and truly in the secular calling as in the pulpit. Converted men can be eminently useful as landlords, magistrates, soldiers, sailors, barristers or merchants. We want

We learn, for another thing, from these verses, that *a believer's own home has the first claims on his attention.* We are taught that in the striking words which our Lord addresses to the man who had been possessed with the devil. "Go home," He says, "to thy friends, and tell them how great things the Lord hath done for thee." The friends of this man had probably not seen him for some years, excepting under the influence of Satan. Most likely he had been as one dead to them, or worse than dead, and a constant cause of trouble, anxiety, and sorrow. Here then was the path of duty. Here was the way by which he could most glorify God. Let him go home and tell his friends what Jesus had done for him. Let him be a living witness before their eyes of the compassion of Christ. Let him deny himself the pleasure of being in Christ's bodily presence, in order to do the higher work of being useful to others.

How much there is in these simple words of our Lord !

witnesses for Christ in all these professions.   Colonel Gardiner and Capt. Vicars have probably done more for the cause of Christ, as military men, than they would ever have done if they had left the army and become clergymen.

In steering our course through life, we should carefully look for the call of *providence* as well as the call of *inclination.*   The position that we choose for ourselves is often that which is the worst for our souls,   When two conflicting paths of duty lie before a believer, the path which has least of the cross, and is most agreeable to his own taste, is seldom the right one.

I write all this with a due recollection of many eminent Christians who began in a secular profession, and left it for the office of the minister.   John Newton and Edward Bickersteth are instances. But I apprehend such cases are exceptions.   I apprehend moreover that in every such case there would be found to have been a remarkable call of *providence* as well as an inward call of the Holy Ghost.   As a general rule, I believe that the rule of St. Paul ought to be carefully observed: "Let every man, wherein he is called, therein abide with God."   (1 Cor. vii. 24.)

What thoughts they ought to stir up in the hearts of all true Christians!—"Go home and tell thy friends."—Home is the place above all others where the child of God ought to make his first endeavours to do good. Home is the place where he is most continually seen, and where the reality of his grace ought most truly to appear. Home is the place where his best affections ought to be concentrated. Home is the place where he should strive daily to be a witness for Christ. Home is the place where he was daily doing harm by his example, so long as he served the world. Home is the place where he is specially bound to be a living epistle of Christ, so soon as he has been mercifully taught to serve God. May we all remember these things daily! May it never be said of us, that we are saints abroad but wicked by our own fireside,—talkers about religion abroad, but worldly and ungodly at home!

But after all, Have we anything to tell others? Can we testify to any work of grace in our hearts? Have we experienced any deliverance from the power of the world, the flesh, and the devil? Have we ever tasted the graciousness of Christ? These are indeed serious questions. If we have never yet been born again, and made new creatures, we can of course have nothing to "tell."

If we have anything to tell others about Christ, let us resolve to tell it. Let us not be silent, if we have found peace and rest in the Gospel. Let us speak to our relations, and friends, and families, and neighbours, according as we have opportunity, and tell them what the Lord has done for our souls. All are not called to be ministers. All are not intended to preach. But all can walk in the steps of the man of whom we have been reading, and in the steps of Andrew, and Philip, and the Samaritan woman. (John i. 41, 45 ; iv. 29.) Happy is he who is not ashamed to say to others, "Come and hear what the Lord hath done for my soul." (Psal. lxvi. 16.)

MARK V. 21—34.

21 And when Jesus was passed over again by ship unto the other side, much people gathered unto him : and he was nigh unto the sea.

22 And, behold, there cometh one of the rulers of the synagogue, Jairus by name; and when he saw him, he fell at his feet,

23 And besought him greatly, saying, My little daughter lieth at the point of death : *I pray thee*, come and lay thy hands on her, that she may be healed ; and she shall live.

24 And *Jesus* went with him; and much people followed him, and thronged him.

25 And a certain woman, which had an issue of blood twelve years,

26 And had suffered many things of many physicians, and had spent all that she had, and was nothing bettered, but rather grew worse,

27 When she had heard of Jesus, came in the press behind, and touched his garment.

28 For she said, If I may touch but his clothes, I shall be whole.

29 And straightway the fountain of her blood was dried up; and she felt in *her* body that she was healed of that plague.

30 And Jesus, immediately knowing in himself that virtue had gone out of him, turned him about in the press, and said, Who touched my clothes?

31 And his disciples said unto him, Thou seest the multitude thronging thee, and sayest thou, Who touched me?

32 And he looked round about to see her that had done this thing.

33 But the woman fearing and trembling, knowing what was done in her, came and fell down before him, and told him all the truth.

34 And he said unto her, Daughter, thy faith hath made thee whole; go in peace, and be whole of thy plague.

THE main subject of these verses is the miraculous healing of a sick woman. Great is our Lord's experience in cases of disease ! Great is His sympathy with His sick and ailing members ! The gods of the heathen are generally represented as terrible and mighty in battle, delighting in bloodshed, the strong man's patrons, and the warrior's friends. The Saviour of the Christian is always set before us as gentle, and easy to be entreated, the healer of the broken-hearted, the refuge of the weak and helpless, the comforter of the distressed, the sick man's best friend. And is not this just the Saviour that human nature needs? The world is full of pain and trouble. The weak on earth are far more numerous than the strong.

Let us mark in these verses, *what misery sin has brought into the world*. We read of one who had had a most painful disease "for twelve years." She had "suffered many things of many physicians, and had spent all that she had, and was nothing bettered, but rather grew worse." Means of every kind had been tried in vain. Medical skill had proved unable to cure. Twelve long weary years had been spent in battling with disease, and relief seemed no nearer than at first. "Hope deferred" might well "make her heart sick." (Prov. xiii. 12.)

How marvellous it is that we do not hate sin more than we do! Sin is the cause of all the pain and disease in the world. God did not create man to be an ailing and suffering creature. It was sin, and nothing but sin, which brought in all the ills that flesh is heir to. It was sin to which we owe every racking pain, and every loathsome infirmity, and every humbling weakness to which our poor bodies are liable. Let us keep this ever in mind. Let us hate sin with a godly hatred.

Let us mark, in the second place, *how different are the feelings with which people draw near to Christ*. We are told in these verses that "much people followed" our Lord, "and thronged him." But we are only told of one person who "came in the press behind," and touched Him with faith and was healed. Many followed Jesus from curiosity, and derived no benefit from Him.

One, and only one, followed under a deep sense of her need, and of our Saviour's power to relieve her, and that one received a mighty blessing.

We see the same thing going on continually in the Church of Christ at the present day. Multitudes go to our places of worship, and fill our pews. Hundreds come up to the Lord's table, and receive the bread and wine. But of all these worshippers and communicants, how few really obtain anything from Christ ! Fashion, custom, form, habit, the love of excitement, or an itching ear, are the true motives of the vast majority. There are but a few here and there who touch Christ by faith, and go home "in peace." These may seem hard sayings. But they are unhappily too true !

Let us mark, in the third place, *how immediate and instantaneous was the cure which this woman received.* No sooner did she touch our Lord's clothes than she was healed. The thing that she had sought in vain for twelve years, was done in a moment. The cure that many physicians could not effect, was wrought in an instant of time. " She felt in her body that she was healed of that plague."

We need not doubt that we are meant to see here an emblem of the relief that the Gospel confers on souls. The experience of many a weary conscience has been exactly like that of this woman with her disease. Many a man has spent sorrowful years in search of peace with God, and failed to find it. He has gone to earthly remedies and obtained no relief. He has wearied himself in going from place to place, and church to church, and has felt after all "nothing bettered but rather worse." But

at last he has found rest.—And where has he found it?—
He has found it, where this woman found her's, in Jesus
Christ. He has ceased from his own works. He has
given over looking to his own endeavours and doings for
relief. He has come to Christ Himself, as a humble
sinner, and committed himself to His mercy. At once
the burden has fallen from off his shoulders. Heaviness
is turned to joy, and anxiety to peace.—One touch of
real faith can do more for the soul than a hundred
self-imposed austerities. One look at Jesus is more effi-
cacious than years of sack-cloth and ashes. May we
never forget this to our dying day! Personal application
to Christ is the real secret of peace with God.

Let us mark, in the fourth place, *how much it becomes
Christians to confess before men the benefits they receive from
Christ.* We see that this woman was not allowed to
go home, when cured, without her cure being noticed.
Our Lord inquired who had touched Him, and "looked
round about to see her that had done this thing." No
doubt He knew perfectly the name and history of the
woman. He needed not that any should tell Him. But
He desired to teach her, and all around Him, that healed
souls should make public acknowledgement of mercies
received.

There is a lesson here which all true Christians
would do well to remember. We are not to be ashamed
to confess Christ before men, and to let others know
what He has done for our souls. If we have found
peace through His blood, and been renewed by His
Spirit, we must not shrink from avowing it, on every
proper occasion. It is not necessary to blow a trumpet

in the streets, and force our experience on every body's notice. All that is required is a willingness to acknowledge Christ as our Master, without flinching from the ridicule or persecution, which by so doing we may bring on ourselves. More than this is not required; but less than this ought not to content us. If we are ashamed of Jesus before men, He will one day be ashamed of us before His Father and the angels.

Let us mark, in the last place, *how precious a grace is faith.* "Daughter," says our Lord to the woman who was healed, "thy faith hath made thee whole: go in peace."

Of all the Christian graces, none is so frequently mentioned in the New Testament as faith, and none is so highly commended.—No grace brings such glory to Christ. Hope brings an eager expectation of good things to come. Love brings a warm and willing heart. Faith brings an empty hand, receives everything, and can give nothing in return.—No grace is so important to the Christian's own soul. By faith we begin. By faith we live. By faith we stand. We walk by faith and not by sight. By faith we overcome. By faith we have peace. By faith we enter into rest.—No grace should be the subject of so much self-inquiry. We should often ask ourselves, Do I really believe? Is my faith true, genuine, and the gift of God?

May we never rest till we can give a satisfactory answer to these questions! Christ is not changed since the day when this woman was healed. He is still gracious and still mighty to save. There is but one thing needful if we want salvation. That one thing is the hand of faith. Let a man only " touch " Jesus, and he shall be made whole.*

MARK V. 35—43.

35 While he yet spake, there came from the ruler of the synagogue's *house certain* which said, Thy daughter is dead: why troublest thou the Master any further?

36 As soon as Jesus heard the word that was spoken, he saith unto the ruler of the synagogue, Be not afraid, only believe.

37 And he suffered no man to follow him, save Peter, and James, and John the brother of James.

38 And he cometh to the house of the ruler of the synagogue, and seeth the tumult, and them that wept and wailed greatly.

39 And when he was come in, he saith unto them, Why make ye this ado, and weep? the damsel is not dead, but sleepeth.

40 And they laughed him to scorn. But when he had put them all out, he taketh the father and the mother of the damsel, and them that were with him, and entereth in where the damsel was lying.

41 And he took the damsel by the hand, and said unto her, Talitha cumi; which is, being interpreted, Damsel, I say unto thee, arise.

42 And straightway the damsel arose, and walked; for she was *of the age* of twelve years. And they were astonished with a great astonishment.

43 And he charged them straitly that no man should know it; and commanded that something should be given her to eat.

A GREAT miracle is recorded in these verses. A dead girl is restored to life. Mighty as the "King of terrors" is, there is One mightier than he. The keys of death are in our Lord Jesus Christ's hands. He will one day "swallow up death in victory." (Isaiah xxv. 8.)

Let us learn from these verses, that *rank places no man*

* Some remarks of Melancthon's on this woman's case are worth reading. We are doubtless to be careful that we do not hastily attach an allegorical and mystical sense to the words of Scripture. Yet we must not forget the depth of meaning which lies in all the acts of our Lord's earthly ministry; and at any rate there is much beauty in the thoughts which the good Reformer expresses. He says, "This woman doth aptly represent the Jewish synagogue vexed a long time with many mischiefs and miseries, especially tortured with unconscionable princes, and unskilful priests, or physicians of the soul, the Pharisees and Sadducees; on whom she had wasted all her goods, and yet she was not a whit better, but rather much worse, till the blessed Lord of Israel in His own person came to ' visit and redeem her.' "

beyond the reach of sorrow. Jairus was a "ruler;" yet
sickness and trouble came to his house. Jairus probably
had wealth, and all the medical help that wealth can
command; yet money could not keep death away from
his child. The daughters of rulers are liable to sickness,
as well as the daughters of poor men. The daughters
of rulers must die.

It is good for us all to remember this. We are too apt
to forget it. We often think and talk as if the possession of riches was the great antidote to sorrow, and as if
money could secure us against sickness and death. But
it is the very extreme of blindness to think so. We
have only to look around us and see a hundred proofs to
the contrary. Death comes to halls and palaces, as well
as to cottages,—to landlords as well as to tenants,—to
rich as well as to poor. It stands on no ceremony. It
tarries no man's leisure or convenience. It will not be
kept out by locks and bars. "It is appointed unto men
once to die, but after this the judgment." (Heb. ix. 27.)
All are going to one place, the grave.

We may be sure there is far more equality in the portions appointed to men than at first sight appears. Sickness is a great leveller. It makes no distinction. Heaven
is the only place where "the inhabitant shall not say, I
am sick." (Isai. xxiii. 24.) Happy are they who set their
affections on things above! They, and they only, have a
treasure which is incorruptible. Yet a little while, and
they will be where they shall hear no more evil tidings.
All tears shall be wiped from their faces. They shall
put on mourning no more. Never again shall they hear
those sorrowful words, "thy daughter,—thy son,—thy

wife,—thy husband,—is dead." The former things will
have passed away.

Let us learn, for another thing, *how almighty is the
power of our Lord Jesus Christ.* That message which
pierced the ruler's heart, telling him that his child was
dead, did not stop our Lord for a moment. At once he
cheered the father's fainting spirits with these gracious
words, "be not afraid, only believe." He comes to the
house where many are weeping and wailing, and enters
the room where the damsel is lying. He takes her by
the hand, and says, "Damsel, I say unto thee arise."
At once the heart begins to beat again, and the breath
returns to the lifeless body. "The damsel arose and
walked." No wonder that we read the words, "they
were astonished with a great astonishment."

Let us think for a moment how wonderful was the
change which took place in that house. From weeping
to rejoicing,—from mourning to congratulation,—from
death to life,—how great and marvellous must have
been the transition! They only can tell that, who have
seen death face to face, and had the light of their households quenched, and felt the iron entering into their own
souls. They, and they only, can conceive what the
family of Jairus must have felt, when they saw their
beloved one given back once more into their bosom by
the power of Christ.—There must have been a happy
family gathering that night!

Let us see in this glorious miracle a proof of what
Jesus can do for dead souls. He can raise our children from the death of trespasses and sins, and make
them walk before Him in newness of life. He can take

our sons and daughters by the hand, and say to them, "arise," and bid them live not to themselves, but to Him that died for them and rose again. Have we a dead soul in our family? Let us call on the Lord to come and quicken him. (Eph. ii. 1.) Let us send to Him message after message, and entreat Him to help. He that came to the succour of Jairus is still plenteous in mercy, and mighty in power.

Finally, let us see in this miracle a blessed pledge of what our Lord will do in the day of His second appearing. He will call His believing people from their graves. He will give them a better, more glorious, and more beautiful body, than they had in the days of their pilgrimage. He will gather together His elect from north, and south, and east, and west, to part no more, and die no more. Believing parents shall once more see believing children. Believing husbands shall once more see believing wives. Let us beware of sorrowing like those who have no hope, over friends who fall asleep in Christ. The youngest and loveliest believer can never die before the right time. Let us look forward. There is a glorious resurrection morning yet to come. "Them which sleep in Jesus will God bring with Him." (1 Thess. iv. 14.) Those words shall one day receive a complete fulfilment, "I will ransom them from the power of the grave : I will redeem them from death : O death, I will be thy plagues: O grave, I will be thy destruction." (Hosea xiii. 14.) He that raised the daughter of Jairus still lives. When He gathers His flock around him at the last day, not one lamb shall be found missing.

MARK. VI. 1—6.

1 And he went out from thence, and came into his own country; and his disciples follow him.

2 And when the sabbath day was come, he began to teach in the synagogue: and many hearing *him* were astonished, saying, From whence hath this *man* these things? and what wisdom *is* this which is given unto him, that even such mighty works are wrought by his hands?

3 Is not this the carpenter, the son of Mary, the brother of James, and Joses, and of Juda, and Simon? and are not his sisters here with us? And they were offended at him.

4 But Jesus said unto them, A prophet is not without honour, but in his own country, and among his own kin, and in his own house.

5 And he could there do no mighty work, save that he laid his hands upon a few sick folk, and healed *them*.

6 And he marvelled because of their unbelief. And he went round about the villages, teaching.

THIS passage shows us our Lord Jesus Christ in "his own country," at Nazareth. It is a melancholy illustration of the wickedness of man's heart, and deserves special attention.

We see, in the first place, *how apt men are to undervalue things with which they are familiar.* The men of Nazareth "were offended" at our Lord. They could not think it possible that one who had lived so many years among themselves, and whose brethren and sisters they knew, could deserve to be followed as a public teacher.

Never had any place on earth such privileges as Nazareth. For thirty years the Son of God resided in this town, and went to and fro in its streets. For thirty years He walked with God before the eyes of its inhabitants, living a blameless, perfect life. But it was all lost upon them. They were not ready to believe the Gospel, when the Lord came among them, and taught in their synagogue. They would not believe that one whose face they knew so well, and who had lived so long, eating, and drinking, and dressing like one of themselves, had any right to claim their attention. They were "offended at Him."

There is nothing in all this that need surprise us. The same thing is going on around us every day, in our own land. The holy Scriptures, the preaching of the Gospel, the public ordinances of religion, the abundant means of grace that England enjoys, are continually undervalued by English people. They are so accustomed to them, that they do not know their privileges. It is an awful truth, that in religion, more than in anything else, familiarity breeds contempt.

There is comfort in this part of our Lord's experience, for some of the Lord's people. There is comfort for faithful ministers of the Gospel, who are cast down by the unbelief of their parishioners or regular hearers. There is comfort for true Christians, who stand alone in their families, and see all around them cleaving to the world. Let both remember that they are drinking the same cup as their beloved Master. Let them remember that He too was despised most by those who knew Him best. Let them learn that the utmost consistency of conduct will not make others adopt their views and opinions, any more than it did the people of Nazareth. Let them know that the sorrowful words of their Lord will generally be fulfilled in the experience of His servants, "a prophet is not without honour, but in his own country, and among his own kin, and in his own house."

We see, in the second place, *how humble was the rank of life which our Lord condescended to occupy, before He began His public ministry.* The people of Nazareth said of Him, in contempt, "Is not this the carpenter?"

This is a remarkable expression, and is only found in the Gospel of St. Mark. It shows us plainly that for the first thirty years of His life, our Lord was not ashamed to work with His own hands. There is something marvellous and overwhelming in the thought! He who made heaven, and earth, and sea, and all that therein is, —He, without whom nothing was made that was made, —the Son of God Himself, took on Him the form of a servant, and "in the sweat of His face ate bread," as a working man. This is indeed that "love of Christ that passeth knowledge." Though He was rich, yet for our sakes He became poor. Both in life and death He humbled Himself, that through Him sinners might live and reign for evermore.

Let us remember when we read this passage, that there is no sin in poverty. We never need be ashamed of poverty, unless our own sins have brought it upon us. We never ought to despise others, because they are poor. It is disgraceful to be a gambler, or a drunkard, or a covetous man, or a liar; but it is no disgrace to work with our own hands, and earn our bread by our own labour. The thought of the carpenter's shop at Nazareth, should cast down the high thoughts of all who make an idol of riches. It cannot be dishonourable to occupy the same position as the Son of God, and Saviour of the world.

We see, in the last place, *how exceedingly sinful is the sin of unbelief.* Two remarkable expressions are used in teaching this lesson. One is, that our Lord "could do no mighty work" at Nazareth, by reason of the hardness of the people's hearts. The other is, that "He marvelled because of their unbelief." The one shows us that unbelief has a power to rob men of the highest blessings. The other shows that it is so suicidal and unreasonable a sin, that even the Son of God regards it with surprise.

We can never be too much on our guard against unbelief. It is the oldest sin in the world. It began in the garden of Eden, when Eve listened to the devil's promises, instead of believing God's words, "ye shall die."— It is the most ruinous of all sins in its consequences. It brought death into the world. It kept Israel for forty years out of Canaan. It is the sin that specially fills hell. "He that believeth not shall be damned."—It is the most foolish and inconsistent of all sins. It makes a man refuse the plainest evidence, shut his eyes against the clearest testimony, and yet believe lies.—Worst of all, it is the commonest sin in the world. Thousands are guilty of it on every side. In profession they are Christians. They know nothing of Paine and Voltaire. But in practice they are really unbelievers. They do not implicitly believe the Bible, and receive Christ as their Saviour.

Let us watch our own hearts carefully in the matter of unbelief. The heart, and not the head, is the seat of its mysterious power. It is neither the want of evidence, nor the difficulties of Christian doctrine, that make men unbelievers.—It is want of will to believe. They love sin. They are wedded to the world. In this state of mind they never lack specious reasons to confirm their will. The humble, child-like heart is the heart that believes.

Let us go on watching our hearts, even after we have believed. The root of unbelief is never entirely destroyed. We have only to leave off watching and praying, and a rank crop of unbelief will soon spring up. No prayer is so important as that of the disciples, "Lord, increase our faith." *

MARK VI. 7—13.

7 And he called *unto him* the twelve, and began to send them forth by two and two; and gave them power over unclean spirits;

8 And commanded them that they should take nothing for *their* journey, save a staff only; no scrip, no bread, no money in *their* purse:

9 But *be* shod with sandals; and not put on two coats.

10 And he said unto them, In what place soever ye enter into an house, there abide till ye depart from that place.

11 And whosoever shall not receive you, nor hear you, when ye depart thence, shake off the dust under your feet for a testimony against them. Verily I say unto you, It shall be more tolerable for Sodom and Gomorrha in the day of judgment, than for that city.

12 And they went out, and preached that men should repent.

13 And they cast out many devils, and anointed with oil many that were sick, and healed *them.*

THESE verses describe the first sending forth of the apostles to preach. The great Head of the church made proof of His ministers, before He left them alone in the world. He taught them to try their own powers of teaching, and to find out their own weaknesses, while He was yet with them. Thus, on the one hand, He was enabled

---

* There is a peculiar expression in this passage, which deserves notice. I refer to the words which say, that our Lord "*could* do no mighty work there, because of their unbelief."

This expression of course cannot mean, that it was "impossible" for our Lord to do a mighty work there, and that although He had the will to do mighty works, He was stopped and prevented by a power greater than His own. Such a view would be dishonouring to our Lord, and in fact would be a practical denial of His divinity. With Jesus nothing is impossible. If He had willed to do works, He had the power.

The meaning evidently must be, that our Lord "*would*" not do any mighty work there, because of the unbelief that He saw. He was prevented by what He perceived was the state of the people's hearts. He would not waste signs and wonders on an unbelieving and hardened generation. He "*could not*" do a mighty work,

to correct their mistakes.   Thus, on the other, they were
trained for the work they were one day to do, and were
not novices, when finally left to themselves.—Well would
it be for the church, if all ministers of the Gospel were
prepared for their duty in like manner, and did not so often
take up their office untried, unproved, and inexperienced.

Let us observe in these verses, *how our Lord Jesus*

without departing from His rule, "according to your faith be it
unto you." He had the power in His hands, but He did not will
to use it.

The distinction I have attempted to draw is doubly useful, because
of the light it throws on another Scriptural expression, which is often
grievously misunderstood.   I refer to the expression, "no man can
come to me, except the Father which hath sent me draw him."
(John vi. 44.)   The words, "no man *can* come," are often much
misapprehended.

The text is a plain declaration of man's natural corruption and
helpless impotence. Man is dead in sin. He cannot come to Christ,
except the Father draws him.   In a word, he is *unable* to come.
But what is the precise nature of his inability ? This is the very
point on which misapprehension exists.

Once for all, let us clearly understand that man's inability to
come to Christ is not physical.   It is utterly untrue to say that a
man can have a strong decided will to come to Christ, and yet be
stopped by some mysterious physical obstacle,—that he can really
and honestly have a will to come, and yet have no power.   Such a
doctrine entirely overthrows man's responsibility, and leads, in
many cases, to wicked continuance in sin.   Thousands of ignorant people will tell you that "they wish to believe, and wish
to come to Christ, and wish to be saved,"—and yet say that "though
they have the will, they have not the power."   It is a fatal delusion, and ruinous to many souls.

The truth is that man's inability to come to Christ, and impotence to that which is good, is *moral*, and not physical.   It is
not true that he has the will to come to Christ, but is unable.   He
is unable, doubtless, and has no power ; but it is simply *because*
he has no will.   His will is the principal cause of his unconverted
state, and until his will is changed by the Holy Ghost, he will
never alter.   He may not like this.   But it is true.   The fault of
his condition is his own will.   Say what he pleases, the blame
lies there.   He may pretend to have many good wishes, but in
reality he has no honest, sincere WILL to be better.   He "will
not come to Christ that he may have life."

Christ sent forth His apostles " two and two."—St. Mark is the only evangelist who mentions this fact. It is one that deserves special notice.

There can be no doubt that this fact is meant to teach us the advantages of Christian company to all who work for Christ. The wise man had good reason for saying, "Two are better than one." (Eccles. iv. 9.) Two men together will do more work than two men singly. They will help one another in judgment, and commit fewer mistakes. They will aid one another in difficulties, and less often fail of success. They will stir one another up when tempted to idleness, and less often relapse into indolence and indifference. They will comfort one another in times of trial, and be less often cast down. "Woe to him that is alone when he falleth; for he hath not another to help him up." (Eccles. iv. 11.)

It is probable that this principle is not sufficiently remembered in the church of Christ in these latter days. The harvest is undoubtedly great all over the world, both at home and abroad. The labourers are unquestionably few, and the supply of faithful men far less than the demand. The arguments for sending out men "one by one," under existing circumstances, are undeniably strong and weighty. But still the conduct of our Lord in this place is a striking fact. The fact that there is hardly a single case in the Acts, where we find Paul or any other apostle working entirely alone, is another remarkable circumstance. It is difficult to avoid the conclusion, that if the rule of going forth "two and two" had been more strictly observed, the missionary field would have yielded larger results than it has.

One thing at all events is clear, and that is the duty of all workers for Christ to work together and help one another whenever they can. " As iron sharpeneth iron, so doth the countenance of a man his friend." Ministers and missionaries, and district visitors, and Sunday school teachers, should make opportunities for meeting, and taking sweet counsel together. The words of St. Paul contain a truth which is too much forgotten : " consider one another, to provoke unto love and good works; not forsaking the assembling of yourselves together." (Heb. x. 24, 25.)

Let us observe, in the second place, *what solemn words our Lord uses about those who will not receive nor hear His ministers.* He says, " it shall be more tolerable for Sodom and Gomorrha in the day of judgment than for that city."

This is a truth which we find very frequently laid down in the Gospels. It is painful to think how entirely it is overlooked by many. Thousands appear to suppose, that so long as they go to church, and do not murder, or steal, or cheat, or openly break any of God's commandments, they are in no great danger. They forget that it needs something more than mere abstinence from outward irregularities to save a man's soul. They do not see that one of the greatest sins a man can commit in the sight of God, is to hear the Gospel of Christ and not believe it,—to be invited to repent and believe, and yet remain careless and unbelieving. In short, to reject the Gospel will sink a man to the lowest place in hell.

Let us never turn away from a passage like this without asking ourselves, What are we doing with the Gospel? We live in a Christian land. We have the Bible in our houses. We hear of the salvation of the Gospel frequently every year. But have we received it into our hearts? Have we really obeyed it in our lives? Have we, in short, laid hold on the hope set before us, taken up the cross, and followed Christ?—If not, we are far worse than the heathen, who bow down to stocks and stones. We are far more guilty than the people of Sodom and Gomorrah. They never heard the Gospel, and therefore never rejected it. But as for us, we hear the Gospel, and yet will not believe. May we search our own hearts, and take heed that we do not ruin our own souls!

Let us observe, in the last place, *what was the doctrine which our Lord's apostles preached.* We read that "they went out and preached that men should repent."

The necessity of repentance may seem at first sight a very simple and elementary truth. And yet volumes might be written to show the fulness of the doctrine, and the suitableness of it to every age and time, and to every rank and class of mankind. It is inseparably connected with right views of God, of human nature, of sin, of Christ, of holiness, and of heaven. All have sinned and come short of the glory of God. All need to be brought to a sense of their sins,—to a sorrow for them,—to a willingness to give them up,—and to a hunger and thirst after pardon. All, in a word, need to be born again and to flee to Christ. This is repentance unto life. Nothing less than this is required for the salvation of any man. Nothing less than this ought to be pressed on men, by every one who professes to teach Bible religion. We must bid men repent, if we would walk in the steps of the apostles, and when they have repented, we must bid them repent more and more to their last day.

Have we ourselves repented? This, after all, is the question that concerns us most. It is well to know what the apostles taught. It is well to be familiar with the whole system of Christian doctrine. But it is far better to know repentance by experience and to feel it inwardly in our own hearts. May we never rest till we know and feel that we have repented! There are no impenitent people in the kingdom of heaven. All who enter in there have felt, mourned over, forsaken, and sought pardon for sin. This must be our experience, if we hope to be saved.*

MARK VI. 14—29.

14 And king Herod heard *of him ;* (for his name was spread abroad :) and he said, That John the Baptist was risen from the dead, and therefore mighty works do shew forth themselves in him.

15 Others said, That it is Elias. And others said, That it is a prophet, or as one of the prophets.

16 But when Herod heard *thereof,* he said, It is John, whom I beheaded : he is risen from the dead.

* The concluding verse in this passage, together with one in the Epistle of James, (James v. 14.) is generally quoted by Roman Catholics, in support of their pretended sacrament of extreme unction. A moment's reflection will show that neither this text nor the other referred to, is any proof at all.

In both cases, the anointing with oil is expressly connected with the *healing* of those anointed. Extreme unction on the contrary is an anointing administered to a *dying* person, when there is no hope of his recovery.

This discrepancy between the anointing of the apostolic times and the anointing practised by the Church of Rome, is so glaring, that some of the ablest Romish controversialists have been obliged to acknowledge, that " extreme unction " is founded on church authority, and not on the authority of Scripture.—Lombardus, Bonaventura, Bellarmine, Jansenius, and Tirinus, are all mentioned by Calovius as being of this opinion.

17 For Herod himself had sent forth and laid hold upon John, and bound him in prison for Herodias' sake, his brother Philip's wife : for he had married her.

18 For John had said unto Herod, It is not lawful for thee to have thy brother's wife.

19 Therefore Herodias had a quarrel against him, and would have killed him ; but she could not :

20 For Herod feared John, knowing that he was a just man and an holy, and observed him ; and when he heard him, he did many things, and heard him gladly.

21 And when a convenient day was come, that Herod on his birthday made a supper to his lords, high captains, and chief *estates* of Galilee ;

22 And when the daughter of the said Herodias came in, and danced, and pleased Herod and them that sat with him, the king said unto the damsel, Ask of me whatsoever thou wilt, and I will give *it* thee.

23 And he sware unto her, What-

soever thou shalt ask of me, I will give *it* thee, unto the half of my kingdom.

24 And she went forth, and said unto her mother, What shall I ask ? And she said, The head of John the Baptist.

25 And she came in straightway with haste unto the king, and asked, saying, I will that thou give me by and by in a charger the head of John the Baptist.

26 And the king was exceeding sorry ; *yet* for his oath's sake, and for their sakes which sat with him, he would not reject her.

27 And immediately the king sent an executioner, and commanded his head to be brought : and he went and beheaded him in the prison,

28 And brought his head in a charger, and gave it to the damsel . and the damsel gave it to her mother.

29 And when his disciples heard *of it,* they came and took up his corpse, and laid it in a tomb.

THESE verses describe the death of one of the most eminent saints of God. They relate the murder of John the Baptist. Of all the evangelists none tells this melancholy story so fully as St. Mark. Let us see what practical lessons the passage contains for our own souls.

We see, in the first place, *the amazing power of truth over the conscience.* Herod "fears" John the Baptist while he lives, and is troubled about him after he dies. A friendless, solitary preacher, with no other weapon than God's truth, disturbs and terrifies a king.

Every body has a conscience. Here lies the secret of a faithful minister's power. This is the reason why Felix "trembled," and Agrippa was "almost persuaded," when Paul the prisoner spoke before them. God has not left Himself without witness in the hearts of unconverted people. Fallen and corrupt as man is, there are thoughts within him accusing or excusing, according as he lives,—thoughts that will not be shut out,—thoughts that can make even kings, like Herod, restless and afraid.

None ought to remember this so much as ministers and teachers. If they preach and teach Christ's truth, they may rest assured that their work is not in vain. Children may seem inattentive in schools. Hearers may seem careless in congregations. But in both cases there is often far more going on in the conscience than our eyes see. Seeds often spring up and bear fruit, when the sower, like John the Baptist, is dead or gone.

We see, in the second place, *how far people may go in religion, and yet miss salvation by yielding to one master-sin.*

King Herod went further than many. He "feared John." He "knew that he was a just man and a holy." He "observed" him. He "heard him, and did many things" in consequence. He even "heard him gladly." But there was one thing Herod would not do. He would not cease from adultery. He would not give up Herodias. And so he ruined his soul for evermore.

Let us take warning from Herod's case. Let us keep back nothing,—cleave to no favourite vice,—spare nothing that stands between us and salvation. Let us often look within, and make sure that there is no darling lust or pet transgression, which, Herodias-like, is murdering our souls. Let us rather cut off the right hand, and pluck out the right eye, than go into hell-fire. Let us not be content with admiring favourite preachers, and gladly hearing evangelical sermons. Let us not rest till we can say with David, " I esteem all Thy commandments concerning all things to be right, and I hate every false way." (Psalm. cxix. 128.)

We see, in the third place, *how boldly a faithful minister of God ought to rebuke sin.* John the Baptist spoke plainly to Herod about the wickedness of his life. He did not excuse himself under the plea that it was imprudent, or impolitic, or untimely, or useless to speak out. He did not say smooth things, and palliate the king's ungodliness by using soft words to describe his offence. He told his royal hearer the plain truth, regardless of all consequences,—"It is not lawful for thee to have thy brother's wife."

Here is a pattern that all ministers ought to follow. Publicly and privately, from the pulpit and in private visits, they ought to rebuke all open sin, and deliver a faithful warning to all who are living in it. It may give offence. It may entail immense unpopularity. With all this they have nothing to do. Duties are theirs. Results are God's.

No doubt it requires great grace and courage to do this. No doubt a reprover, like John the Baptist, must go to work wisely and lovingly in carrying out his master's commission, and rebuking the wicked. But it is a matter in which his character for faithfulness and charity are manifestly at stake. If he believes a man is injuring his soul, he ought surely to tell him so. If he loves him truly and tenderly, he ought not to let him ruin himself unwarned. Great as the present offence may be, in the long run the faithful reprover will generally be respected. "He that rebuketh a man, afterwards shall find more

favour than he that flattereth him with his tongue."
(Prov. xxviii. 23.)

We see, in the fourth place, *how bitterly people hate a
reprover, when they are determined to keep their sins.*
Herodias, the king's unhappy partner in iniquity, seems
to have sunk even deeper in sin than Herod. Hardened
and seared in conscience by her wickedness, she hated
John the Baptist for his faithful testimony, and never
rested till she had procured his death.

We need not wonder at this. When men and women
have chosen their line, and resolved to have their own
wicked way, they dislike any one who tries to turn them.
They would fain be let alone. They are irritated by opposition. They are angry when they are told the truth.
The prophet Elijah was called a "man that troubled
Israel." The prophet Micaiah was hated by Ahab, "because he never prophesied good of him, but evil." The
prophets and faithful preachers of every age have been
treated in like manner. They have been hated by some,
as well as not believed.

Let it never surprise us when we hear of faithful
ministers of the Gospel being spoken against, hated, and
reviled. Let us rather remember that they are ordained
to bear witness against sin, the world, and the devil, and
that if they are faithful they cannot help giving offence.
It is no disgrace to a minister's character to be disliked
by the wicked and ungodly. It is no real honour
to a minister to be thought well of by everybody.
Those words of our Lord are not enough considered,—
" Woe unto you when all men speak well of you."

We see, in the fifth place, *how much sin may sometimes follow from feasting and revelling.* Herod keeps his birthday with a splendid banquet. Company, drinking, dancing, fill up the day. In a moment of excitement, he grants a wicked girl's request to have the head of John the Baptist cut off. Next day, in all probability, he repented bitterly of his conduct. But the deed was done. It was too late.

This is a faithful picture of what often results from feasting and merry-making. People do things at such seasons from heated feelings, which they afterwards deeply repent. Happy are they who keep clear of temptations, and avoid giving occasion to the devil! Men never know what they may do, when they once venture off safe ground. Late hours, and crowded rooms, and splendid entertainments, and mixed company, and music, and dancing, may seem harmless to many people. But the Christian should never forget, that to take part in these things is to open a wide door to temptation.

We see, finally, in these verses, *how little reward some of God's best servants receive in this world.* An unjust imprisonment and a violent death, were the last fruit that John the Baptist reaped, in return for his labour. Like Stephen and James and others, of whom the world was not worthy, he was called to seal his testimony with his blood.

Histories like these are meant to remind us, that the true Christian's best things are yet to come. His rest, his crown, his wages, his reward, are all on the other side of the grave. Here, in this world, he must

walk by faith and not by sight; and if he looks for
the praise of man, he will be disappointed. Here, in this
life, he must sow, and labour, and fight, and endure persecution; and if he expects a great earthly reward, he
expects what he will not find.—But this life is not all.
There is to be a day of retribution. There is a glorious
harvest yet to come. Heaven will make amends for all.
Eye hath not seen, and ear hath not heard the glorious
things that God has laid up for all that love Him. The
value of real religion is not to be measured by the things
seen, but the things unseen. "The sufferings of this
present time are not worthy to be compared with the
glory which shall be revealed." "Our light affliction,
which is but for a moment, worketh for us a far more
exceeding and eternal weight of glory." (Rom. viii. 18;
2 Cor. iv. 17.)

MARK VI. 30—34.

30 And the apostles gathered themselves together unto Jesus, and told
him all things, both what they had
done, and what they had taught.

31 And he said unto them, Come
ye yourselves apart into a desert place,
and rest a while: for there were many
coming and going, and they had no
leisure so much as to eat.

32 And they departed into a desert
place by ship privately.

33 And the people saw them departing, and many knew him, and ran
afoot thither out of all cities, and out-
went them, and came together unto
him.

34 And Jesus, when he came out,
saw much people, and was moved with
compassion toward them, because they
were as sheep not having a shepherd:
and he began to teach them many
things.

LET us mark in this passage, *the conduct of the apostles
when they returned from their first mission as preachers.*
We read that they "gathered themselves together unto
Jesus, and told Him all things, both what they had done,
and what they had taught."

These words are deeply instructive. They are a bright example to all ministers of the Gospel, and to all labourers in the great work of doing good to souls. All such should daily do as the apostles did on this occasion. They should tell all their proceedings to the great Head of the Church. They should spread all their work before Christ, and ask of Him counsel, guidance, strength, and help.

Prayer is the main secret of success in spiritual business. It moves Him who can move heaven and earth. It brings down the promised aid of the Holy Ghost, without whom the finest sermons, the clearest teaching, and the most diligent working, are all alike in vain. It is not always those who have the most eminent gifts who are most successful labourers for God. It is generally those who keep up closest communion with Christ and are most instant in prayer. It is those who cry with the prophet Ezekiel, "Come from the four winds, O breath, and breathe upon these slain that they may live." (Ezek. xxxvii. 9.) It is those who follow most exactly the apostolic model, and "give themselves to prayer and the ministry of the word." (Acts vi. 4.) Happy is that church which has a praying as well as a preaching ministry! The question we should ask about a new minister, is not merely "Can he preach well?" but "Does he pray much for his people and his work?"

Let us mark, in the second place, *the words of our Lord to the apostles, when they returned from their first public ministry.* "He said unto them, come ye apart yourselves into a desert place, and rest a while."

These words are full of tender consideration. Our

Lord knows well that His servants are flesh as well as spirit, and have bodies as well as souls. He knows that at best they have a treasure in earthen vessels, and are themselves compassed with many infirmities. He shows them that He does not expect from them more than their bodily strength can do. He asks for what we *can* do, and not for what we cannot do. "Come ye apart," He says, " and rest awhile."

These words are full, of deep wisdom. Our Lord knows well that His servants must attend to their own souls as well as the souls of others. He knows that a constant attention to public work is apt to make us forget our own private soul-business, and that while we are keeping the vineyards of others, we are in danger of neglecting our own. (Cant. i. 6.) He reminds us that it is good for ministers to withdraw occasionally from public work, and look within. "Come ye apart," He says, "into a desert place."

There are few unhappily in the Church of Christ, who need these admonitions. There are but few in danger of overworking themselves, and injuring their own bodies and souls by excessive attention to others. The vast majority of professing Christians are indolent and slothful, and do nothing for the world around them. There are few comparatively who need the bridle nearly so much as the spur.—Yet these few ought to lay to heart the lessons of this passage. They should economize their health as a talent, and not squander it away like gamblers. They should be content with spending their daily income of strength, and should not draw recklessly on their principal. They should remember that to do a

little, and do it well, is often the way to do most in the
long run.   Above all they should never forget to watch
their own hearts jealously, and to make time for regular
self-examination, and calm meditation.   The prosperity
of a man's ministry and public work is intimately bound
up with the prosperity of his own soul.   Occasional retire-
ment is one of the most useful ordinances.

Finally, let us mark the *feelings of our Lord Jesus
Christ towards the people who came together to Him.*   We
read that He " was moved with compassion toward them,
because they were as sheep without a shepherd."   They
were destitute of teachers.   They had no guides but the
blind Scribes and Pharisees.   They had no spiritual food
but man-made traditions.   Thousands of immortal souls
stood before our Lord, ignorant, helpless, and on the high-
road to ruin.   It touched the gracious heart of our Lord
Jesus Christ.   He was " moved with compassion toward
them.   He began to teach them many things."

Let us never forget that our Lord is the same yester-
day, to-day, and for ever.   He never changes.   High in
heaven, at God's right hand, He still looks with compassion on the children of men.   He still pities the
ignorant, and them that are out of the way.   He is still
willing to " teach them many things."   Special as His
love is towards His own sheep who hear His voice, He
still has a mighty general love towards all mankind,—a
love of real pity, a love of compassion.   We must not
overlook this.   It is a poor theology which teaches that
Christ cares for none except believers.   There is warrant in Scripture for telling the chief of sinners, that
Jesus pities them, and cares for their souls, that Jesus is

willing to save them, and invites them to believe and be saved.

Let us ask ourselves, as we leave the passage, whether we know anything of the mind of Christ? Are we like Him, tenderly concerned about the souls of the unconverted? Do we, like Him, feel deep compassion for all who are yet as sheep without a shepherd? Do we care about the impenitent and ungodly near our own doors? Do we care about the Heathen, the Jew, the Mahometan, and the Roman Catholic in foreign lands? Do we use every means, and give our money willingly, to spread the Gospel in the world? These are serious questions and demand a serious reply. The man who cares nothing for the souls of other people is not like Jesus Christ. It may well be doubted whether he is converted himself, and knows the value of his own soul.

MARK VI. 35—46.

35 And when the day was now far spent, his disciples came unto him, and said, This is a desert place, and now the time is far passed:

36 Send them away that they may go into the country round about, and into the villages, and buy themselves bread: for they have nothing to eat.

37 He answered and said unto them, Give ye them to eat. And they say unto him, Shall we go and buy two hundred penny worth of bread, and give them to eat?

38 He saith unto them, How many loaves have ye? go and see. And when they knew, they say, Five, and two fishes.

39 And he commanded them to make all sit down by companies upon the green grass.

40 And they sat down in ranks, by hundreds, and by fifties.

41 And when he had taken the five loaves and the two fishes, he looked up to heaven, and blessed, and brake the loaves, and gave them to his disciples to set before them; and the two fishes divided he among them all.

42 And they did all eat, and were filled.

43 And they took up twelve baskets full of the fragments, and of the fishes.

44 And they that did eat of the loaves were about five thousand men.

45 And straightway he constrained his disciples to get into the ship, and to go to the other side before unto Bethsaida, while he sent away the people.

46 And when he had sent them away, he departed into a mountain to pray.

OF all our Lord Jesus Christ's miracles, none is so frequently described in the Gospels, as that which we have now read. Each of the four Evangelists was inspired to record it. It is evident that it demands a more than ordinary attention from every reader of God's word.

Let us observe, for one thing, in this passage, *what an example this miracle affords of our Lord Jesus Christ's almighty power*. We are told that He fed five thousand men, with five loaves and two fishes. We are distinctly told that this multitude had nothing to eat. We are no less distinctly told that the whole provision for their sustenance consisted of only five loaves and two fishes. And yet we read that our Lord took these loaves and fishes, blessed, brake, and gave them to His disciples to set before the people. And the conclusion of the narrative tells us, that "they did all eat, and were filled," and that " twelve baskets full of fragments " were taken up.

Here was creative power, beyond all question. Something real, solid, substantial, must manifestly have been called into being, which did not before exist. There is no room left for the theory, that the people were under the influence of an optical delusion, or a heated imagination. Five thousand hungry people would never have been satisfied, if they had not received into their mouths material bread. Twelve baskets full of fragments would never have been taken up, if the five loaves had not been miraculously multiplied. In short, it is plain that the hand of Him who made the world out of nothing was present on this occasion. None but He who at the first created all things, and sent down manna in the desert, could thus have "spread a table in the wilderness."

It becomes all true Christians to store up facts like

these in their minds, and to remember them in time of need. We live in the midst of an evil world, and see few with us, and many against us. We carry within us a weak heart, too ready at any moment to turn aside from the right way. We have near us, at every moment, a busy devil, watching continually for our halting, and seeking to lead us into temptation. Where shall we turn for comfort? What shall keep faith alive, and preserve us from sinking in despair?—There is only one answer. We must look to Jesus. We must think on His almighty power, and His wonders of old time. We must call to mind how He can create food for His people out of nothing, and supply the wants of those who follow Him, even in the wilderness.—And as we think these thoughts, we must remember that this Jesus still lives, never changes, and is on our side.

Let us observe, for another thing, in this passage, *our Lord Jesus Christ's conduct, when the miracle of feeding the multitude had been performed.* We read, that "when He had sent them away, He departed into a mountain to pray."

There is something deeply instructive in this circumstance. Our Lord sought not the praise of man. After one of His greatest miracles, we find Him immediately seeking solitude, and spending His time in prayer. He practised what He had taught elsewhere, when He said, "enter into thy closet, and shut thy door, and pray to thy Father which is in secret." None ever did such mighty works as He did. None ever spake such words. None ever was so instant in prayer.

Let our Lord's conduct in this respect be our example.

We cannot work miracles as He did; in this He stands alone. But we can walk in His steps, in the matter of private devotion. If we have the Spirit of adoption, we can pray. Let us resolve to pray more than we have done hitherto. Let us strive to make time, and place, and opportunity for being alone with God. Above all, let us not only pray, before we attempt to work for God, but pray also after our work is done.

It would be well for us all, if we examined ourselves more frequently as to our habits about private prayer. What time do we give to it in the twenty-four hours of the day? What progress can we mark, one year with another, in the fervency, fulness, and earnestness of our prayers? What do we know by experience, of "labouring fervently in prayer?" (Col. iv. 12.) These are humbling inquiries, but they are useful for our souls. There are few things, it may be feared, in which Christians come so far short of Christ's example, as they do in the matter of prayer. Our Master's strong crying and tears,—His continuing all night in prayer to God,—His frequent withdrawal to private places, to hold close communion with the Father, are things more talked of and admired than imitated. We live in an age of hurry, bustle, and so-called activity. Men are tempted continually to cut short their private devotions, and abridge their prayers. When this is the case, we need not wonder that the Church of Christ does little in proportion to its machinery. The Church must learn to copy its Head more closely. Its members must be more in their closets. "We have little," because little is asked. (James iv. 2.)

MARK VI. 47—56.

47 And when even was come, the ship was in the midst of the sea, and he alone on the land.

48 And he saw them toiling in rowing; for the wind was contrary unto them : and about the fourth watch of the night he cometh unto them, walking upon the sea, and would have passed by them.

49 But when they saw him walking upon the sea, they supposed it had been a spirit, and cried out :

50 For they all saw him, and were troubled. And immediately he talked with them, and saith unto them, Be of good cheer: it is I; be not afraid.

51 And he went up unto them into the ship; and the wind ceased : and they were sore amazed in themselves beyond measure, and wondered.

52 For they considered not *the miracle* of the loaves : for their heart was hardened.

53 And when they had passed over, they came into the land of Gennesaret, and drew to the shore.

54 And when they were come out of the ship, straightway they knew him.

55 And ran through that whole region round about, and began to carry about in beds those that were sick, where they heard he was.

56 And whithersoever he entered, into villages, or cities, or country, they laid the sick in the streets, and besought him that they might touch if it were but the border of his garment : and as many as touched him were made whole.

THE event first recorded in these verses, is a beautiful emblem of the position of all believers, between the first and second advents of Jesus Christ. Like the disciples, we are now tossed to and fro by storms, and do not enjoy the visible presence of our Lord. Like the disciples, we shall see our Lord face to face again, though it may be a time of great extremity, when He returns. Like the disciples, we shall see all things changed for the better, when our Master comes to us. We shall no longer be buffeted by storms. There will be a great calm.

There is nothing fanciful in such an application of the passage. We need not doubt that there is a deep meaning in every step of His life, who was "God manifest in the flesh." For the present, however, let us confine ourselves to the plain, practical lessons which these verses contain.

Let us notice, in the first place, how *our Lord sees the troubles of His believing people, and in due time will help them.* We read that when "the ship was in the midst of the sea, and He alone on the land," He "saw His disciples toiling in rowing,"—came to them walking on the sea,—cheered them with the gracious words, "It is I, be not afraid,"—and changed the storm into a calm.

There are thoughts of comfort here for all true believers. Wherever they may be, or whatsoever their circumstances, the Lord Jesus sees them. Alone, or in company, —in sickness or in health,—by sea or by land,—in perils in the city,—in perils in the wilderness,—the same eye which saw the disciples tossed on the lake, is ever looking at us. We are never beyond the reach of His care. Our way is never hid from Him. He knows the path that we take, and is still able to help. He may not come to our aid at the time we like best, but He will never allow us utterly to fail. He that walked upon the water never changes. He will always come at the right time to uphold His people. Though He tarry, let us wait patiently. Jesus sees us, and will not forsake us.

Let us notice, in the second place, *the fears of the disciples, when they first saw our Lord walking upon the sea.* We are told that "they supposed it had been a spirit, and cried out. For they all saw Him, and were afraid."

What a faithful picture of human nature we have in these words! How many thousands in the present day, if they had seen what the disciples saw, would have behaved in the same manner! How few, if they were on board a ship, in a storm at midnight, and suddenly saw one walking on the water, and drawing near to the ship, —how few would preserve their composure, and be altogether free from fears! Let men laugh, if they

please, at the superstitious fears of these unlearned disciples. Let them boast, if they like, of the march of
intellect, and the spread of knowledge, in these latter
times. There are few, we may confidently assert, who,
placed in the same position as the apostles, would have
shown more courage than they. The boldest sceptics
have sometimes proved the greatest cowards, when appearances have been seen at night, which they could not
explain.

The truth is, there is an instinctive feeling in all
men, which makes them shrink from anything which
seems to belong to another world. There is a consciousness which many try in vain to conceal by affected
carelessness, that there are beings unseen, as well as seen,
and that the life which we now live in the flesh, is not
the only life in which man has a portion. The common
stories about ghosts and apparitions, are undoubtedly
foolish and superstitious. They are almost always trace-
able to the fears and imaginations of weak-minded people.
Yet the universal currency which such stories obtain, all
over the world, is a fact that deserves notice. It is
an indirect evidence of latent belief in unseen things, just
as counterfeit coin is an evidence that there is true
money. It forms a peculiar testimony which the
infidel would find it hard to explain away. It proves
that there is something within men, which testifies of a
world beyond the grave, and that when men feel it, they
are afraid.

The plain duty of the true Christian is, to live provided
with an antidote against all fears of the great unseen
world. That antidote is faith in an unseen Saviour,

and constant communion with Him. Armed with that antidote, and seeing Him who is invisible, nothing need make us afraid. We travel on towards a world of spirits. We are surrounded even now by many dangers. But with Jesus for our Shepherd, we have no cause for alarm. With Him for our Shield, we are safe.

Let us notice, in the conclusion of the chapter, *what a bright example we have of our duty to one another.* We are told that when our Lord came into the land of Gennesaret, the people "ran through that whole region," and brought to Him in beds "those that were sick." We read that "whithersoever he entered, into villages, or cities, or country, they laid the sick in the streets, and besought him, that they might touch if it were but the border of his garment."

Let us see here a pattern for ourselves. Let us go and do likewise. Let us strive to bring all around us who are in need of spiritual medicine, to Jesus the great Physician, that they may be healed. Souls are dying every day. Time is short. Opportunities are rapidly passing away. The night cometh when no man can work. Let us spare no pains in labouring to bring men and women to the knowledge of Jesus Christ, that they may be saved. It is a comfortable thought, that "as many as touch him will be made whole."

MARK VII. 1—13.

1 Then came together unto him the Pharisees, and certain of the Scribes, which came from Jerusalem.

2 And when they saw some of his disciples eat bread with defiled, that is to say, with unwashen hands, they found fault.

3 For the Pharisees, and all the Jews, except they wash *their* hands oft, eat not, holding the tradition of the elders.

4 And *when they come* from the market, except they wash, they eat not. And many other things there be,

which they have received to hold, *as* the washing of cups, and pots, brasen vessels, and of tables.

5 Then the Pharisees and Scribes asked him, Why walk not thy disciples according to the tradition of the elders, but eat bread with unwashen hands?

6 He answered and said unto them, Well hath Esaias prophesied of you hypocrites, as it is written, This people honoureth me with *their* lips, but their heart is far from me.

7 Howbeit in vain do they worship me, teaching *for* doctrines the commandments of men.

8 For laying aside the commandment of God, ye hold the tradition of men, *as* the washing of pots and cups:

and many other such like things ye do.

9 And he said unto them, Full well ye reject the commandment of God, that ye may keep your own traditions.

10 For Moses said, Honour thy father and thy mother; and, Whoso curseth father or mother, let him die the death:

11 But ye say, If a man shall say to his father or mother, *It is* Corban, that is to say, a gift, by whatsoever thou mightest be profited by me; *he shall be free.*

12 And ye suffer him no more to do ought for his father or his mother;

13 Making the word of God of none effect through your tradition, which ye have delivered: and many such like things do ye.

THIS passage contains a humbling picture of what human nature is capable of doing in religion. It is one of those Scriptures which ought to be frequently and diligently studied by all who desire the prosperity of the Church of Christ.

The first thing, which demands our attention in these verses, is *the low and degraded condition of Jewish religion, when our Lord was upon earth.* What can be more deplorable than the statement now before us? We find the principal teachers of the Jewish nation finding fault, "because our Lord's disciples ate bread with unwashen hands!" We are told that they attached great importance to the "washing of cups, and pots, and brazen vessels, and tables!" In short, the man who paid most rigid attention to mere external observances of human invention was reckoned the holiest man!

The nation, be it remembered, in which this state of things existed, was the most highly favoured in the world. To it was given the law on Mount Sinai, the service of God, the priest-hood, the covenants, and the

promises.   Moses, and Samuel, and David, and the prophets, lived and died among its people.   No nation upon
earth ever had so many spiritual privileges.   No nation
ever misused its privileges so fearfully, and so thoroughly
forsook its own mercies.   Never did fine gold become so
dim !   From the religion of the books of Deuteronomy
and Psalms, to the religion of washing hands, and pots,
and cups, how great was the fall !   No wonder that in
the time of our Lord's earthly ministry, He found the
people like sheep without a shepherd.   External observances alone feed no consciences and sanctify no
hearts.

Let the history of the Jewish church be a warning to
us never to trifle with false doctrine. If we once tolerate
it we never know how far it may go, or into what degraded state of religion we may at last fall.   Once leave
the King's highway of truth, and we may end with washing pots and cups, like Pharisees and Scribes.   There is
nothing too mean, trifling, or irrational for a man, if he
once turns his back on God's word.   There are branches
of the Church of Christ at this day in which the Scriptures are never read, and the Gospel never preached,—
branches in which the only religion now remaining consists in using a few unmeaning forms and keeping certain
man-made fasts and feasts,—branches which began well,
like the Jewish church, and like the Jewish church, have
now fallen into utter barrenness and decay.   We can
never be too jealous about false doctrine.   A little leaven
leaveneth the whole lump.   Let us earnestly contend for
the whole faith once delivered to the saints.*

* Absurd and ridiculous as the customs and traditions of the

The second thing, that demands our attention, is *the uselessness of mere lip-service in the worship of God.* Our Lord enforces this lesson by a quotation from the Old Testament : " Well hath Esaias prophesied of you hypocrites, This people honoureth me with their lips, but their heart is far from me."

The heart is the part of man which God chiefly notices in religion. The bowed head, and the bended knee,— the grave face and the rigid posture,—the regular response, and the formal amen,—all these together do not make up a spiritual worshipper. The eyes of God look further and deeper. He requires the worship of the heart. " My son," He says to every one of us, " Give me thy heart."

Let us remember this in the public congregation. It must not content us to take our bodies to Church, if we leave our hearts at home. The eye of man may detect no flaw in our service. Our minister may look at us with approbation. Our neighbours may think us patterns of

Pharisees appear at first sight, it is a humbling fact that the Pharisees have never wanted imitators and successors. Zeal about washing pots, and cups, and tables, may seem almost ludicrous, and worthy of none but children ; but we need not look far to find an exact parallel near home. What can we say to the gravity and seriousness with which men argue on behalf of chasubles, albs, tunicles, piscinas, sedilia, credence-tables, rood-screens, and the like, in the present day ?—What can we say to the exaggerated attention paid by many to ceremonies, ornaments, gestures, and postures, in the worship of God, about which it is enough to say that Scripture is totally silent ?—What is it all but Pharisaism over again? What is it but a melancholy repetition of disproportioned zeal about men's traditional usages ? What single argument can be used in defence of these things that the Pharisees might not have used with equal force ? Eighteen hundred years have passed away, and yet the generation that made so much ado about washing pots, cups, and tables, is still amongst us. The succession of the Pharisees has never ceased.

what a Christian ought to be. Our voice may be heard foremost in the praise and prayer. But it is all worse than nothing in God's sight, if our hearts are far away. It is only wood, hay, and stubble before Him who discerns thoughts, and reads the secrets of the inward man.

Let us remember this in our private devotions. It must not satisfy us to say good words, if our heart and our lips do not go together. What does it profit us to be fluent and lengthy, if our imaginations are roving far away, while we are upon our knees?—It profits us nothing at all. God sees what we are about, and rejects our offering. Heart-prayers are the prayers He loves to hear. Heart-prayers are the only prayers that He will answer. Our petitions may be weak, and stammering, and mean in our eyes. They may be presented with no fine words, or well-chosen language, and might seem almost unintelligible, if they were written down. But if they come from a right heart, God understands them. Such prayers are His delight.

The last thing that demands our attention in these verses, is *the tendency of man's inventions in religion to supplant God's word.* Three times we find this charge brought forward by our Lord against the Pharisees. " Laying aside the commandments of God, ye hold the traditions of men."—" Full well ye reject the commandment of God, that ye may keep your own traditions." —" Making the Word of God of none effect through your traditions."—The first step of the Pharisees, was to add their traditions to the Scriptures, as useful supplements. The second was to place them on a level with the Word of God, and give them equal authority. The last was to honour them above the Scripture, and to degrade Scripture from its lawful position. This was the state of things which our Lord found when He was upon earth. Practically, the traditions of man were everything, and the Word of God was nothing at all. Obedience to the traditions constituted true religion. Obedience to the Scriptures was lost sight of altogether.

It is a mournful fact, that Christians have far too often walked in the steps of Pharisees in this matter. The very same process has taken place over and over again. The very same consequences have resulted. Religious observances of man's invention, have been pressed on the acceptance of Christians,—observances to all appearance useful, and at all events well-meant, but observances nowhere commanded in the word of God. These very observances have by and bye been enjoined with more vigour than God's own commandments, and defended with more zeal than the authority of God's own word. We need not look far for examples. The history of our own church will supply them.*

Let us beware of attempting to add any thing to the word of God, as necessary to salvation. It provokes

* The persecution of the Puritans in the time of the Stewarts, on account of canons and rubrics was, in too many cases, neither more nor less than zeal for traditions. An enormous amount of zeal was expended in enforcing conformity to the Church of England, while drunkenness, swearing, and open sin were comparatively let alone. Obedience to man-made ecclesiastical rules was required, on pain of fine or imprisonment, while open disobedience to God's ten commandments was overlooked. Experience supplies painful proof, that traditions once called into being are first called *useful*. Then they become *necessary*. At last they are too often made *idols*, and all must bow down to them, or be punished.

God to give us over to judicial blindness. It is as good as saying that His Bible is not perfect, and that we know better than He does what is necessary for man's salvation. It is just as easy to destroy the authority of God's word by addition as by subtraction, by burying it under man's inventions as by denying its truth. The whole Bible, and nothing but the Bible, must be our rule of faith,—nothing added and nothing taken away.

Finally, let us draw a broad line of distinction between those things in religion which have been devised by man, and those which are plainly commanded in God's word. What God commands is necessary to salvation. What man commands is not. What man devises may be useful and expedient for the times; but salvation does not hinge on obedience to it. What God requires is essential to life eternal. He that wilfully disobeys it ruins his own soul.*

* The subtle way in which the Pharisees evaded the requirements of the fifth commandment, to which our Lord refers in this passage, calls for a few words of explanation.

We must remember that the Pharisees did not openly deny the obligation of the fifth commandment. In all probability they professed to attach as much importance to it as any men. And yet they contrived to make it void! How did they effect this?

They taught that a man might dedicate to God's service, as sacred, any part of his property which might be applied to the relief of his parents, and so discharge himself from any further expense about them. He had only to say that all his money was "corban,"—that is, given over to holy purposes,—and no further claim could be made upon him for his father's or mother's support. Under pretence of giving God a prior claim, he set himself free from the burden of maintaining them for ever. He did not flatly deny his duty to minister of his worldly substance to his parents' necessities. But he evaded it by setting up a human tradition, and asserting a higher call of duty, even duty to God.

The likeness between the traditions and sophistries of the Pharisees, making void God's word under a pretended zeal for God's glory, and those of the Jesuits, and other advocates of the Roman

MARK VII. 14—23.

14 And when he had called all the people *unto him*, he said unto them, Hearken unto me every one *of you*, and understand :

15 There is nothing from without a man, that entering into him can defile him : but the things which come out of him, those are they that defile the man.

16 If any man have ears to hear, let him hear.

17 And when he was entered into the house from the people, his disciples asked him concerning the parable.

18 And he saith unto them, Are ye so without understanding also ? Do ye not perceive, that whatsoever thing from without entereth into the man, *it* cannot defile him ;

19 Because it entereth not into his heart, but into the belly, and goeth out into the draught, purging all meats ?

20 And he said, That which cometh out of the man, that defileth the man.

21 For from within, out of the heart of men, proceed evil thoughts, adulteries, fornications, murders,

22 Thefts, covetousness, wickedness, deceit, lasciviousness, an evil eye, blasphemy, pride, foolishness :

23 All these evil things come from within, and defile the man.

WE see in the beginning of this passage, *how slow of understanding men are in spiritual things.* " Hearken," says our Lord to the people, " hearken unto me every one of you and understand."—" Are ye so without understanding ? " He says to His disciples,—" Do ye not perceive ? "

Catholic Church, is painfully striking. The following passage from an old commentator is worth reading :

" The Scriptures teach that there is no difference to be put between meats, in regard of holiness, but that every creature of God is good. This the Papists make void by teaching that it is matter of religion and conscience to abstain from flesh meats at certain seasons.—The Scripture teacheth that we should pray to God alone. This they make void by their manifold prayers to saints departed.—The Scripture teacheth Christ alone to be our mediator, both of redemption and intercession. This they make void by making saints intercessors.—The Scripture teacheth Christ to be the only head of the church. This they abrogate by their doctrine of the Pope's supremacy.—The Scripture teacheth that every soul should be subject to the higher power. This they abrogate by exempting the Pope and popish clergy from subjection to the civil power of princes and magistrates.—Lastly, to instance in the same kind as our Saviour here against the Pharisees, whereas the word of God commands children to honour their parents, the Papists teach that if the child have vowed a monastical life, he is exempted from duty to parents."—*Petter on St. Mark.*

The corruption of human nature is an universal disease. It affects not only a man's heart, will, and conscience, but his mind, memory, and understanding. The very same person who is quick and clever in worldly things, will often utterly fail to comprehend the simplest truths of Christianity. He will often be unable to take in the plainest reasonings of the Gospel. He will see no meaning in the clearest statements of evangelical doctrine. They will sound to him either foolish or mysterious. He will listen to them like one listening to a foreign language, catching a word here and there, but not seeing the drift of the whole. "The world by wisdom knows not God." (1 Cor. i. 21.) It hears, but does not understand.

We must pray daily for the teaching of the Holy Ghost, if we would make progress in the knowledge of divine things. Without Him, the mightiest intellect and the strongest reasoning powers will carry us but a little way. In reading the Bible and hearing sermons, everything depends on the spirit in which we read and hear. A humble, teachable, child-like frame of mind is the grand secret of success. Happy is he who often says with David, "Teach me thy statutes." (Psalm cxix. 64.) Such an one will understand as well as hear.

We see, in the second place, from this passage, *that the heart is the chief source of defilement and impurity in God's sight.* Moral purity does not depend on washing or not washing,—touching things or not touching them,—eating things or not eating them, as the Scribes and Pharisees taught. "There is nothing from without a man, that entering into him can defile him: but the things which come out of him, these are they that defile the man."

There is a deep truth in these words which is frequently
overlooked.   Our original sinfulness and natural inclination to evil are seldom sufficiently considered.   The
wickedness of men is often attributed to bad examples,
bad company, peculiar temptations, or the snares of the
devil.   It seems forgotten that every man carries
within him a fountain of wickedness.   We need no bad
company to teach us, and no devil to tempt us, in order
to run into sin.   We have within us the beginning of
every sin under heaven.

We ought to remember this in the training and education of children.   In all our management we must
never forget, that the seeds of all mischief and wickedness
are in their hearts.   It is not enough to keep boys and
girls at home, and shut out every outward temptation.
They carry within them a heart ready for any sin, and
until that heart is changed they are not safe, whatever
we do.   When children do wrong, it is a common practice
to lay all the blame on bad companions.   But it is
mere ignorance, blindness, and foolishness to do so.
Bad companions are a great evil no doubt, and an evil
to be avoided as much as possible.   But no bad companion teaches a boy or girl half as much sin as their
own hearts will suggest to them, unless they are renewed
by the Spirit.   The beginning of all wickedness is within.   If parents were half as diligent in praying for
their children's conversion, as they are in keeping them
from bad company, their children would turn out far
better than they do.*

* The common arguments against " public school " education, appear to me based on forgetfulness of our Lord's teaching about the

We see, in the last place, from this passage, *what a black catalogue of evils the human heart contains.* "Out of the heart of men," says our Lord, "proceed evil thoughts, adulteries, fornications, murders, thefts, covetousness, an evil eye, blasphemy, pride, foolishness: all these evil things come from within."

Let us distinctly understand, when we read these words, that our Lord is speaking of the human heart generally. He is not speaking only of the notorious profligate, or the prisoner in the jail. He is speaking of all mankind. All of us, whether high or low, rich or poor, masters or servants, old or young, learned or un-learned,—all of us have by nature such a heart as Jesus here describes. The seeds of all the evils here mentioned lie hid within us all. They may lie dormant all our lives. They may be kept down by the fear of consequences,— the restraint of public opinion,—the dread of discovery, —the desire to be thought respectable,—and, above all, by the almighty grace of God. But every man has within him the root of every sin.

How humble we ought to be, when we read these verses! "We are all as an unclean thing" in God's

heart. Unquestionably there are many evils in " public schools," however carefully conducted. It must needs be so. We must expect it. But it is no less true that there are great dangers in private education, and dangers in their kind quite as formidable as any which beset a boy at public school. Of course no universal rule can be laid down. Regard must be had to individual character and temperament. But to suppose, as some seem to do, that boys educated at public schools must turn out ill, and boys educated at home must turn out well, is surely not wise. It is forgetting our Lord's doctrine, that the heart is the principal source of evil. Without a change of heart a boy may be kept at home, and yet learn all manner of sin.

sight. (Isai. lxiv. 6.) He sees in each one of us count-less evils, which the world never sees at all, for He reads our hearts. Surely of all sins to which we are liable, self-righteousness is the most unreasonable and unbe-coming.

How thankful we ought to be for the Gospel, when we read these verses! That Gospel contains a complete provision for all the wants of our poor defiled natures. The blood of Christ can "cleanse us from all sin." The Holy Ghost can change even our sinful hearts, and keep them clean, when changed. The man that does not glory in the Gospel, can surely know little of the plague that is within him.

How watchful we ought to be, when we remember these verses! What a careful guard we ought to keep over our imaginations, our tongues, and our daily be-haviour! At the head of the black list of our heart's contents, stand "evil thoughts." Let us never forget that. Thoughts are the parents of words and deeds. Let us pray daily for grace to keep our *thoughts* in order, and let us cry earnestly and fervently, "lead us not into temptation."

MARK VII. 24—30.

24 And from thence he arose, and went into the borders of Tyre and Sidon, and entered into an house, and would have no man know *it :* but he could not be hid.

25 For a *certain* woman, whose young daughter had an unclean spirit, heard of him, and came and fell at his feet:

26 The woman was a Greek, a Sy-rophenician by nation; and she be-sought him that he would cast forth the devil out of her daughter.

27 But Jesus said unto her, Let the children first be filled: for it is not meet to take the children's bread, and to cast *it* unto the dogs.

28 And she answered and said unto him, Yes, Lord: yet the dogs under the table eat of the children's crumbs.

29 And he said unto her, For this saying go thy way; the devil is gone out of thy daughter.

30 And when she was come to her house, she found the devil gone out, and her daughter laid upon the bed.

WE know nothing of the woman, who is here mentioned, beyond the facts that we here read. Her name, her former history, the way in which she was led to seek our Lord, though a Gentile, and dwelling in the borders of Tyre and Sidon,—all these things are hidden from us. But the few facts that are related about this woman are full of precious instruction. Let us observe them, and learn wisdom.

In the first place, *this passage is meant to encourage us to pray for others.* The woman who came to our Lord, in the history now before us, must doubtless have been in deep affliction. She saw a beloved child possessed by an unclean spirit. She saw her in a condition in which no teaching could reach the mind, and no medicine could heal the body,—a condition only one degree better than death itself. She hears of Jesus, and beseeches Him to " cast forth the devil out of her daughter." She prays for one who could not pray for herself, and never rests till her prayer is granted. By prayer she obtains the cure which no human means could obtain. Through the prayer of the mother, the daughter is healed. On her own behalf that daughter did not speak a word; but her mother spoke for her to the Lord, and did not speak in vain. Hopeless and desperate as her case appeared, she had a praying mother, and where there is a praying mother there is always hope.

The truth here taught is one of deep importance. The case here recorded is one that does not stand alone. Few duties are so strongly recommended by Scriptural example, as the duty of intercessory prayer. There is a long catalogue of instances in Scripture, which show the

benefits that may be conferred on others by praying for
them. The nobleman's son at Capernaum,—the centurion's servant,—the daughter of Jairus, are all striking
examples. Wonderful as it may seem, God is pleased to
do great things for souls, when friends and relations are
moved to pray for them. "The effectual fervent prayer of
a righteous man availeth much." (James v. 16.)

Fathers and mothers are especially bound to remember
the case of this woman. They cannot give their children
new hearts. They can give them Christian education,
and show them the way of life ; but they cannot give
them a will to choose Christ's service, and a mind to love
God. Yet there is one thing they can always do ;—they
can pray for them. They can pray for the conversion
of profligate sons, who will have their own way, and
run greedily into sin. They can pray for the conversion of worldly daughters, who set their affections
on things below, and love pleasure more than God.
Such prayers are heard on high. Such prayers will
often bring down blessings. Never, never let us forget
that the children for whom many prayers have been
offered, seldom finally perish. Let us pray more for
our sons and daughters. Even when they will not let
us speak to them about religion, they cannot prevent us
speaking for them to God.

In the second place, *this passage is meant to teach us to
persevere in praying for others.* The woman whose
history we are now reading, appeared at first to obtain
nothing by her application to our Lord. On the contrary,
our Lord's reply was discouraging. Yet she did not
give up in despair. She prayed on, and did not faint.

She pressed her suit with ingenious arguments. She would take no refusal. She pleaded for a few "crumbs" of mercy, rather than none at all. And through this holy importunity she succeeded. She heard at last these joyful words : "For this saying go thy way ; the devil is gone out of thy daughter."

Perseverance in prayer is a point of great moment. Our hearts are apt to become cool and indifferent, and to think that it is no use to draw near to God. Our hands soon hang down, and our knees wax faint. Satan is ever labouring to draw us off from our prayers, and filling our minds with reasons why we may give them up.—These things are true with respect to all prayers, but they are especially true with respect to intercessory prayer. It is always far more meagre than it ought to be. It is often attempted for a little season, and then left off. We see no immediate answer to our prayers. We see the persons for whose souls we pray, going on still in sin. We draw the conclusion that it is useless to pray for them, and allow our intercession to come to an end.

In order to arm our minds with arguments for perseverance in intercessory prayer, let us often study the case of this woman. Let us remember how she prayed on and did not faint, in the face of great discouragement. Let us mark how at last she went home rejoicing, and let us resolve, by God's grace, to follow her example.

Do we know what it is to pray for ourselves ? This, after all, is the first question for self-inquiry. The man who never speaks to God about his own soul, can know nothing of praying for others. He is as yet

Godless, Christless, and hopeless, and has to learn the very rudiments of religion. Let him awake, and call upon God.

But do we pray for ourselves ? Then let us take heed that we pray for others also. Let us beware of selfish prayers,—prayers which are wholly taken up with our own affairs, and in which there is no place for other souls beside our own. Let us name all whom we love before God continually. Let us pray for all,—the worst, the hardest, and the most unbelieving. Let us continue praying for them year after year, in spite of their continued unbelief. God's time of mercy may be a distant one. Our eyes may not see an answer to our intercessions. The answer may not come for ten, fifteen, or twenty years. It may not come till we have exchanged prayer for praise, and are far away from this world. But while we live, let us pray for others. It is the greatest kindness we can do to any one, to speak for him to our Lord Jesus Christ. The day of judgment will show that one of the greatest links in drawing some souls to God, has been the intercessory prayer of friends.

MARK VII. 31—37.

31 And again, departing from the coasts of Tyre and Sidon, he came unto the sea of Galilee, through the midst of the coasts of Decapolis.

32 And they bring unto him one that was deaf, and had an impediment in his speech ; and they beseech him to put his hand upon him.

33 And he took him aside from the multitude, and put his fingers into his ears, and he spit, and touched his tongue ;

34 And looking up to heaven, he sighed, and saith unto him, Ephphatha, that is, Be opened.

35 And straightway his ears were opened, and the string of his tongue was loosed, and he spake plain.

36 And he charged them that they should tell no man : but the more he charged them, so much the more a great deal they published it ;

37 And were beyond measure astonished, saying, He hath done all things well : he maketh both the deaf to hear, and the dumb to speak.

THE first thing that demands our notice in these verses, is *the mighty miracle which is here recorded.* We read that they brought unto our Lord "one that was deaf and had an impediment in his speech," and besought him that He would "put His hand upon Him." At once the petition is granted, and the cure is wrought. Speech and hearing are instantaneously given to the man by a word and a touch. "Straightway his ears were opened, and the string of his tongue was loosed, and he spake plain."

We see but half the instruction of this passage, if we only regard it as an example of our Lord's divine power. It is such an example, beyond doubt, but it is something more than that. We must look further, deeper, and lower than the surface, and we shall find in the passage precious spiritual truths.

Here we are meant to see our Lord's power to heal the spiritually deaf. He can give the chief of sinners a hearing ear. He can make him delight in listening to the very Gospel which he once ridiculed and despised.

Here also we are meant to see our Lord's power to heal the spiritually dumb. He can teach the hardest of transgressors to call upon God. He can put a new song in the mouth of him whose talk was once only of this world. He can make the vilest of men speak of spiritual things, and testify the Gospel of the grace of God.

When Jesus pours forth His Spirit, nothing is impossible. We must never despair of others. We must never regard our own hearts as too bad to be changed. He that healed the deaf and dumb still lives. The cases which moral philosophy pronounces hopeless, are not incurable if they are brought to Christ.

The second thing which demands our notice in these verses, is *the peculiar manner in which our Lord thought good to work the miracle here recorded.* We are told that when the deaf and dumb person was brought to Jesus, " He took him aside from the multitude, and put his fingers into his ears, and he spit and touched his tongue ; and looking up to heaven, he sighed,"—and then, and not till then, came the words of commanding power, " Ephphatha, that is, be opened."

There is undoubtedly much that is mysterious in these actions. We know not why they were used. It would have been as easy to our Lord to speak the word, and command health to return at once, as to do what He here did. His reasons for the course He adopted are not recorded. We only know that the result was the same as on other occasions ;—the man was cured.

But there is one simple lesson to be learned from our Lord's conduct on this occasion. That lesson is, that Christ was not tied to the use of any one means in doing His works among men. Sometimes He thought fit to work in one way, sometimes in another. His enemies were never able to say, that unless He employed certain invariable agency He could not work at all.

We see the same thing going on still in the Church of Christ. We see continual proof that the Lord is not tied to the use of any one means exclusively in conveying grace to the soul. Sometimes He is pleased to work by the word preached publicly, sometimes by the word read privately. Sometimes He awakens people by sickness and affliction, sometimes by the rebukes or counsel of friends. Sometimes He employs means of grace to turn people out of the way of sin. Sometimes He arrests their attention by some providence, without any means of grace at all. He will not have any means of grace made an idol and exalted, to the disparagement of other means. He will not have any means despised as useless, and neglected as of no value. All are good and valuable. All are in their turn employed for the same great end, the conversion of souls. All are in the hands of Him who "giveth not account of His matters," and knows best which to use, in each separate case that He heals.

The last thing which demands our notice in these verses, is *the remarkable testimony which was borne by those who saw the miracle here recorded.* They said of our Lord, " He hath done all things well ! "

It is more than probable that those who said these words were little sensible of their full meaning, when applied to Christ. Like Caiaphas, they "spoke not of themselves." (John xi. 51.) But the truth to which they gave utterance is full of deep and unspeakable comfort, and ought to be daily remembered by all true Christians.

Let us remember it as we look back over the days past of our lives, from the hour of our conversion. "Our Lord hath done all things well." In first bringing us out of darkness into marvellous light,—in humbling us and teaching us our weakness, guilt, and folly,—in stripping us of our idols, and choosing all our portions, —in placing us where we are, and giving us what we have,—how well everything has been done ! How great the mercy that we have not had our own way !

Let us remember it as we look forward to the days yet to come. We know not what they may be, bright or dark, many or few. But we know that we are in the hands of Him who "doeth all things well." He will not err in any of his dealings with us. He will take away and give,—He will afflict and bereave,—He will move and He will settle, with perfect wisdom, at the right time, in the right way. The great Shepherd of the sheep makes no mistakes. He leads every lamb of His flock by the right way to the city of habitation.

We shall never see the full beauty of these words till the resurrection morning. We shall then look back over our lives, and know the meaning of everything that happened from first to last. We shall remember all the way by which we were led, and confess that all was "well done." The why and the wherefore, the causes and the reasons of every thing which now perplexes, will be clear and plain as the sun at noon-day. We shall wonder at our own past blindness, and marvel that we could ever have doubted our Lord's love. "Now we see through a glass darkly, but then face to face. Now we know in part, but then shall we know even as we are known." * (1 Cor. xiii. 13.)

---

* The reason why our Lord made use of the previous actions recorded in this miracle,—spitting, looking up to heaven, and sighing,—is a question that has often perplexed commentators. Some observations of Luther, quoted by Stier, are worth reading:

"This sigh was not drawn from Christ on account of the single tongue and ear of this poor man; but it is a common sigh over all tongues and ears, yea over all hearts, bodies, and souls, and over all men from Adam to his last descendant."

"Our beloved Lord saw well what an amount of suffering and sorrow would be occasioned by tongues and ears. For the greatest

MARK VIII. 1—13.

1 In those days the multitude being very great, and having nothing to eat, Jesus called his disciples *unto him*, and saith unto them,

2 I have compassion on the multitude, because they have now been with me three days, and have nothing to eat:

3 And if I send them away fasting, to their own houses, they will faint by the way: for divers of them came from far.

4 And his disciples answered him, From whence can a man satisfy these *men* with bread here in the wilderness?

5 And he asked them, How many loaves have ye? And they said, Seven.

6 And he commanded the people to sit down on the ground: and he took the seven loaves, and gave thanks, and brake, and gave to his disciples to set before *them ;* and they did set *them* before the people.

7 And they had a few small fishes: and he blessed, and commanded to set them also before *them*.

8 So they did eat, and were filled: and they took up of the broken *meat* that was left seven baskets.

9 And they that had eaten were about four thousand : and he sent them away.

10 And straightway he entered into a ship with his disciples, and came into the parts of Dalmanutha.

11 And the Pharisees came forth, and began to question with him, seeking of him a sign from heaven, tempting him.

12 And he sighed deeply in his spirit, and saith, Why doth this generation seek after a sign? verily I say unto you, There shall no sign be given unto this generation.

13 And he left them, and entering into the ship again departed to the other side.

ONCE more we see our Lord feeding a great multitude with a few loaves and fishes. He knew the heart of man. He foresaw the rise of cavillers and sceptics, who would question the reality of the wonderful works He performed. By repeating the mighty miracle here recorded, He stops the mouth of all who are not wilfully blind to evidence. Publicly, and before four thousand witnesses, He shows His almighty power a second time.

Let us observe in this passage *how great is the kindness and compassion of our Lord Jesus Christ.* He saw around Him a " very great multitude," who had nothing to eat. He knew that the great majority were following

mischief which has been inflicted on Christianity, has not arisen from tyrants, (with persecution, murder, and pride against the word,) but from that little bit of flesh which abides between the jaws. This it is that inflicts the greatest injury upon the kingdom of God."

Him from no other motive than idle curiosity, and had no claim whatever to be regarded as His disciples. Yet when He saw them hungry and destitute, He pitied them:—"I have compassion on the multitude, because they have now been with me three days, and have nothing to eat."

The feeling heart of our Lord Jesus Christ appears in these words. He has compassion even on those who are not His people,—the faithless, the graceless, the followers of this world. He feels tenderly for them, though they know it not. He died for them, though they care little for what He did on the cross. He would receive them graciously, and pardon them freely, if they would only repent and believe on Him. Let us ever beware of measuring the love of Christ by any human measure. He has a special love, beyond doubt, for His own believing people. But He has also a general love of compassion, even for the unthankful and the evil. His love "passeth knowledge." (Ephes. iii. 19.)

Let us strive to make Jesus our pattern in this, as well as in everything else. Let us be kind, and compassionate, and pitiful, and courteous to all men. Let us be ready to do good to all men, and not only to friends and the household of faith. Let us carry into practice our Lord's injunction, "Love your enemies, bless them that curse you, do good to them that hate you." (Matt. v. 44.) This is to show the mind of Christ. This is the right way to heap coals of fire on an enemy's head, and to melt foes into friends. (Rom. xii. 20.)

Let us observe, in the second place, from this passage, *that with Christ nothing is impossible.* The disciples said,

" from whence can a man satisfy these men with bread here in the wilderness?" They might well say so. Without the hand of Him who first made the world out of nothing, the thing could not be. But in the almighty hands of Jesus seven loaves and a few fishes were made sufficient to satisfy four thousand men. Nothing is too hard for the Lord.

We must never allow ourselves to doubt Christ's power to supply the spiritual wants of all His people. He has " bread enough and to spare" for every soul that trusts in Him. Weak, infirm, corrupt, empty as believers feel themselves, let them never despair, while Jesus lives. In Him there is a boundless store of mercy and grace, laid up for the use of all His believing members, and ready to be bestowed on all who ask in prayer. "It pleased the Father that in Him should all fulness dwell." (Coloss. i. 19.)

Let us never doubt Christ's providential care for the temporal wants of all His people. He knows their circumstances. He is acquainted with all their necessities. He will never allow them to lack anything that is really for their good. His heart is not changed since He ascended up on high, and sat down on the right hand of God. He still lives who had compassion on the hungry crowd in the wilderness, and supplied their need. How much more, may we suppose, will He supply the need of those who trust Him? He will supply them without fail. Their faith may occasionally be tried. They may sometimes be kept waiting, and be brought very low. But the believer shall never be left entirely destitute. " Bread shall be given him ; his water shall be sure." (Isaiah xxxiii. 16.)

Let us observe, in the last place, *how much sorrow unbelief occasions to our Lord Jesus Christ.* We are told that when "the Pharisees began to question with Him, seeking of Him a sign from heaven, tempting Him, He sighed deeply in His spirit." There was a deep meaning in that sigh! It came from a heart which mourned over the ruin that these wicked men were bringing on their own souls. Enemies as they were, Jesus could not behold them hardening themselves in unbelief without sorrow.

The feeling which our Lord Jesus Christ here expressed, will always be the feeling of all true Christians. Grief over the sins of others is one leading evidence of true grace. The man who is really converted, will always regard the unconverted with pity and concern. This was the mind of David: "I beheld the transgressors, and was grieved." (Psalm cxix. 158.) This was the mind of the godly in the days of Ezekiel: "They sighed and cried for the abominations done in the land." (Ezek. ix. 4.) This was the mind of Lot: "He vexed his righteous soul with the unlawful deeds" of those around him. (2 Peter ii. 8.) This was the mind of Paul: "I have great heaviness and continual sorrow for my brethren." (Rom. ix. 2.) In all these cases we see something of the mind of Christ. As the great Head feels, so feel the members. They all grieve when they see sin.

Let us leave the passage with solemn self-inquiry. Do we know anything of likeness to Christ, and fellow-feeling with Him? Do we feel hurt, and pained, and sorrowful, when we see men continuing in sin and unbelief? Do

we feel grieved and concerned about the state of the unconverted? These are heart-searching questions, and
demand serious consideration. There are few surer marks
of an unconverted heart, than carelessness and indifference about the souls of others.

Finally, let us never forget that unbelief and sin are
just as great a cause of grief to our Lord now, as they
were eighteen hundred years ago. Let us strive and
pray that we may not add to that grief by any act or
deed of ours. The sin of grieving Christ is one which
many commit continually without thought or reflection.
He that sighed over the unbelief of the Pharisees is still
unchanged. Can we doubt that when He sees some
persisting in unbelief at the present day, He is grieved?
From such sin may we be delivered!

MARK VIII. 14—21.

14 Now *the disciples* had forgotten to take bread, neither had they in the ship with them more than one loaf.

15 And he charged them, saying, Take heed, beware of the leaven of the Pharisees, and *of* the leaven of Herod.

16 And they reasoned among themselves, saying, *It is* because we have no bread.

17 And when Jesus knew *it*, he saith unto them, Why reason ye, because ye have no bread? perceive ye not yet, neither understand? have ye your heart yet hardened?

18 Having eyes, see ye not? and having ears, hear ye not? and do ye not remember?

19 When I brake the five loaves among five thousand, how many baskets full of fragments took ye up? They say unto him, Twelve.

20 And when the seven among four thousand, how many baskets full of fragments took ye up? And they said, Seven.

21 And he said unto them, How is it that ye do not understand?

LET us notice *the solemn warning* which our Lord gives to
His disciples at the beginning of this passage. He says,
"take heed, beware of the leaven of the Pharisees,
and of the leaven of Herod."

We are not left to conjecture the meaning of this warning. This is made clear by the parallel passage in St. Matthew's Gospel. We there read that Jesus did not mean the leaven of " bread," but the leaven of " doctrine." The self-righteousness and formalism of the Pharisees,— the worldliness and scepticism of the courtiers of Herod, were the objects of our Lord's caution. Against both He bids His disciples be on their guard.

Such warnings are of deep importance. It would be well for the Church of Christ, if they had been more remembered. The assaults of persecution from without have never done half so much harm to the Church, as the rise of false doctrines within. False prophets and false teachers within the camp have done far more mischief in Christendom than all the bloody persecutions of the emperors of Rome.—The sword of the foe has never done such damage to the cause of truth as the tongue and the pen.

The doctrines which our Lord specify, are precisely those which have always been found to inflict most injury on the cause of Christianity. Formalism on the one hand, and scepticism on the other, have been chronic diseases in the professing Church of Christ. In every age multitudes of Christians have been infected by them. In every age men need to watch against them, and be on their guard.

The expression used by our Lord in speaking of false doctrine is singularly forcible and appropriate. He calls it "leaven." No word more suitable could have been employed. It exactly describes the small beginnings of false doctrine,—the subtle quiet way in which it insensibly pervades a man's religion,—the deadly power with which it changes the whole character of his Christianity. Here, in fact, lies the great danger of false doctrine. If it approached us under its true colours, it would do little harm. The great secret of its success is its subtlety and likeness to truth. Every error in religion has been said to be a truth abused.

Let us often "examine ourselves whether we be in the faith," and beware of "leaven." Let us no more trifle with a little false doctrine, than we would trifle with a little immorality or a little lie. Once admit it into our hearts, and we never know how far it may lead us astray. The beginning of departure from the pure truth is like the letting out of waters,—first a drop, and at last a torrent. A little leaven leaveneth the whole lump. (Gal. v. 9.)

Let us notice *the dull understanding of the disciples,* when our Lord gave the warning of this passage. They thought that the "leaven" of which He spoke must be the leaven of bread. It never struck them that He was speaking of doctrine. They drew from Him the sharp reproof: "Perceive ye not yet, neither understand? have ye your heart yet hardened? How is it that ye do not understand?" Believers, converted, renewed, as the disciples were, they were still dull of apprehension in spiritual things. Their eyes were still dim, and their perception slow in the matters of the kingdom of God.

We shall find it useful to ourselves to remember what is here recorded of the disciples. It may help to correct the high thoughts which we are apt to entertain of our own wisdom, and to keep us humble and lowly-minded.

We must not fancy that we know everything as soon as we are converted. Our knowledge, like all our graces, is always imperfect, and never so far from perfection as at our first beginning in the service of Christ. There is more ignorance in our hearts than we are at all aware of. "If any man think that he knoweth anything, he knoweth nothing yet as he ought to know." (1 Cor. viii. 2.)

Above all, we shall find it useful to remember what is here recorded, in dealing with young Christians. We must not expect perfection in a new convert. We must not set him down as graceless and godless and a false professor, because at first he sees but half the truth and commits many mistakes. His heart may be right in the sight of God, and yet, like the disciples, he may be very slow of understanding in the things of the Spirit. We must bear with him patiently, and not cast him aside. We must give him time to grow in grace and knowledge, and his latter end may find him ripe in wisdom, like Peter and John. It is a blessed thought that Jesus, our Master in heaven, despises none of His people. Marvellous and blameworthy as their slowness to learn undoubtedly is, His patience never gives way. He goes on teaching them, "line upon line, precept upon precept." Let us do likewise. Let it be a rule with us never to despise the weakness and dulness of young Christians. Wherever we see a spark of true grace, however dim and mixed with infirmity, let us be helpful and kind. Let us do as we would be done by.

MARK VIII. 22—26.

22 And he cometh to Bethsaida; and they bring a blind man unto him, and besought him to touch him.
23 And he took the blind man by

the hand, and led him out of the town; and when he had spit on his eyes, and put his hands upon him, he asked him if he saw ought.

24 And he looked up, and said, I see men as trees, walking.

25 After that he put *his* hands again upon his eyes, and made him look up: and he was restored, and saw every man clearly.

26 And he sent him away to his house, saying, Neither go into the town, nor tell *it* to any in the town.

WE do not know the reason of the peculiar means employed by our Lord Jesus Christ, in working the miracle recorded in these verses. We see a blind man miraculously healed. We know that a word from our Lord's mouth, or a touch of His hand would have been sufficient to effect a cure. But we see Jesus taking this blind man by the hand,—leading him out of the town,—spitting on his eyes,—putting His hands on him, and then, and not till then, restoring his sight. And the meaning of all these actions, the passage before us leaves entirely unexplained.

But it is well to remember, in reading passages of this kind, that the Lord is not tied to the use of any one means. In the conversion of men's souls there are diversities of operation, but it is the same Spirit which converts. So also in the healing of men's bodies there were varieties of agency employed by our Lord, but it was the same divine power that effected the cure. In all His works God is a sovereign. He giveth not account of any of His matters.

One thing in the passage demands our special observation. That thing is the gradual nature of the cure, which our Lord performed on this blind man. He did not deliver him from his blindness at once, but by degrees. He might have done it in a moment, but He chose to do it step by step. First the blind man said that he only saw " men as trees walking." Afterwards his eyesight was restored completely, and he " saw every man clearly." In this respect the miracle stands entirely alone.

We need hardly doubt that this gradual cure was meant to be an emblem of spiritual things. We may be sure that there was a deep meaning in every word and work of our Lord's earthly ministry, and here, as in other places, we shall find a useful lesson.

Let us see then in this gradual restoration to sight, a vivid illustration of *the manner in which the Spirit frequently works in the conversion of souls.* We are all naturally blind and ignorant in the matters which concern our souls. Conversion is an illumination, a change from darkness to light, from blindness to seeing the kingdom of God. Yet few converted people see things distinctly at first. The nature and proportion of doctrines, practices, and ordinances of the Gospel are dimly seen by them, and imperfectly understood. They are like the man before us, who at first saw men as trees walking. Their vision is dazzled and unaccustomed to the new world into which they have been introduced. It is not till the work of the Spirit has become deeper and their experience been somewhat matured, that they see all things clearly, and give to each part of religion its proper place. This is the history of thousands of God's children. They begin with seeing men as trees walking,—they end with seeing all clearly. Happy is he who has learned this lesson well, and is humble and distrustful of his own judgment.

Finally, let us see in the gradual cure of this blind

man, a striking picture of *the present position of Christ's believing people in the world,* compared with that which is to come. We see in part and know in part in the present dispensation. We are like those that travel by night. We know not the meaning of much that is passing around us. In the providential dealings of God with His children, and in the conduct of many of God's saints, we see much that we cannot understand,—and cannot alter. In short, we are like him that saw "men as trees walking."

But let us look forward and take comfort. The time comes when we shall see all "clearly." The night is far spent. The day is at hand. Let us be content to wait, and watch, and work, and pray. When the day of the Lord comes, our spiritual eye-sight will be perfected. We shall see as we have been seen, and know as we have been known.

MARK VIII. 27—33.

27 And Jesus went out, and his disciples, into the towns of Cæsarea Philippi: and by the way he asked his disciples, saying unto them, Whom do men say that I am?

28 And they answered, John the Baptist: but some *say,* Elias; and others, One of the prophets.

29 And he saith unto them, But whom say ye that I am? And Peter answereth and saith unto him, Thou art the Christ.

30 And he charged them that they should tell no man of him.

31 And he began to teach them,

that the Son of man must suffer many things, and be rejected of the elders, and *of* the Chief Priests, and Scribes, and be killed, and after three days rise again.

32 And he spake that saying openly. And Peter took him, and began to rebuke him.

33 But when he had turned about and looked on his disciples, he rebuked Peter, saying, Get thee behind me, Satan : for thou savourest not the things that be of God, but the things that be of men.

The circumstances here recorded are of great importance. They took place during a journey, and arose

out of a conversation "by the way." Happy are those
journeys, in which time is not wasted on trifles, but
redeemed as far as possible for the consideration of
serious things.

Let us observe *the variety of opinions about Christ,*
which prevailed among the Jews. Some said that he
was John the Baptist,—some Elias,—and others one of
the prophets. In short every kind of opinion appears to
have been current, excepting that one which was true.

We may see the same thing on every side at the
present day. Christ and his Gospel are just as little
understood in reality, and are the subject of just as many
different opinions as they were eighteen hundred years
ago. Many know the name of Christ, acknowledge Him
as one who came into the world to save sinners, and
regularly worship in buildings set apart for His service.
Few thoroughly realize that He is very God,—the one
Mediator,—the one High Priest,—the only source of life
and peace,—their own Shepherd and their own Friend.
Vague ideas about Christ are still very common. In-
telligent experimental acquaintance with Christ is still
very rare. May we never rest till we can say of Christ,
"My beloved is mine and I am His." (Cant. ii. 16.)
This is saving knowledge. This is life eternal.

Let us observe *the good confession of faith which the
apostle Peter witnessed.* He replied to our Lord's question,
"Whom say ye that I am?" "Thou art the Christ."

This was a noble answer, when the circumstances
under which it was made are duly considered. It was
made when Jesus was poor in condition, without honour,
majesty, wealth, or power. It was made when the

heads of the Jewish nation, both in church and state, refused to receive Jesus as the Messiah. Yet even then Simon Peter says, "Thou art the Christ." His strong faith was not stumbled by our Lord's poverty and low estate. His confidence was not shaken by the opposition of Scribes and Pharisees, and the contempt of rulers and priests. None of these things moved Simon Peter. He believed that He whom he followed, Jesus of Nazareth, was the promised Saviour, the true Prophet greater than Moses, the long-predicted Messiah. He declared it boldly and unhesitatingly, as the creed of himself and his few companions : "Thou art the Christ."

There is much that we may profitably learn from Peter's conduct on this occasion. Erring and unstable as he sometimes was,—the faith he exhibited in the passage now before us is well worthy of imitation. Such bold confessions as his, are the truest evidence of living faith, and are required in every age, if men will prove themselves to be Christ's disciples. We too must be ready to confess Christ, even as Peter did. We shall never find our Master and His doctrine popular. We must be prepared to confess Him, with few on our side, and many against us. But let us take courage and walk in Peter's steps, and we shall not fail of receiving Peter's reward. Jesus takes notice of those who confess Him before men, and will one day confess them as His servants before an assembled world.

Let us observe *the full declaration which our Lord makes of His own coming death and resurrection.* We read that "He began to teach them, that the Son of man must suffer many things, and be rejected of the elders,

and of the chief priests, and scribes, and be killed, and
after three days rise again."

The events here announced must have sounded strange
to the disciples. To be told that their beloved Master,
after all His mighty works, would soon be put to death,
must have been heavy tidings and past their understanding. But the words which convey the announcement are scarcely less remarkable than the event;—"He
must suffer,—He *must* be killed,—He *must* rise again."

Why did our Lord say "must?" Did He mean that
He was unable to escape suffering,—that He must die
by compulsion of a stronger power than His own?
Impossible. This could not have been His meaning.—
Did He mean that He must needs die to give a great
example to the world of self-sacrifice and self-denial, and
that this, and this alone, made His death necessary?
Once more it may be replied, "Impossible."—There is a
far deeper meaning in the word "must" suffer and be
killed. He meant that His death and passion were
necessary in order to make atonement for man's sin.
Without shedding His blood, there could be no remission.
Without the sacrifice of His body on the cross, there
could be no satisfaction to God's holy law. He "must"
suffer to make reconciliation for iniquity. He "must" die,
because without His death as a propitiatory offering, sinners could never have life. He "must" suffer, because
without His vicarious sufferings, our sins could never be
taken away. In a word, He "must" be delivered for our
offences, and raised again for our justification.

Here is the centre truth of the Bible. Let us never
forget that. All other truths compared to this are of

secondary importance. Whatever views we hold of religious truth, let us see that we have a firm grasp upon the atoning efficacy of Christ's death. Let the truth so often proclaimed by our Lord to His disciples, and so diligently taught by the disciples to the world, be the foundation truth in our Christianity. In life and in death, in health and in sickness, let us lean all our weight on this mighty fact,—that though we have sinned Christ hath died for sinners,—and that though we deserve nothing, Christ hath suffered on the cross for us, and by that suffering purchased heaven for all that believe in Him.

Finally, let us observe in this passage *the strange mixture of grace and infirmity which may be found in the heart of a true Christian.* We see that very Peter who had just witnessed so noble a confession, presuming to rebuke his Master because He spoke of suffering and dying. We see Him drawing down on Himself the sharpest rebuke which ever fell from our Lord's lips during His earthly ministry :—" Get thee behind me, Satan : thou savourest not the things that be of God, but the things that be of man."

We have here a humbling proof that the best of saints is a poor fallible creature.—Here was *ignorance* in Simon Peter. He did not understand the necessity of our Lord's death, and would have actually prevented His sacrifice on the cross.—Here was *self-conceit* in Simon Peter. He thought he knew what was right and fitting for his Master better than his Master himself, and actually undertook to show the Messiah a more excellent way.—And last, but not least, Simon Peter did it all with the *best intentions!* He meant well. His motives were pure. But zeal and earnestness are no excuse for error. A man may mean well and yet fall into tremendous mistakes.

Let us learn humility from the facts here recorded. Let us beware of being puffed up with our own spiritual attainments, or exalted by the praise of others. Let us never think that we know everything and are not likely to err. We see that it is but a little step from making a good confession to being a "Satan" in Christ's way. Let us pray daily, "Hold thou me up,—keep me,—teach me,—let me not err."

Lastly, let us learn charity towards others from the facts here recorded. Let us not be in a hurry to cast off our brother as graceless because of errors and mistakes. Let us remember that his heart may be right in the sight of God, like Peter's, though like Peter he may for a time turn aside. Rather let us call to mind St. Paul's advice and act upon it. "If a man be overtaken in a fault, ye which are spiritual, restore such an one in the spirit of meekness; considering thyself, lest thou also be tempted." (Gal. vi. 1.)

MARK VIII. 34—38.

34 And when he had called the people *unto him* with his disciples also, he said unto them, Whosoever will come after me, let him deny himself, and take up his cross, and follow me.

35 For whosoever will save his life shall lose it; but whosoever shall lose his life for my sake and the Gospel's, the same shall save it.

36 For what shall it profit a man, if he shall gain the whole world, and lose his own soul?

37 Or what shall a man give in exchange for his soul?

38 Whosoever therefore shall be ashamed of me and of my words in this adulterous and sinful generation; of him also shall the Son of man be ashamed, when he cometh in the glory of his Father with the holy angels.

THE words of our Lord Jesus Christ in this passage are peculiarly weighty and solemn. They were spoken to correct the mistaken views of His disciples, as to the nature of His kingdom. But they contain truths of the deepest importance to Christians in every age of the Church. The whole passage is one which should often form the subject of private meditation.

We learn, for one thing, from these verses, *the absolute necessity of self-denial, if we would be Christ's disciples, and be saved.* What saith our Lord? "Whosoever will come after me, let him deny himself, and take up his cross, and follow me."

Salvation is undoubtedly all of grace. It is offered freely in the Gospel to the chief of sinners, without money and without price. "By grace are ye saved through faith, and that not of yourselves; it is the gift of God: not of works, lest any man should boast." (Ephes. ii. 8, 9.) But all who accept this great salvation, must prove the reality of their faith by carrying the cross after Christ. They must not think to enter heaven without trouble, pain, suffering, and conflict on earth. They must be content to take up the cross of doctrine, and the cross of practice,—the cross of holding a faith which the world despises, and the cross of living a life which the world ridicules as too strict and righteous overmuch. They must be willing to crucify the flesh, to mortify the deeds of the body, to fight daily with the devil, to come out from the world, and to lose their lives, if needful, for Christ's sake and the Gospel's.—These are hard sayings, but they admit of no evasion. The words of our Lord are plain and unmistakeable. If we will not carry the cross, we shall never wear the crown.

Let us not be deterred from Christ's service by fear of the cross. Heavy as that cross may seem, Jesus will give us grace to bear it. "I can do all things through Christ which strengtheneth me." (Phil. iv. 13.) Thousands and tens of thousands have borne it before us, and have found Christ's yoke easy, and Christ's burden light. No good thing on earth was ever attained without trouble. We cannot surely expect that without trouble we can enter the kingdom of God. Let us go forward boldly, and allow no difficulty to keep us back. The cross by the way is but for a few years. The glory at the end is for evermore.

Let us often ask ourselves whether our Christianity costs us anything? Does it entail any sacrifice? Has it the true stamp of heaven? Does it carry with it any cross?—If not, we may well tremble and be afraid. We have everything to learn. A religion which costs nothing, is worth nothing. It will do us no good in the life that now is. It will lead to no salvation in the life to come.

We learn, for another thing, from these verses, *the unspeakable value of the soul*. What saith our Lord? "What shall it profit a man if he shall gain the whole world, and lose his own soul?" These words were meant to stir us up to exertion and self-denial. They ought to ring in our ears like a trumpet, every morning when we rise from our beds, and every night when we lie down. May they be deeply graven in our memories, and never effaced by the devil and the world!

We have all souls that will live for evermore. Whether we know it or not, we all carry about with us something which will live on when our bodies are mouldering in the grave. We have all souls, for which we shall have to give account to God. It is an awful thought, when we consider how little attention most men give to anything except this world. But it is true.

Any man may lose his own soul. He cannot save it : Christ alone can do that. But he can lose it, and that in many different ways. He may murder it, by loving sin and cleaving to the world.—He may poison it by choosing a religion of lies, and believing man-made superstitions.—He may starve it, by neglecting all means of grace, and refusing to receive into his heart the Gospel. —Many are the ways that lead to the pit. Whatever way a man takes, he, and he alone, is accountable for it. Weak, corrupt, fallen, impotent as human nature is, man has a mighty power of destroying, ruining, and losing his own soul.

The whole world cannot make up to a man the loss of his soul. The possession of all the treasures that the world contains, would not compensate for eternal ruin. They would not satisfy us, and make us happy while we had them. They could only be enjoyed for a few years, at best, and must then be left for evermore. Of all un-profitable and foolish bargains that man can make, the worst is that of giving up his soul's salvation for the sake of this present world. It is a bargain of which thousands, like Esau, who sold his birthright for a mess of pottage, have repented,—but many, unhappily, like Esau, have repented too late.

Let these sayings of our Lord sink deep into our hearts. Words are inadequate to express their importance. May we remember them in the hour of temptation, when the

soul seems a small and unimportant thing, and the world
seems very bright and great. May we remember them
in the hour of persecution, when we are tried by the fear
of man, and half inclined to forsake Christ. In hours
like these, let us call to mind this mighty question of our
Lord, and repeat it to ourselves, "What shall it profit a
man if he gain the whole world, and lose his own soul?"

We learn, in the last place, from these verses, *the great
danger of being ashamed of Christ.* What saith our
Lord? "Whosoever shall be ashamed of me and of my
words in this adulterous and sinful generation, of him
also shall the Son of Man be ashamed when He cometh
in the glory of His Father with the holy angels."

When can it be said of any one, that he is ashamed
of Christ? We are guilty of it, when we are ashamed
of letting people see that we believe and love the doctrines
of Christ, that we desire to live according to the commandment of Christ, and that we wish to be reckoned
among the people of Christ. Christ's doctrine, laws, and
people were never popular, and never will be. The man
who boldly confesses that he loves them, is sure to bring
on himself ridicule and persecution. Whosoever shrinks
from this confession from fear of this ridicule and persecution, is ashamed of Christ, and comes under the
sentence of the passage before us.

Perhaps there are few of our Lord's sayings which are
more condemning than this. "The fear of man" does
indeed " bring a snare." (Prov. xxix. 25.) There are
thousands of men who would face a lion, or storm a
breach, if duty called them, and fear nothing,—and yet
would be ashamed of being thought "religious,"—and

would not dare to avow that they desired to please Christ rather than man. Wonderful indeed is the power of ridicule! Marvellous is the bondage in which men live to the opinion of the world!

Let us all pray daily for faith and courage to confess Christ before men. Of sin, or worldliness, or unbelief, we may well be ashamed. We ought never to be ashamed of Him who died for us on the cross. In spite of laughter, mockery, and hard words, let us boldly avow that we serve Christ. Let us often look forward to the day of His second coming, and remember what He says in this place. Better a thousand times confess Christ now, and be despised by man, than be disowned by Christ before His Father in the day of judgment.

MARK IX. 1—13.

1 And he said unto them, Verily I say unto you, That there be some of them that stand here, which shall not taste of death, till they have seen the kingdom of God come with power.

2 And after six days Jesus taketh *with him* Peter, and James, and John, and leadeth them up into an high mountain apart by themselves: and he was transfigured before them.

3 And his raiment became shining, exceeding white as snow; so as no fuller on earth can white them.

4 And there appeared unto them Elias with Moses: and they were talking with Jesus.

5 And Peter answered and said to Jesus, Master, it is good for us to be here: and let us make three tabernacles; one for thee, and one for Moses, and one for Elias.

6 For he wist not what to say; for they were sore afraid.

7 And there was a cloud that overshadowed them: and a voice came out of the cloud, saying, This is my beloved Son: hear him.

8 And suddenly, when they had looked round about, they saw no man any more, save Jesus only with themselves.

9 And as they came down from the mountain, he charged them that they should tell no man what things they had seen, till the Son of man was risen from the dead.

10 And they kept that saying with themselves, questioning one with another what the rising from the dead should mean.

11 And they asked him, saying, Why say the Scribes that Elias must first come?

12 And he answered and told them, Elias verily cometh first, and restoreth all things; and how it is written of the Son of man, that he must suffer many things, and be set at nought.

13 But I say unto you, That Elias is indeed come, and they have done unto him whatsoever they listed, as it is written of him.

THE connection of this passage with the end of the last chapter ought never to be overlooked. Our Lord had been speaking of His own coming death and passion,—of the necessity of self-denial, if men would be His disciples, —of the need of losing our lives, if we would have them saved.—But in the same breath He goes on to speak of His future kingdom and glory. He takes off the edge of His "hard sayings," by promising a sight of that glory to some of those who heard Him. And in the history of the transfiguration, which is here recorded, we see that promise fulfilled.

The first thing which demands our notice in these verses, is *the marvellous vision they contain of the glory which Christ and His people shall have at His second coming.*

There can be no doubt that this was one of the principal purposes of the transfiguration. It was meant to teach the disciples, that though their Lord was lowly and poor in appearance now, He would one day appear in such royal majesty as became the Son of God. It was meant to teach them, that when their Master came the second time, His saints, like Moses and Elias, would appear with Him. It was meant to remind them, that though reviled and persecuted now, because they belonged to Christ, they would one day be clothed with honour, and be partakers of their Master's glory.*

* The analogy between the glory assumed by our Lord at His transfiguration, and the glory which the saints shall receive at His resurrection, is well pointed out by Victor Antiochenus in a passage quoted by Du Veil. He says, "We must not suppose that there is to be any change of the natural form of man in the kingdom of heaven. For as the appearance of Christ was not in

We have reason to thank God for this vision. We are often tempted to give up Christ's service, because of the cross and affliction which it entails. We see few with us, and many against us. We find our names cast out as evil, and all manner of evil said of us, because we believe and love the Gospel. Year after year we see our companions in Christ's service removed by death, and we feel as if we knew little about them, except that they are gone to an unknown world, and that we are left alone. All these things are trying to flesh and blood. No wonder that the faith of believers sometimes languishes, and their eyes fail while they look for their hope.

Let us see in the story of the transfiguration, a remedy for such doubting thoughts as these. The vision of the holy mount is a gracious pledge that glorious things are in store for the people of God. Their crucified Saviour shall come again in power and great glory. His saints shall all come with Him, and are in safe keeping until that happy day. We may wait patiently. "When Christ, who is our life shall appear, then shall ye also appear with Him in glory." (Colos. iii. 4.)

The second thing which demands our notice in this passage, is *the strong expression of the apostle Peter, when he saw his Lord transfigured.* "Master," he said, "it is good for us to be here."

No doubt there was much in this saying, which cannot be commended. It showed an ignorance of the purpose

itself changed, but only illumined, (or glorified)—so, also, the just who will be conformed to His glorious body, will not be changed as to their outward form. Their bodies will only receive a certain accession of splendour and light, which St. Paul calls a change, (1 Cor. xv. 52.) but the evangelists, a transfiguration."

for which Jesus came into the world, to suffer and to die.
It showed a forgetfulness of his brethren, who were not
with him, and of the dark world which so much needed
his Master's presence. Above all, the proposal which he
made at the same time to "build three tabernacles" for
Moses, Elias, and Christ, shewed a low view of his
Master's dignity, and implied that he did not know that
a greater than Moses and Elias was there. In all these
respects the apostle's exclamation is not to be praised,
but to be blamed.

But having said this, let us not fail to remark what
joy and happiness this glorious vision conferred on this
warm-hearted disciple.* Let us see in his fervent cry,
"It is good to be here," what comfort and consolation
the sight of glory can give to a true believer. Let us
look forward, and try to form some idea of the pleasure
which the saints shall experience, when they shall at last
meet the Lord Jesus at His second coming, and meet to
part no more. A vision of a few minutes was sufficient
to warm and stir Peter's heart. The sight of two saints
in glory was so cheering and quickening, that he would
fain have enjoyed more of it. What then shall we say,
when we see our Lord appear at the last day with all His
saints? What shall we say, when we ourselves are

* The remark of Brentius on the glorious nature of the whole
vision of the transfiguration is well worth quoting. Like most of
that admirable commentator's expositions, it contains much in few
words.

"No Synod on earth was ever more gloriously attended than
this. No assembly was ever more illustrious. Here is God the
Father, God the Son, and God the Holy Ghost. Here are Moses
and Elias, the chief of the prophets. Here are Peter, James, and
John, the chief of the apostles."

allowed to share in His glory, and join the happy company, and feel that we shall go out no more from the joy of our Lord?—These are questions that no man can answer. The happiness of that great day of gathering together is one that we cannot now conceive. The feelings of which Peter had a little foretaste, will then be our's in full experience. We shall all say with one heart and one voice, when we see Christ and all His saints, "It is good to be here."

The last thing which demands our notice in this passage is *the distinct testimony which it bears to Christ's office and dignity, as the promised Messiah.* We see this testimony first in the appearance of Moses and Elias, the representatives of the law and the prophets. They appear as witnesses that Jesus is He of whom they spoke in old times, and of whom they wrote that He would come. They disappear after a few minutes, and leave Jesus alone, as though they would show that they were only witnesses, and that our Master having come, the servants resign to Him the chief place.—We see this testimony, secondly, in the miraculous voice from heaven, saying, "this is my beloved Son : hear Him." The same voice of God the Father, which was heard at our Lord's baptism, was heard once more at His transfiguration. On both occasions there was the same solemn declaration, "this is my beloved Son." On this last occasion, there was an addition of two most important words, "Hear Him."

The whole conclusion of the vision was calculated to leave a lasting impression on the minds of the three disciples. It taught them in the most striking manner, that their Lord was as far above them and the prophets, as the master of the house is above the servants, and that they must in all things believe, follow, obey, trust, and hear Him.

Finally, the last words of the voice from heaven, are words that should be ever before the minds of all true Christians. They should "*hear Christ.*" He is the great Teacher; they that would be wise must learn of Him. He is the light of the world: they that would not err must follow Him. He is the Head of the Church: they that would be living members of His mystical body must ever look to Him. The grand question that concerns us all is not so much what man says, or ministers say, — what the Church says, or what councils say,—but What says Christ?—Him let us hear. In Him let us abide. On Him let us lean. To Him let us look. He and He only will never fail us, never disappoint us, and never lead us astray. Happy are they who know experimentally the meaning of the text, "my sheep hear my voice, and I know them, and they follow me: and I give unto them eternal life; and they shall never perish, neither shall any man pluck them out of my hand." (John x. 27, 28.)*

* The coming of Elias, or Elijah, which forms the topic of conversation between our Lord and His disciples in the latter part of the passage now expounded, is a deep and mysterious subject.

1. According to one class of interpreters, the ministry of John the Baptist was the coming of Elias. They consider that the prophecy of Malachi, (Mal. iv. 5, 6) that Elijah the prophet should be sent before the great and dreadful day of the Lord, was completely accomplished in John the Baptist, and that no other coming of Elias is to be expected. This is the view maintained by the great majority of Protestant Commentators, both English and Foreign, from the time of the Reformation to the present day.

2. According to another class of interpreters, a literal coming of

MARK IX. 14—29.

14 And when he came to *his* disciples, he saw a great multitude about them, and the Scribes questioning with them.

15 And straightway all the people, when they beheld him, were greatly amazed, and running to *him* saluted him.

16 And he asked the Scribes, What question ye with them?

17 And one of the multitude answered and said, Master, I have brought thee my son, which hath a dumb spirit;

18 And wheresoever he taketh him, he teareth him: and he foameth, and gnasheth with his teeth, and pineth away: and I spake to thy disciples that they should cast him out; and they could not.

19 He answereth him, and saith, O faithless generation, how long shall I be with you? how long shall I suffer you? bring him unto me.

20 And they brought him unto him: and when he saw him, straightway the spirit tare him; and he fell on the ground, and wallowed foaming.

21 And he asked his father, How long is it ago since this came unto him? And he said, Of a child.

22 And ofttimes it hath cast him into the fire, and into the waters, to destroy him: but if thou canst do any thing, have compassion on us, and help us.

23 Jesus said unto him, If thou canst believe, all things *are* possible to him that believeth.

24 And straightway the father of the child cried out, and said with tears, Lord, I believe; help thou mine unbelief.

25 When Jesus saw that the people came running together, he rebuked the foul spirit, saying unto him, *Thou* dumb and deaf spirit, I charge thee, come out of him, and enter no more into him.

26 And *the spirit* cried, and rent him sore, and came out of him: and he was as one dead; insomuch that many said, He is dead.

27 But Jesus took him by the hand, and lifted him up; and he arose.

28 And when he was come into the house, his disciples asked him privately, Why could not we cast him out?

29 And he said unto them, This kind can come forth by nothing, but by prayer and fasting.

THE contrast between these verses and those which precede them in the chapter is very striking. We pass from the mount of transfiguration to a melancholy history of the work of the devil. We come down from the vision

Elias is yet to take place. They consider that John the Baptist only went before our Lord in the "spirit and power of Elias," (Luke i. 17.) and that the words of Malachi are yet to be fulfilled. This is the view maintained by nearly all the Fathers, by the great majority of the Roman Catholic Commentators, and by not a few modern Protestant divines both English and continental at the present time.

If I must express an opinion, when great and learned divines differ so widely, I must honestly confess that I decidedly incline to the second of the two interpretations above given. I believe that a literal appearing of Elijah the prophet before the second coming of Christ may be expected. Dark and incomprehensible as the subject is, the scriptural arguments in favour of this view appear to of glory, to a conflict with Satanic possession. We change the blessed company of Moses and Elias, for the rude intercourse of unbelieving Scribes. We leave the foretaste of millennial glory, and the solemn voice of God the Father testifying to God the Son, and return once more to a scene of pain, weakness, and misery,—a boy in agony of body, a father in deep distress, and a little band of feeble disciples baffled by Satan's power, and unable to give relief.—The contrast, we must all feel, is very great. Yet it is but a faint emblem of the change of scene that Jesus voluntarily undertook to witness, when He first laid aside His glory and came into the world. And it is after all a vivid picture of the life of all true Christians. With them, as with their Master, work, conflict, and scenes of weakness and sor- row will always be the rule. With them too, visions of glory, foretastes of heaven, seasons on the mount, will always be the exception.

Let us learn from these verses, *how dependent Christ's disciples are on the company and help of their Master.*

me unanswerable. Any other view seems to do violence to the plain meaning of the words of Malachi iv. 5, 6; Matt. xvii. 11; John i. 21. There seems no reason why there should not be a double "coming of Elias,"—the first, "in spirit and power," when John the Baptist preached,—the second, "literal and in person," when He shall come at the end of the world,—immediately before the great and dreadful day of the Lord.

The whole question is undoubtedly surrounded with difficulties, whatever view we adopt. I can only say that after patient and calm investigation, I see much fewer difficulties in the way of the interpretation to which I lean, than in the way of the other. I hold with Augustine, Jerome, Chrysostom, Hilary, Jansenius, Brenius, Greswell, Alford, and Stier, that Malachi iv. 5, 6, is not yet completely fulfilled, and that Elijah the prophet will yet come. Those who can read Greek will find an interesting note on this subject, in Cramer's Catena on St. Mark.

We see this truth brought out in a striking manner in the scene which meets our Lord's eyes, when He came down from the mount. Like Moses, when he came down from Mount Sinai, he finds his little flock in confusion. He sees His nine apostles beset by a party of malicious Scribes, and baffled in an attempt to heal one who had been brought to them possessed with a devil. The very same disciples who a short time before had done many miracles and " cast out many devils," had now met with a case too hard for them. They were learning by humbling experience the great lesson, " without me ye can do nothing." (John xv. 5.)—It was a useful lesson, no doubt, and over-ruled to their spiritual good. It would probably be remembered all the days of their lives. The things that we learn by smarting experience, abide in our memories, while truths heard with the ear are often forgotten. But we may be sure it was a bitter lesson at the time.—We do not love to learn that we can do nothing without Christ.

We need not look far to see many illustrations of this truth in the history of Christ's people in every age. The very men who at one time have done great exploits in the cause of the Gospel, at another time have failed entirely, and proved weak and unstable as water. The temporary recantations of Cranmer and Jewell are striking examples. The holiest and best of Christians has nothing to glory of. His strength is not his own. He has nothing but what he has received. He has only to provoke the Lord to leave him for a season, and he will soon discover that his power is gone. Like Samson, when his hair was shorn, he is weak as any other man.

Let us learn a lesson of humility from the failure of the disciples. Let us strive to realize every day our need of the grace and presence of Christ. With Him we may do all things. Without Him we can do nothing at all. With Him we may overcome the greatest temptations. Without Him the least may overcome us. Let our cry be every morning, "leave us not to ourselves,— we know not what a day may bring forth,—if thy presence go not with us we cannot go up."

Let us learn, in the second place, from these verses, *how early in life we are liable to be injured by Satan.* We read a fearful description of the miseries inflicted by Satan on the young man, whose case is here recorded. And we are told that he had been under this awful visitation from his very infancy. It came to him, "of a child."

There is a lesson of deep importance here which we must not overlook. We must labour to do good to our children, even from their earliest years. If Satan begins so early to do them harm, we must not be behind him in diligence to lead them to God. How soon in life a child becomes responsible and accountable, is a difficult question to solve. Perhaps far sooner than many of us suppose. One thing, at all events, is very clear: it is never too soon to strive and pray for the salvation of the souls of children,—never too soon to speak to them as moral beings, and tell them of God, and Christ, and right, and wrong. The devil, we may be quite sure, loses no time in endeavouring to influence the minds of young people. He begins with them even "of a child." Let us work hard to counteract him. If young hearts can be filled by Satan, they can also be filled with the Spirit of God.

Let us learn, in the third place, from these verses, *how faith and unbelief can be mixed together in the same heart*. The words of the child's father set this truth before us in a touching way. "Lord," he cried, "I believe ; help thou mine unbelief."

We see in those words a vivid picture of the heart of many a true Christian. Few indeed are to be found among believers, in whom trust and doubt, hope and fear, do not exist side by side. Nothing is perfect in a child of God, so long as he is in the body. His knowledge, and love, and humility, are all more or less defective, and mingled with corruption. And as it is with his other graces, so it is with his faith. He believes, and yet has about him a remainder of unbelief.

What shall we do with our faith ? We must *use it*. Weak, trembling, doubting, feeble as it may be, we must use it. We must not wait till it is great, perfect, and mighty, but like the man before us, turn it to account, and hope that one day it will be more strong. "Lord," he said, "I believe."

What shall we do with our unbelief ? We must *resist it*, and pray against it. We must not allow it to keep us back from Christ. We must take it to Christ, as we take all other sins and infirmities, and cry to Him for deliverance. Like the man before us, we must cry, "Lord, help mine unbelief."

These are experimental truths. Happy are they who know something of them. The world is ignorant of them. Faith and unbelief, doubts and fears, are all foolishness to the natural man. But let the true Christian study these things well, and thoroughly understand them. It is of the utmost importance to our comfort to know, that a true believer may be known by his inward warfare, as well as by his inward peace.

Let us mark, in the last place, *the complete dominion which our Lord exercises over Satan and all his agents.* The spirit who was too strong for the disciples, is at once cast out by the Master. He speaks with mighty authority, and Satan at once is obliged to obey, " I charge thee, come out of him, and enter no more into him."

We may leave the passage with comfortable feelings. Greater is He that is for us than all they that are against us. Satan is strong, busy, active, malicious. But Jesus is able to save to the uttermost all that come unto God by Him,—from the devil, as well as from sin,—from the devil, as well as from the world. Let us possess our souls in patience. Jesus still lives, and will not let Satan pluck us out of His hand. Jesus still lives, and will soon come again to deliver us entirely from the fiery darts of the wicked one. The great chain is prepared. (Rev. xx. 1.) Satan shall one day be bound. The God of peace shall bruise Satan under our feet shortly.* (Rom. xvi. 20.)

MARK IX. 30—37.

30 And they departed thence, and passed through Galilee ; and he would not that any man should know *it.*

31 For he taught his disciples, and said unto them, The Son of man is delivered into the hands of men, and they shall kill him ; and after that he is killed, he shall rise the third day.

32 But they understood not that saying, and were afraid to ask him.

33 And he came to Capernaum : and being in the house he asked them,

* The expression, " greatly amazed," in the fifteenth verse of the passage now expounded, deserves some notice. The Greek word

What was it that ye disputed among yourselves by the way?

34 But they held their peace: for by the way they had disputed among themselves, who *should be* the greatest.

35 And he sat down, and called the twelve, and saith unto them, If any man desire to be first, *the same* shall be last of all, and servant of all.

36 And he took a child, and set him in the midst of them: and when he had taken him in his arms, he said unto them,

37 Whosoever shall receive one of such children in my name, receiveth me: and whosoever shall receive me, receiveth not me, but him that sent me.

LET us mark, in these verses, *our Lord's renewed announcement of His own coming, death, and resurrection.* "He taught his disciples, and said unto them, The Son of man is delivered into the hands of men, and they shall kill him; and after that he is killed, he shall rise the third day."

The dullness of the disciples in spiritual things appears once more, as soon as this announcement was made. There was good in the tidings as well as seeming evil, —sweet as well as bitter,—life as well as death,—the resurrection as well as the cross. But it was all darkness to the bewildered twelve. "They understood not that saying, and were afraid to ask." Their minds were still full of their mistaken ideas of their Master's reign upon earth. They thought that His earthly kingdom was immediately to appear. Never are we so slow to understand, as when prejudice and pre-conceived opinions darken our eyes.

The immense importance of our Lord's death and resurrection comes out strongly in this fresh announce-

is exceedingly strong, and implies a feeling much beyond that which the English word "amazed" conveys to our minds. It certainly seems as if some traces of visible glory, or, at any rate, some expression of extraordinary majesty appeared in our Lord's countenance, after the transfiguration. It reminds us of the face of Moses shining when he came down from the mount.

ment which He makes. It is not for nothing that He reminds us again that He must die. He would have us know that His death was the great end for which He came into the world. He would remind us that by that death the great problem was to be solved, how God could be just, and yet justify sinners. He did not come upon earth merely to teach, and preach, and work miracles. He came to make satisfaction for sin, by His own blood and suffering on the cross. Let us never forget this. The incarnation, and example, and words of Christ are all of deep importance. But the grand object which demands our notice in the history of His earthly ministry, is His death on Calvary.

Let us mark, in the second place, in these verses, *the ambition and love of preeminence which the apostles exhibited.* "By the way they disputed among themselves who should be greatest."

How strange this sounds! Who would have thought that a few fishermen and publicans could have been overcome by emulation, and the desire of supremacy? Who would have expected that poor men, who had given up all for Christ's sake, would have been troubled by strife and dissension, as to the place and precedence which each one deserved? Yet so it is. The fact is recorded for our learning. The Holy Ghost has caused it to be written down for the perpetual use of Christ's Church. Let us take care that it is not written in vain.

It is an awful fact, whether we like to allow it or not, that pride is one of the commonest sins which beset human nature. We are all born Pharisees. We all naturally think far better of ourselves than we ought.

We all naturally fancy that we deserve something better than we have.—It is an old sin. It began in the garden of Eden, when Adam and Eve thought they had not got everything that their merits deserved.—It is a subtle sin. It rules and reigns in many a heart without being detected, and can even wear the garb of humility.—It is a most soul-ruining sin. It prevents repentance,—keeps men back from Christ,—checks brotherly love, and nips in the bud spiritual anxiety.—Let us watch against it, and be on our guard. Of all garments, none is so graceful, none wears so well, and none is so rare, as true humility.

Let us mark, in the third place, *the peculiar standard of true greatness which our Lord sets before His disciples.* He says to them, "If any man desire to be first, the same shall be last of all, and servant of all."

These words are deeply instructive. They show us that the maxims of the world are directly contrary to the mind of Christ. The world's idea of greatness is to rule, but Christian greatness consists in serving. The world's ambition is to receive honour and attention, but the desire of the Christian should be to give rather than receive, and to attend on others rather than be attended on himself. In short, the man who lays himself out most to serve his fellow men, and to be useful in his day and generation, is the greatest man in the eyes of Christ.*

Let us strive to make a practical use of this heart-searching maxim. Let us seek to do good to our fellow

---

* The words of Augustine on this point are worth reading. He says,

" A Bishop's office is a name of labour rather than of honour ; so that he who coveteth preeminence rather than usefulness may understand that he is not a bishop."—*De Civit. Dei.*

men, and to mortify that self-pleasing and self-indulgence, to which we are all so prone. Is there any service that we can render to our fellow Christians? Is there any kindness that we can do them, to help them and promote their happiness? If there is, let us do it without delay. Well would it be for Christendom, if empty boasts of Churchmanship and orthodoxy were less frequent, and practical attention to our Lord's words in this passage more common. The men who are willing to be last of all, and servants of all, for Christ's sake, are always few. Yet these are the men who do good, break down prejudices, convince infidels that Christianity is a reality, and shake the world.

Let us mark, in the last place, *what encouragement our Lord gives us to shew kindness to the least and lowest who believe in His name.* He teaches this lesson in a very touching manner. He took a child in His arms, and said to His disciples, "whosoever shall receive one of such children in my name, receiveth me, and whosoever shall receive me, receiveth Him that sent me."

The principle here laid down is a continuation of that which we have just considered. It is one which is foolishness to the natural man. Flesh and blood can see no other way to greatness than crowns, and rank, and wealth, and high position in the world. The Son of God declares that the way lies in devoting ourselves to the care of the weakest and lowest of His flock. He enforces His declaration by marvellous words, which are often read and heard without thought. He tells us that to "receive one child in His name, is to receive Christ, and to receive Christ is to receive God."

There is rich encouragement here for all who devote themselves to the charitable work of doing good to neglected souls. There is encouragement for every one who labours to restore the outcast to a place in society,—to raise the fallen,—to gather together the ragged children, whom no man cares for,—to pluck the worst of characters from a life of sin, like brands from the burning,—and to bring the wanderers home. Let all such take comfort when they read these words. Their work may often be hard and discouraging. They may be mocked, ridiculed, and held up to scorn by the world. But let them know that the Son of God marks all they do, and is well pleased. Whatever the world may think, these are they whom Jesus will delight to honour at the last day.

MARK IX. 38—50.

38 And John answered him, saying, Master, we saw one casting out devils in thy name, and he followeth not us: and we forbad him, because he followeth not us.

39 But Jesus said, Forbid him not: for there is no man which shall do a miracle in my name, that can lightly speak evil of me.

40 For he that is not against us is on our part.

41 For whosoever shall give you a cup of water to drink in my name, because ye belong to Christ, verily I say unto you, he shall not lose his reward.

42 And whosoever shall offend one of *these* little ones that believe in me, it is better for him that a millstone were hanged about his neck, and he were cast into the sea.

43 And if thy hand offend thee, cut it off: it is better for thee to enter into life maimed, than having two hands to go into hell, into the fire that never shall be quenched:

44 Where their worm dieth not, and the fire is not quenched.

45 And if thy foot offend thee, cut it off: it is better for thee to enter halt into life, than having two feet to be cast into hell, into the fire that never shall be quenched:

46 Where their worm dieth not, and the fire is not quenched.

47 And if thine eye offend thee, pluck it out: it is better for thee to enter into the kingdom of God with one eye, than having two eyes to be cast into hell fire:

48 Where their worm dieth not, and the fire is not quenched.

49 For every one shall be salted with fire, and every sacrifice shall be salted with salt.

50 Salt *is* good: but if the salt have lost his saltness, wherewith will ye season it? Have salt in yourselves, and have peace one with another.

WE see in these verses, *the mind of Christ on the great*

subject of toleration in religion. The apostle John said to Him, "Master, we saw one casting out devils in Thy name, and he followeth not us : and we forbad him, because he followeth not us." The man was doing a good work without doubt. He was warring on the same side as the apostles, beyond question. But this did not satisfy John. He did not work in the company of the apostles. He did not fight in line with them. And therefore John had forbidden him.—But let us hear now what the great Head of the Church decides ! "Jesus said, forbid him not ; for there is no man which shall do a miracle in my name that can ligthly speak evil of me. For he that is not against us, is on our part."

Here is a golden rule indeed, and one that human nature sorely needs, and has too often forgotten. Men of all branches of Christ's Church are apt to think that no good can be done in the world, unless it is done by their own party and denomination. They are so narrow-minded, that they cannot conceive the possibility of working on any other pattern but that which they follow. They make an idol of their own peculiar ecclesiastical machinery, and can see no merit in any other. They are like him who cried when Eldad and Medad prophesied in the camp, "My lord Moses forbid them." (Num. xi. 28.)

To this intolerant spirit we owe some of the blackest pages of Church history. Christians have repeatedly persecuted Christians for no better reason than that which is here given by John. They have practically proclaimed to their brethren, "you shall either follow us, or not work for Christ at all."

Let us be on our guard against this feeling. It is only too near the surface of all our hearts. Let us study to realize that liberal, tolerant spirit which Jesus here recommends, and be thankful for good works wheresoever and by whomsoever done. Let us beware of the slightest inclination to stop and check others, merely because they do not choose to adopt our plans, or work by our side. We may think our fellow Christians mistaken in some points. We may fancy that more would be done for Christ, if they would join us, and if all worked in the same way. We may see many evils arising from religious dissensions and divisions.—But all this must not prevent us rejoicing if the works of the devil are destroyed and souls are saved. Is our neighbour warring against Satan? Is he really trying to labour for Christ? This is the grand question. Better a thousand times that the work should be done by other hands than not done at all. Happy is he who knows something of the spirit of Moses, when he said, "Would God that all the Lord's people were prophets;"—and of Paul, when he says, " If Christ is preached, I rejoice, yea, and will rejoice." * (Num. xi. 29 ; Phil. i. 18.

* The remarks of Quesnel on this passage are interesting,—and doubly so when we remember that the writer was a Roman Catholic. He says, "That which John here does, is an example of an indiscreet zeal for the interests of Christ. The most holy persons have sometimes occasion to secure themselves from secret emulations. We very easily mingle our own interests with those of God; and our vanity uses the glory of His name only as a veil. A preacher sometimes imagines that his only desire is, that men should follow Christ, and adhere to His word; and it is himself whom he desires they should follow, and to whom he is very glad to find them adhere."

"Christ suffers many things in His Church, which are done without His mission; but He makes them contribute to the

192

We see, for another thing, in these verses, *the need of giving up anything that stands between us and the salvation of our souls.* The "hand" and the "foot" are to be cut off, and the "eye" to be plucked out, if they offend, or are occasions of falling. The things that are dear to us as eye, foot, or hand, are to be cast off and given up, if they injure our souls, whatever pain the sacrifice may cost us.

This is a rule that sounds stern and harsh at first sight. But our loving Master did not give the rule without cause. Compliance with it is absolutely necessary, since neglect of it is the sure way to hell. Our bodily senses are the channels through which many of our most formidable temptations approach us. Our bodily members are ready instruments of evil, but slow to that which is good. The eye, the hand, and the foot are good servants, when under right direction. But they need daily watching, lest they lead us into sin.

Let us resolve by God's grace to make a practical use of our Lord's solemn injunction in this place. Let us regard it as the advice of a wise physician, the counsel of a tender father, the warning of a faithful friend. However men may ridicule us for our strictness and preciseness, let us habitually "crucify our flesh with its affections and lusts." Let us deny ourselves any enjoyment, rather than incur peril of sinning against God. Let us walk in Job's steps: He says, " I made a covenant with mine eyes." (Job xxxi. 1.) Let us remember Paul: He says, "I keep

establishment of His kingdom. Whatever reason we may have to fear that some persons will not persevere in goodness, we must notwithstanding suffer them to continue their endeavours, when they appear to be any ways useful. God Himself authorizes such persons, since it is He who performs the good in them."

under my body, and bring it into subjection, lest that by any means, when I have preached to others, I myself should be a cast away." (1 Cor. ix. 27.)

We see, in the last place, in these verses, *the reality, awfulness, and eternity of future punishment.* Three times the Lord Jesus speaks of "hell." Three times He men tions the "worm that never dies." Three times He says that "the fire is not quenched."

These are awful expressions. They call for reflection rather then exposition. They should be pondered, considered, and remembered by all professing Christians. It matters little whether we regard them as figurative and emblematic. If they are so, one thing at least is very clear. The worm and the fire are emblems of real things. There is a real hell, and that hell is eternal.

There is no mercy in keeping back from men the subject of hell. Fearful and tremendous as it is, it ought to be pressed on all, as one of the great truths of Christianity. Our loving Saviour speaks frequently of it. The apostle John, in the book of Revelation, often describes it. The servants of God in these days must not be ashamed of confessing their belief in it. Were there no boundless mercy in Christ for all that believe in Him, we might well shrink from the awful topic. Were there no precious blood of Christ able to cleanse away all sin, we might well keep silence about the wrath to come. But there is mercy for all who ask in Christ's name. There is a fountain open for all sin. Let us then boldly and unhesitatingly maintain that there is a hell, and beseech men to flee from it, before it be too late. "Knowing the terrors of the Lord," the worm, and the fire, let us "persuade men." (1 Cor. v. 11.)   It is not possible to say too much aboutChrist.   But it is quite possible to say too little about hell.

Let the concluding words of our Lord ring in our ears, as we leave the passage:—"Have salt in yourselves, and have peace one with another."   Let us make sure that we have in our hearts the saving grace of the Holy Ghost, sanctifying, purifying, preserving from corruption, our whole inward man.   Let us watch the grace given to us with daily watchfulness, and pray to be kept from carelessness and sin, lest we be overtaken in faults, bring misery on our consciences, and discredit on our profession. Above all let us live in peace one with another, not seeking great things, or striving for the preeminence, but clothed with humility, and loving all who love Christ in sincerity.   These seem simple things.   But in attending to them is great reward.*

* The last verse but one in the passage now expounded, appears to baffle all the commentators.   I allude of course to the words, " Every one shall be salted with fire, and every sacrifice shall be salted with salt."   The true meaning of these words and their connexion with the context, are problems which seem not yet solved. At all events, not one of the many interpretations which have been hitherto proposed is entirely satisfactory.   We must confess that it is one of those knots which are yet untied in the exposition of Scripture.

1.   Some think that our Lord is speaking only of the wicked and their future punishment, and that He means,—" every lost soul shall be salted with the fire of hell, even as every sacrifice under the law of Moses is salted with salt."   This appears to be the view held by Whitby.

2.   Some think that our Lord is speaking only of the righteous and their fiery trials in this life, by which they are purified and preserved from corruption, and that He means,—" every true disciple of mine shall be as it were salted and passed through the fire of tribulation, even as every sacrifice is salted with salt."   Of those who think that our Lord speaks only of the righteous, some think

1 And he arose from thence, and cometh into the coasts of Judæa, by the farther side of Jordan: and the people resort unto him again; and, as he was wont, he taught them again.

2 And the Pharisees came to him, and asked him, Is it lawful for a man to put away *his* wife? tempting him.

3 And he answered and said unto them, What did Moses command you?

4 And they said, Moses suffered to write a bill of divorcement, and to put *her* away.

5 And Jesus answered and said unto them, For the hardness of your heart he wrote you this precept.

6 But from the beginning of the creation God made them male and female.

7 For this cause shall a man leave his father and mother, and cleave to his wife;

8 And they twain shall be one flesh: so then they are no more twain, but one flesh.

9 What therefore God hath joined together, let not man put asunder.

10 And in the house his disciples asked him again of the same *matter*.

11 And he saith unto them, Whosoever shall put away his wife, and marry another, committeth adultery against her.

12 And if a woman shall put away her husband, and be married to another, she committeth adultery.

THE opening verse of this passage shows us *the patient perseverance of our Lord Jesus Christ as a teacher.* We

that the "fire" means not tribulation, and some the work of the Holy Spirit. Cartwright holds the last of these opinions, Junius the first.

3. Some think that in the first clause of the verse, our Lord is speaking of all members of His church, both good and bad, and that His meaning is the same as that of St. Paul, where He says "The fire shall try every man's work of what sort it is." (1 Cor. iii. 13.) The second clause, they think, describes the preserving effect of grace on the hearts of true believers. According to this view, the meaning of the verse would be,—"every one shall be finally salted, tried, and tested by the fire of the last day; and every one who has offered himself as a living sacrifice to God, shall be salted with grace, and so finally preserved from death and corruption."

4. Some think that in the first clause of the verse our Lord is speaking of the wicked, and in the second clause of the righteous. According to this view, the sense would be,—"every wicked man shall be salted with fire and punished for evermore;—and every living sacrifice to God, or godly man, shall be salted with grace, kept from the power of death, and saved for evermore."—This is the view of Hammond and Manton.

I offer no opinion and make no comment on any of the above views. The objections which might be made against every one of them are neither few nor small. Whether these objections are insuperable or not, is a point on which learned theologians differ widely, and a conclusion will perhaps never be attained until the Lord appears. My own conviction is, that we must wait for more light, and regard the text at present as one of the "deep things" of God'

are told that He came "into the coasts of Judæa by the
farther side of Jordan : and the people resort unto Him
again ; and as He was wont, He taught them again."

Wherever our Lord went, He was always about His
Father's business, preaching, teaching, and labouring to
do good to souls. He threw away no opportunity. In
the whole history of His earthly ministry, we never read
of an idle day. Of Him it may be truly said, that He
"sowed beside all waters," and that "in the morning He
sowed His seed, and in the evening withheld not His
hand." (Isaiah xxxii. 20. Eccles. xi. 6.)

And yet our Lord knew the hearts of all men. He knew
perfectly well that the great proportion of His hearers
were hardened and unbelieving. He knew, as He spoke,
that most of His words fell to the ground uncared for
and unheeded, and that so far as concerned the salvation
of souls, most of His labour was in vain. He knew all
this, and yet He laboured on.

Let us see in this fact a standing pattern to all who try
to do good to others, whatever their office may be. Let
it be remembered by every minister and every missionary,
—by every schoolmaster and every Sunday-school teacher,
—by every district visitor and every lay agent,—by every
head of a house who has family prayers,—and by every
nurse who has the charge of children. Let all such
remember Christ's example, and resolve to do likewise.
We are not to give up teaching, because we see no good
done. We are not to relax our exertions, because we see
no fruit of our toil. We are to work on steadily, keeping before us the great principle, that duty is our's and
results are God's. There must be ploughmen and sowers,

as well as reapers and binders of sheaves. The honest master pays his labourers according to the work they do, and not according to the crops that grow on his land. Our Master in heaven will deal with all His servants at the last day in like manner. He knows that success is not in their hands. He knows that they cannot change hearts. He will reward them according to their labour, and not according to the fruits which have resulted from their labour. It is not "the good and *successful* servant," but the "good and *faithful* servant," to whom He will say, "enter thou into the joy of thy Lord."* (Matt. xxv. 21.)

The greater portion of this passage is meant to show us *the dignity and importance of the relation of marriage*. It is plain that the prevailing opinions of the Jews upon this subject, when our Lord was upon earth, were lax and low in the extreme. The binding character of the marriage tie was not recognized. Divorce for slight and trivial

* Some remarks of Bishop Latimer on this point are well worth reading. They occur in a passage in one of his sermons on the parable of the wedding garment. He says, "the man who had not the wedding garment was blamed because he professed one thing, and was indeed another. Why did not the king blame the preachers? There was no fault in them, they did their duties: they had no further commandment but to call men to the marriage. The garment he should have provided himself. Therefore he quarrelleth not with the preachers, 'What doth this fellow here? why suffered ye him to enter?' For their commission extended no further but only to call him. Many are grieved that there is so little fruit of their preaching. And when they are asked, 'Why do you not preach, having so great gifts given you of God?' 'I would preach, say they, but I see so little fruit, so little amendment of life, that it maketh me weary:' a naughty answer: a very naughty answer. Thou art troubled with that which God gave thee no charge of: and leavest undone that which thou art charged with."—*Latimer's Works. Parker Society. Vol. I. p.* 286.

causes was allowable and common.* The duties of husbands towards wives, and of wives towards husbands, as
a natural consequence, were little understood. To correct
this state of things, our Lord sets up a high and holy
standard of principles. He refers to the original institution of marriage at the creation, as the union of one
man and one woman. He quotes and endorses the
solemn words used at the marriage of Adam and Eve,
as words of perpetual significance, "a man shall leave
his father and mother, and cleave to his wife : and they
twain shall be one flesh." He adds a solemn comment
to these words,—"What God hath joined together, let
not man put asunder." And finally, in reply to the
inquiry of His disciples, he declares that divorce followed
by re-marriage, except for the cause of unfaithfulness, is
a breach of the seventh commandment. †

*The extent to which the Jews allowed divorce for absurd and
frivolous causes, would be almost incredible, if we had not the
evidence of their own Rabbinical writings on the subject. A full
account of the matter will be found in Lightfoot's Horæ Hebraicæ
on St. Matthew v. 31. One passage quoted by him will be sufficient to give the reader an idea of Jewish customs about divorce :
"The school of Hillel saith, If the wife cooks her husband's food
ill by over-salting it, or over-roasting it, she is to be put away."

†I am aware that the opinions I have expressed at the close of
this paragraph are contrary to that of some learned divines. I
can only say that I have arrived at them deliberately, after calm
investigation of the parallel passage in Matt. xix. 9, and of the
words of our Lord in Matt. v. 32. I decidedly believe that the re-
marriage forbidden by Christ, is re-marriage after a divorce for
trivial and frivolous causes, and that His words do not apply to
re-marriage after divorce on account of unfaithfulness. Re-marriage after divorce for frivolous causes is clearly adultery, for one
simple reason ;—the divorce never ought to have taken place, and
the divorced party is still a married person in the sight of God.—
Re-marriage after divorce for unfaithfulness, by the same process
of reasoning, is not adultery. Unfaithfulness dissolves the marriage
tie altogether, and place the husband and wife once more in the
position of unmarried people, or of a widower or widow.

The importance of the whole subject, on which our Lord here pronounces judgment, can hardly be overrated. We ought to be very thankful that we have so clear and full an exposition of His mind upon it. The marriage relation lies at the very root of the social system of nations. The public morality of a people, and the private happiness of the families which compose a people, are deeply involved in the whole question of the law of marriage. The experience of all nations confirms the wisdom of our Lord's decision in this passage in the most striking manner. It is a fact clearly ascertained, that polygamy, and permission to obtain divorce on slight grounds, have a direct tendency to promote immorality. In short, the nearer a nation's laws about marriage approach to the law of Christ, the higher has the moral tone of that nation always proved to be.

It becomes all those who are married, or purpose marriage, to ponder well the teaching of our Lord Jesus Christ in this passage. Of all relations of life, none ought to be regarded with such reverence, and none taken in hand so cautiously as the relation of husband and wife. In no relation is so much earthly happiness to be found, if it be entered upon discreetly, advisedly, and in the fear of God. In none is so much misery seen to follow, if it be taken in hand unadvisedly, lightly, wantonly, and without thought.—From no step in life does so much benefit come to the soul, if people marry "in the Lord." From none does the soul take so much harm, if fancy, passion, or any mere worldly motive is the only cause which produce the union. Solomon was the wisest of men. "Nevertheless even him did outlandish women cause to sin." (Neh. xiii. 26.)

There is, unhappily, only too much necessity for impressing these truths upon people. It is a mournful fact, that few steps in life are generally taken with so much levity, self-will, and forgetfulness of God as marriage. Few are the young couples who think of inviting Christ to their wedding! It is a mournful fact that unhappy marriages are one great cause of the misery and sorrow of which there is so much in the world. People find out too late, that they have made a mistake, and go in bitterness all their days. Happy are they, who in the matter of marriage observe three rules. The *first* is to marry only in the Lord, and after prayer for God's approval and blessing. The *second* is not to expect too much from their partners, and to remember that marriage is, after all, the union of two sinners, and not of two angels. The *third* rule is to strive first and foremost for one another's sanctification. The more holy married people are, the happier they are. "Christ loved the church, and gave Himself for it, that He might *sanctify* it." * (Eph. v. 25, 26.)

* There is an expression in this passage which claims special observation. The Pharisees told our Lord, that " Moses suffered to write a bill of divorcement, and to put her away." The answer of our Lord is very remarkable. He says, "*For the hardness of your hearts he wrote you this precept.*" And He then goes on to show that this permission to divorce was a proof that their forefathers had fallen below the original standard of marriage, and were dealt with as being in a weak and diseased state of soul. For He says, " But from the beginning of the creation God made them male and female."

The expression throws much light on some portions of the civil law of Moses. It shows us that it was an institution which in some of its requirements was specially adapted to the state of mind in which the Israelites were, on first leaving the land of Egypt. It was not intended in all its minute particulars to be a code of perpetual obligation. It was meant to lead on to something better and higher, when the people were able to bear it. The possession

13 And they brought young children to him, that he should touch them : and *his* disciples rebuked those that brought *them*.

14 But when Jesus saw *it*, he was much displeased, and said unto them, Suffer the little children to come unto me, and forbid them not; for of such is the kingdom of God.

15 Verily I say unto you, Whosoever shall not receive the kingdom of God as a little child, he shall not enter therein.

16 And he took them up in his arms, put *his* hands upon them, and blessed them.

THE scene brought before us in these four verses is deeply, interesting.—We see young children brought to Christ, "that He should touch them," and the disciples rebuking those that brought them. We are told that when Jesus saw this He was "much displeased," and rebuked His disciples in words of a very remarkable tenor. And finally we are told, that "He took them up in His arms, put His hands upon them and blessed them."

of it was undoubtedly a great privilege, and one of which the Jews might justly glory. Yet in glorying they were to remember also, that their law contained some grounds for humiliation. Its very permission to obtain divorce on light grounds, was a standing witness of the hardness and cruelty of the people. It was thought better to tolerate such divorces, than to have the nation filled with murder, adultery, cruelty, and desertion. In short, the very law of which the Jew boasted, was shown by our Lord to contain permissive statutes, which were in reality written to his shame.

The expression throws light on the position of God's people in this world of sin. It shows us that there may be things *tolerated* and permitted by God, both in churches and states, not because they are the best things, but because they are the things best suited to the church or state in which they are found. It is vain to expect perfection in any government, or in any church. If we have the essentials of justice in the one, and of truth in the other, we may be content. God tolerated many things in the government of Israel, until the time of reformation. Surely we may tolerate many things too. To spend our lives in searching after an imaginary state of perfection, either civil or ecclesiastical, is at best a waste of time. If God was pleased to suffer some things in Israel "for the hardness of their hearts," we may well endure some things in churches and states which we do not quite like. There is a balance of evil in every position in the world. There are imperfections every where. The state of perfection is yet to come.

Let us learn, for one thing, from this passage, *how much attention the souls of children should receive from the Church of Christ.* The Great Head of the Church found time to take special notice of children. Although His time on earth was precious, and grown up men and women were perishing on every side for lack of knowledge, He did not think little boys and girls of small importance. He had room in His mighty heart even for them. He declared by His outward gesture and deed, His good will toward them. And not least, He has left on record words concerning them, which His Church should never forget, "Of such is the kingdom of God."

We must never allow ourselves to suppose that little children's souls may be safely let alone. Their characters for life depend exceedingly on what they see and hear during their first seven years. They are never too young to learn evil and sin. They are never too young to receive religious impressions. They think in their childish way about God, and their souls, and a world to come, far sooner and far more deeply than most people are aware. They are far more ready to respond to appeals to their feeling of right and wrong than many suppose. They have each a conscience. God has mercifully not left Himself without a witness in their hearts, fallen and corrupt as their natures are. They have each a soul which will live for ever in heaven or in hell. We cannot begin too soon to endeavour to bring them to Christ.

These truths ought to be diligently considered by every branch of the Church of Christ. It is the bounden duty of every Christian congregation to make provision for the spiritual training of its children. The boys and girls of every family should be taught as soon as they can learn,—should be brought to public worship as soon as they can behave with propriety,—should be regarded with affectionate interest as the future congregation, which will fill our places when we are dead. We may confidently expect Christ's blessing on all attempts to do good to children. No church can be regarded as being in a healthy state which neglects its younger members, and lazily excuses itself on the plea, that "young people will be young," and that it is useless to try to do them good. Such a church shows plainly that it has not the mind of Christ. A congregation which consists of none but grown up people, whose children are idling at home or running wild in the streets or fields, is a most deplorable and unsatisfactory sight. The members of such a congregation may pride themselves on their numbers, and on the soundness of their own views. They may content themselves with loud assertions that they cannot change their children's hearts, and that God will convert them some day if He thinks fit. But they have yet to learn that Christ regards them as neglecting a solemn duty, and that Christians who do not use every means to bring children to Christ are committing a great sin.

Let us learn, for another thing, from this passage, *how much encouragement there is to bring young children to be baptized.* Of course it is not pretended that there is any mention of baptism, or even any reference to it in the verses before us. All we mean to say is that the expressions and gestures of our Lord in this passage, are a strong indirect argument in favour of infant baptism. It is on this account that the passage occupies a prominent place in the baptismal service of the Church of England.

The subject of infant baptism is undoubtedly a delicate and difficult one. Holy and praying men are unable to see alike upon it. Although they read the same Bible, and profess to be led by the same Spirit, they arrive at different conclusions about this sacrament. The great majority of Christians hold, that infant baptism is Scriptural and right. A comparatively small section of the Protestant Church, but one containing many eminent saints among its members, regards infant baptism as unscriptural and wrong. The difference is a melancholy proof of the blindness and infirmity which remain even in the saints of God.

But the difference now referred to, must not make members of the Church of England shrink from holding decided opinions on the subject. That church has declared plainly in its Articles, that "The baptism of young children is in any wise to be retained, as most agreeable with the institution of Christ." To this opinion we need not be afraid to adhere.

It is allowed on all sides that infants my be elect and chosen of God unto salvation,—may be washed in Christ's blood, born again of the Spirit, have grace, be justified, sanctified, and enter heaven. If these things be so, it is hard to see why they may not receive the outward sign of baptism.

It is allowed furthermore that infants are members of Christ's visible church, by virtue of their parent's Christianity. What else can we make of St. Paul's words, "now are they holy." (1 Cor. vii. 14.) If this be so, it is difficult to understand why an infant may not receive the outward sign of admission into the church, just as the Jewish child received the outward sign of circumcision.

The objection that baptism ought only to be given to those who are old enough to repent and believe, does not appear a convincing one. We read in the New Testament that the "houses" of Lydia and Stephanas were baptized, and that the jailer of Philippi and "all his" were baptized. It is very difficult to suppose that in no one of these three cases were there any children. (Acts xvi. 15, 33. 1 Cor. i. 16.)

The objection that our Lord Jesus Christ Himself never directly commanded infants to be baptized is not a weighty one. The church of the Jews, to which He came, had always been accustomed to admit children into the church by the sign of circumcision. The very fact that Jesus says nothing about the age for baptizing, goes far to prove that He intended no change to be made.*

* In considering the arguments in favour of infant baptism, there are two facts which ought to be duly pondered. They are extra-scriptural facts, and I have therefore purposely omitted them in the Expository Thoughts on this passage. But they are weighty facts, and may help some minds in coming to a conclusion.

1. One fact is the testimony of history to the almost universal practice of infant baptism in the early church. The proof of this is to be found in Wall's History of Infant Baptism. If infant baptism is so entirely opposed to the mind of Christ, as some say that it is, it is at least a curious circumstance, that the early church should have been so ignorant on the subject.

2. The other fact is the notorious practice of baptizing the infant children of proselytes in the Jewish Church. The proof of this is to be found in Lightfoot's Horæ Hebraicæ on St. Matthew iii. 6. He says, for instance, "The Anabaptists object, 'it is not commanded to baptize infants,—therefore they are not to be baptized.' To whom I answer, 'it is not forbidden to baptize infants,—therefore they are to be baptized.' And the reason is plain. For when

The subject may be safely left here. Few controversies have done so much harm, and led to so little spiritual fruit as the controversy about baptism. On none has so much been said and written without producing conviction. On none does experience seem to show that Christians had better leave each other alone, and agree to differ.

The baptism that it concerns us all to know, is not so much the baptism of water as the baptism of the Holy Ghost. Thousands are washed in baptismal waters, who are never renewed by the Spirit. Have we been born again? Have we received the Holy Spirit, and been made new creatures in Jesus Christ? If not, it matters little when, and where, and how we have been baptized; we are yet in our sins. Without a new birth there can be no salvation. May we never rest till we know and feel that we have passed from death to life, and are indeed born of God!

Pædobaptism in the Jewish Church was so known, usual and frequent in the admission of proselytes, there was no need to strengthen it with any precept, when baptism passed into an evangelical sacrament. For Christ took baptism into His own hands, and into evangelical use as He found it; this only added that He might promote it to a worthier end, and larger use. The whole nation knew well enough that little children used to be baptized: there was no need of a precept for that which had ever, by common use, prevailed."

"On the other hand, there was need of a plain and open prohibition, that infants and little children should not be baptized, if our Saviour would not have had them baptized. For since it was most common, in all ages foregoing that, little children should be baptized, if Christ had minded to abolish the custom He would have openly forbidden it. Therefore His silence and the silence of Scripture confirms Pædobaptism, and continues it unto all ages."— *Lightfoot's Works. Vol.* xi. *p.* 59. *Pitman's edition.*

MARK X. 17—27.

17 And when he was gone forth into the way, there came one running, and kneeled to him, and asked him, Good Master, what shall I do that I may inherit eternal life?

18 And Jesus said unto him, Why callest thou me good? *there is* none good but one, *that is,* God.

19 Thou knowest the commandments, Do not commit adultery, Do not kill, Do not steal, Do not bear false witness, Defraud not, Honour thy father and mother.

20 And he answered and said unto him, Master, all these have I observed from my youth.

21 Then Jesus beholding him loved him, and said unto him, One thing thou lackest: go thy way, sell whatsoever thou hast, and give to the poor, and thou shalt have treasure in heaven: and come, take up the cross, and follow me.

22 And he was sad at that saying, and went away grieved: for he had great possessions.

23 And Jesus looked round about, and saith unto his disciples, How hardly shall they that have riches enter into the kingdom of God!

24 And the disciples were astonished at his words. But Jesus answereth again, and saith unto them, Children, how hard is it for them that trust in riches to enter into the kingdom of God!

25 It is easier for a camel to go through the eye of a needle, than for a rich man to enter into the kingdom of God.

26 And they were astonished out of measure, saying among themselves, Who then can be saved?

27 And Jesus looking upon them saith, With men *it is* impossible, but not with God: for with God all things are possible.

THE story we have now read is recorded no less than three times in the New Testament. Matthew, Mark, and Luke were all inspired by one Spirit to write it for our learning. There is no doubt a wise purpose in this three-fold repetition of the same simple facts. It is intended to show us that the lessons of the passage deserve particular notice from the Church of Christ.

Let us learn for one thing from this passage, *the self-ignorance of man.*

We are told of one who "came running" to our Lord, and kneeled to him and asked" the solemn question, "what shall I do that I may inherit eternal life?" At first sight there was much that was promising in this man's case. He showed anxiety about spiritual things, while most around him were careless and indifferent. He showed a disposition to reverence our Lord, by kneeling to Him, while Scribes and Pharisees despised Him. Yet all this time this man was profoundly ignorant of his own heart. He hears our Lord recite those commandments which make up our duty to our neighbour, and at once declares, "All these have I observed from my youth." The searching nature of the moral law, its application to our thoughts, and words, as well as actions, are matters with which he is utterly unacquainted.

The spiritual blindness here exhibited is unhappily most common. Myriads of professing Christians at the present day have not an idea of their own sinfulness and guilt in the sight of God. They flatter themselves that they have never done anything very wicked.—"They have never murdered, or stolen, or committed adultery, or borne false witness. They cannot surely be in much danger of missing heaven."—They forget the holy nature of that God with whom they have to do. They forget how often they break His law in temper, or imagination, even when their outward conduct is correct. They never study such portions of Scripture as the fifth chapter of St. Matthew, or at any rate they study it with a thick veil over their hearts, and do not apply it to themselves. The result is that they are wrapped up in self-righteousness. Like the church of Laodicea, they are "rich and increased with goods, and have need of nothing." (Rev. iii. 17.) Self-satisfied they live, and self-satisfied too often they die.

Let us beware of this state of mind. So long as we think that we can keep the law of God, Christ profits us nothing. Let us pray for self-knowledge. Let us ask for the Holy Spirit to convince us of sin, to show us our own hearts, to show us God's holiness, and so to show us our need of Christ. Happy is he who has learned by experience the meaning of St. Paul's words, " I was alive without the law once ; but when the commandment came, sin revived, and I died." (Rom. vii. 9.) Ignorance of the law and ignorance of the Gospel will generally be found together. He whose eyes have really been opened to the spirituality of the commandments, will never rest till he has found Christ.

Let us learn, for another thing, from this passage, *the love of Christ towards sinners.*

This is a truth which is brought out in the expression used by St. Mark, when in his account of this man's story, he says, that " Jesus beholding him, loved him." That love beyond doubt, was a love of pity and compassion. Our Lord beheld with pity the strange mixture of earnestness and ignorance which the case before Him presented. He saw with compassion a soul struggling with all the weakness and infirmity entailed by the fall,—the conscience ill at ease, and sensible that it wanted relief,—the understanding sunk in darkness and blinded as to the first principles of spiritual religion. Just as we look with sorrow at some noble ruin, roofless, and shattered, and unfit for man's use, yet showing many a mark of the skill with which it was designed and reared at first, so may we suppose that Jesus looked with tender concern at this man's soul.

We must never forget that Jesus feels love and compassion for the souls of the ungodly. Without controversy He feels a peculiar love for those who hear His voice and follow Him. They are His sheep, given to

Him by the Father, and watched with a special care. They are His bride, joined to Him in an everlasting covenant, and dear to Him as part of Himself. But the heart of Jesus is a wide heart. He has abundance of pity, compassion, and tender concern even for those who are following sin and the world. He who wept over unbelieving Jerusalem is still the same. He would still gather into his bosom the ignorant and self-righteous, the faithless and impenitent, if they were only willing to be gathered. (Matt. xxiii. 37.) We may boldly tell the chief of sinners that Christ loves him. Salvation is ready for the worst of men, if they will only come to Christ. If men are lost, it is not because Jesus does not love them, and is not ready to save. His own solemn words unravel the mystery, " Men love darkness rather than light." " Ye will not come unto me that ye might have life." (John iii. 19 ; v. 40.)

Let us learn, in the last place, from this passage, *the immense danger of the love of money.* This is a lesson which is twice enforced on our notice. Once it comes out in the conduct of the man whose history is here related. With all his professed desire after eternal life, he loved his money better than his soul. " He went away grieved."—Once it comes out in the solemn words of our Lord to his disciples; " How hard is it for them that have riches to enter into the kingdom of God." " It is easier for a camel to go through the eye of a needle than for a rich man to enter into the kingdom of God." The last day alone will fully prove how true those words are.

Let us watch against the love of money. It is a snare to the poor as well as to the rich. It is not so much the

having money, as the trusting in it, which ruins the soul.
Let us pray for contentment with such things as we
have. The highest wisdom is to be of one mind with
St. Paul, "I have learned, in whatsoever state I am,
therewith to be content." (Phil. iv. 11.)

MARK X. 28—34.

28 Then Peter began to say unto him, Lo, we have left all, and have followed thee.

29 And Jesus answered and said, Verily I say unto you, There is no man that hath left house, or brethren, or sisters, or father, or mother, or wife, or children, or lands, for my sake, and the Gospel's,

30 But he shall receive an hundred-fold now in this time, houses, and brethren, and sisters, and mothers, and children, and lands, with persecutions; and in the world to come eternal life.

31 But many that are first shall be last; and the last first.

32 And they were in the way going up to Jerusalem; and Jesus went before them: and they were amazed; and as they followed, they were afraid. And he took again the twelve, and began to tell them what things should happen unto him,

33 Saying, Behold, we go up to Jerusalem; and the Son of man shall be delivered unto the Chief Priests, and unto the Scribes; and they shall condemn him to death, and shall deliver him to the Gentiles:

34 And they shall mock him, and shall scourge him, and shall spit upon him, and shall kill him: and the third day he shall rise again.

THE first thing which demands our attention in these
verses, is *the glorious promise which they contain.* The
Lord Jesus says to His apostles, "Verily I say unto you,
There is no man that hath left house, or brethren, or
sisters, or father, or mother, or wife, or children, or lands,
for my sake, and the Gospel's; but he shall receive an
hundred-fold now in this time, houses, and brethren, and
sisters, and mothers, and children, and lands, with persecutions; and in the world to come eternal life.

There are few wider promises than this in the word of
God. There is none certainly in the New Testament
which holds out such encouragement for the life that now
is. Let every one that is fearful and faint-hearted in

Christ's service look at this promise. Let all who are enduring hardness and tribulation for Christ's sake, study this promise well, and drink out of it comfort.

To all who make sacrifices on account of the Gospel, Jesus promises " an hundred-fold now in this time." They shall have not only pardon and glory in the world to come. They shall have even here upon earth, hopes, and joys, and sensible comforts sufficient to make up for all that they lose. They shall find in the communion of saints, new friends, new relations, new companions, more loving, faithful, and valuable than any they had before their conversion. Their introduction into the family of God shall be an abundant recompense for exclusion from the society of this world. This may sound startling and incredible to many ears. But thousands have found by experience that it is true.

To all who make sacrifices on account of the Gospel, Jesus promises " eternal life in the world to come." As soon as they put off their earthly tabernacle, they shall enter upon a glorious existence, and in the morning of the resurrection shall receive such honour and joy as pass man's understanding. Their light affliction for a few years shall end in an everlasting reward. Their fights and sorrows while in the body, shall be exchanged for perfect rest and a conqueror's crown. They shall dwell in a world where there is no death, no sin, no devil, no cares, no weeping, no parting, for the former things will have passed away. God has said it, and it shall all be found true.

Where is the saint who will dare to say in the face of these glorious promises, that there is no encouragement to serve Christ? Where is the man or woman whose hands are beginning to hang down, and whose knees are beginning to faint in the Christian race? Let all such ponder this passage, and take fresh courage. The time is short. The end is sure. Heaviness may endure for a night, but joy cometh in the morning. Let us wait patiently on the Lord.

The second thing, which demands our attention in these verses, is *the solemn warning which they contain*. The Lord Jesus saw the secret self-conceit of His apostles. He gives them a word in season to check their high thoughts. "Many that are first shall be last, and the last first."

How true were these words, when applied to the twelve apostles! There stood among those who heard our Lord speak, a man who at one time seemed likely to be one of the foremost of the twelve. He was one who appeared more careful and trustworthy than any. He had the charge of the bag, and kept what was put in it. And yet that man fell away and came to a disgraceful end. His name was Judas Iscariot.—Again, there did not stand among our Lord's hearers that day one who at a later period did more for Christ than any of the twelve. At the time when our Lord spoke he was a young Pharisee, brought up at the feet of Gamaliel, and zealous for nothing so much as the law. And yet that young man in the end was converted to the faith of Christ, was not behind the chiefest apostles, and laboured more abundantly than all. His name was Saul. Well might our Lord say, "the first shall be last; and the last first."

How true were these words, when we apply them to

the history of Christian churches! There was a time when Asia Minor, and Greece, and Northern Africa, were full of professing Christians, while England and America were heathen lands. Sixteen hundred years have made a mighty change. The churches of Africa and Asia have fallen into complete decay. The English and American churches are labouring to spread the Gospel over the world. Well might our Lord say, "the first shall be last, and the last first."

How true these words appear to believers, when they look back over their own lives, and remember all they have seen from the time of their own conversion! How many began to serve Christ at the same time with themselves, and seemed to run well for a season. But where are they now? The world has got hold of one. False doctrine has beguiled another. A mistake in marriage has spoiled a third. Few indeed are the believers who cannot call to mind many such cases. Few have failed to discover, by sorrowful experience, that "the last are often first, and the first last."

Let us learn to pray for humility, when we read texts like this. It is not enough to begin well. We must persevere, and go on, and continue in well-doing. We must not be content with the fair blossoms of a few religious convictions, and joys, and sorrows, and hopes, and fears. We must bear the good fruit of settled habits of repentance, faith, and holiness. Happy is he who counts the cost, and resolves, having once begun to walk in the narrow way, by God's grace never to turn aside.

The last thing that demands our attention in this passage, is *our Lord's clear foreknowledge of His own sufferings and death.* Calmly and deliberately He tells His disciples of His coming passion at Jerusalem. One after another He describes all the leading circumstances which would attend His death. Nothing is reserved. Nothing is kept back.

Let us mark this well. There was nothing involuntary and unforeseen in our Lord's death. It was the result of His own free, determinate, and deliberate choice. From the beginning of His earthly ministry He saw the cross before Him, and went to it a willing sufferer. He knew that His death was the needful payment that must be made to reconcile God and man. That payment He had covenanted and engaged to make at the price of His own blood. And so, when the appointed time came, like a faithful surety, He kept His word, and died for our sins on Calvary.

Let us ever bless God that the Gospel sets before us such a Saviour, so faithful to the terms of the covenant, —so ready to suffer,—so willing to be reckoned sin, and a curse in our stead. Let us not doubt that He who fulfilled His engagement to suffer, will also fulfil His engagement to save all who come to Him. Let us not only accept Him gladly as our Redeemer and Advocate, but gladly give ourselves, and all we have, to His service. Surely if Jesus cheerfully died for us, it is a small thing to require Christians to live for Him.

MARK X. 35—45.

35 And James and John, the sons of Zebedee, come unto him, saying, Master, we would that thou shouldest do for us whatsoever we shall desire. 36 And he said unto them, What would ye that I should do for you?

37 They said unto him, Grant unto us, that we may sit, one on thy right hand, and the other on thy left hand, in thy glory.

38 But Jesus said unto them, Ye know not what ye ask : can ye drink of the cup that I drink of? and be baptized with the baptism that I am baptized with?

39 And they said unto him, We can. And Jesus said unto them, Ye shall indeed drink of the cup that I drink of; and with the baptism that I am baptized withal shall ye be baptized :

40 But to sit on my right hand and on my left hand is not mine to give ; but *it shall be given to them* for whom it is prepared.

41 And when the ten heard *it*, they began to be much displeased with James and John.

42 But Jesus called them *to him*, and saith unto them, Ye know that they which are accounted to rule over the Gentiles exercise lordship over them ; and their great ones exercise authority upon them.

43 But so shall it not be among you : but whosoever will be great among you, shall be your minister :

44 And whosoever of you will be the chiefest, shall be servant of all.

45 For even the Son of man came not to be ministered unto, but to minister, and to give his life a ransom for many.

LET us mark in this passage, *the ignorance of our Lord's disciples.* We find James and John petitioning for the first places in the kingdom of glory. We find them confidently declaring their ability to drink of their Master's cup, and be baptized with their Master's baptism. In spite of all the plain warnings of our Lord, they clung obstinately to the belief that Christ's kingdom on earth was immediately going to appear. Notwithstanding their many shortcomings in Christ's service, they had no misgivings as to their power to endure anything which might come upon them. With all their faith, and grace, and love to Jesus, they neither knew their own hearts, nor the nature of the path before them. They still dreamed of temporal crowns, and earthly rewards. They still knew not what manner of men they were.

There are few true Christians who do not resemble James and John, when they first begin the service of Christ. We are apt to expect far more present enjoyment from our religion, than the Gospel warrants us to expect. We are apt to forget the cross, and the tribula-

tion, and to think only of the crown. We form an
incorrect estimate of our own patience and power of
endurance. We misjudge our own ability to stand temptation and trial. And the result of all is, that we often
buy wisdom dearly, by bitter experience, after many disappointments, and not a few falls.

Let the case before us teach us the importance of a
solid and calm judgment in our religion. Like James
and John, we are right in coveting the best gifts, and in
telling all our desires to Christ. Like them we are right
in believing that Jesus is King of kings, and will one day
reign upon the earth. But let us not, like them, forget that
there is a cross to be borne by every Christian, and that
" through much tribulation we must enter into the kingdom of God." (Acts xiv. 22.) Let us not, like them, be
over-confident in our own strength, and forward in professing that we can do any thing that Christ requires.
Let us, in short, beware of a boastful spirit, when we first
begin to run the Christian course. If we remember this,
it may save us many a humbling fall.

Let us mark, secondly, in this passage, *what praise our
Lord bestows on lowliness, and devotion to the good of others.*
It seems that the ten were much displeased with James
and John, because of the petition which they made to
their Master. Their ambition and love of preeminence
were once more excited at the idea of any one being
placed above themselves. Our Lord saw their feelings,
and, like a wise physician, proceeded at once to supply a
corrective medicine. He tells them that their ideas of
greatness were built on a mistaken foundation. He
repeats with renewed emphasis, the lesson already laid

down in the preceding chapter, "Whosoever of you will be the chiefest shall be servant of all." And He backs up all by the overwhelming argument of His own example : "Even the Son of Man came not to be ministered unto, but to minister."*

Let all who desire to please Christ, watch and pray against self-esteem. It is a feeling which is deeply rooted in our hearts. Thousands have come out from the world, taken up the cross, professed to forsake their own righteousness, and believe in Christ, who have felt irritated and annoyed, when a brother has been more honoured than themselves. These things ought not so to be. We ought often to ponder the words of St. Paul, "Let nothing be done through strife or vain glory ; but in lowliness of mind, let each esteem others better than themselves." (Philipp. ii. 3.) Blessed is that man who

*The remarks of Quesnel on this passage are worth reading. He says, "The ambition of clergymen is a great scandal in the church, and is frequently an occasion of emulations, enmities, divisions, schisms, and wars ; of all which the displeasure of the apostles gives us an imperfect shadow and resemblance. If apostles, trained up in the school of humility and charity, are not free from this vice, what effects will not ambition produce in souls wholly immersed in flesh and blood, which have no motion but from their passions, no law but that of their own desires?"

"Men strangely forget themselves, when, as a ministry appointed only for the sake of heaven, they are contending with the great ones of the earth in haughtiness and grandeur. It is very difficult to support equally the double character of a spiritual pastor and a temporal prince ; and to join humility with grandeur, meekness with dominion, and the constant application of a pastor with the care of secular affairs."

"The greatest prelate in the church, is he who is most conformable to the example of Christ, by humility, charity, and continual attendance on his flock, and who looks on himself as a servant to the children of God."

can sincerely rejoice when others are exalted, though he himself is overlooked and passed by!

Above all, let all who desire to walk in Christ's steps, labour to be useful to others. Let them lay themselves out to do good in their day and generation. There is always a vast field for doing it, if men have the will and inclination. Let them never forget, that true greatness does not consist in being an admiral, or a general,— a statesman, or an artist. It consists in devoting ourselves, body, and soul, and spirit to the blessed work of making our fellow men more holy and more happy. It is those who exert themselves by the use of Scripture means to lessen the sorrow, and increase the joy, of all around them, — the Howards, the Wilberforces, the Martyns, the Judsons of a country, — who are truly great in the sight of God. While they live they are laughed at, mocked, ridiculed, and often persecuted. But their memorial is on high. Their names are written in heaven. Their praise endureth for ever. Let us remember these things, and while we have time do good unto all men, and be servants of all for Christ's sake. Let us strive to leave the world better, holier, happier than it was when we were born. A life spent in this way is truly Christlike, and brings its own reward.

Let us mark, lastly, in this passage, *the language which our Lord uses in speaking of His own death.* He says, "The Son of Man came to give His life a ransom for many."

This is one of those expressions which ought to be carefully treasured up in the minds of all true Christians. It is one of the texts which prove incontrovertibly the

atoning character of Christ's death.   That death was
no common death, like the death of a martyr, or of
other holy men. It was the public payment by an
Almighty Representative of the debts of sinful man
to a holy God.   It was the ransom which a Divine
Surety undertook to provide, in order to procure liberty for sinners, tied and bound by the chain of their
sins.   By that death Jesus made a full and complete
satisfaction for man's countless transgressions.   He bore
our sins in His own body on the tree.   The Lord laid on
Him the iniquity of us all.   When He died, He died for
us.   When He suffered, He suffered in our stead.   When
He hung on the cross, He hung there as our Substitute.
When His blood flowed, it was the price of our souls.

Let all who trust in Christ take comfort in the thought,
that they build on a sure foundation.   It is true that we
are sinners, but Christ has borne our sins.   It is true
that we are poor helpless debtors, but Christ has paid our
debts.   It is true that we deserve to be shut up for ever
in the prison of hell.   But, thanks be to God, Christ hath
paid a full and complete ransom for us.   The door is
wide open.   The prisoners may go free.   May we all
know this privilege by heartfelt experience, and walk in
the blessed liberty of the children of God.*

* The manner in which our Lord uses the word baptism in the
passage now expounded, deserves careful notice. He says to two
disciples, who were already baptized with water, "Can ye be baptized with the baptism that I am baptized with?"   The expression
is very remarkable.   It is a clear proof that in the New Testament
a sacramental dipping or sprinkling with water is not always
necessarily implied by the word baptism.   It establishes the fact
that there is such a thing as being baptized, in a certain sense,
without the use of any outward ordinance at all.

MARK X. 46—52.

46 And they came to Jericho: and as he went out of Jericho with his disciples and a great number of people, blind Bartimæus, the son of Timæus, sat by the highway side begging.

47 And when he heard that it was Jesus of Nazareth, he began to cry out, and say, Jesus, *thou* Son of David, have mercy on me.

48 And many charged him that he should hold his peace: but he cried the more a great deal, *Thou* Son of David, have mercy on me.

49 And Jesus stood still, and commanded him to be called. And they call the blind man, saying unto him, Be of good comfort, rise; he calleth thee.

50 And he, casting away his garment, rose, and came to Jesus.

51 And Jesus answered and said unto him, What wilt thou that I should do unto thee? The blind man said unto him, Lord, that I might receive my sight.

52 And Jesus said unto him, Go thy way; thy faith hath made thee whole. And immediately he received his sight, and followed Jesus in the way.

WE read in these verses an account of one of our Lord's miracles. Let us see in it, as we read, a vivid emblem of spiritual things. We are not studying a history which concerns us personally any more than the exploits of Cæsar or Alexander. We have before us a picture which ought to be deeply interesting to the soul of every Christian.

This is a point that ought to be remembered in interpreting some of the passages in the Epistles where the words "baptism" and "baptized" are used. In such texts, for instance, as "baptism doth save us," (1 Peter iii. 21.) or "as many as have been baptized into Christ have put on Christ," (Gal. iii. 27.,) it is clear that something more is contained than any mere outward ordinance. In both cases, the baptism of water is undoubtedly meant, but it is no less evident that something is implied also of deeper moment than any ordinance administered by man. In both cases it is a baptism which is accompanied by true faith, and a heart-reception of Christ, such as was the baptism of the Philippian jailer. To quote such texts in support of what is commonly called the baptismal regeneration of infants, is to wrest and pervert them from their proper meaning. The conclusion of the text in St. Peter, for example, seems to place this beyond question. He emphatically warns us not to suppose that he means nothing more than the washing of water, or bodily reception of a sacrament, by the word baptism.

It has been a wise act on the part of translators of the New Testament to adhere to the Greek words "baptize" and "baptism" in rendering the Bible into the vernacular tongue of each nation. No other words could possibly imply all that the two Greek words

In the first place, we have here *an example of strong faith*. We are told that as Jesus went out of Jericho, a blind man named Bartimæus "sat by the wayside begging. And when he heard that it was Jesus of Nazareth, he began to cry out, and say, Jesus, thou Son of David, have mercy on me."

Bartimæus was blind in body, but not in soul. The eyes of his understanding were open. He saw things which Annas and Caiaphas, and hosts of letter-learned Scribes and Pharisees, never saw at all. He saw that Jesus of Nazareth, as our Lord was contemptuously called,—Jesus, who had lived for thirty years in an obscure Galilean village,—this very Jesus was the Son of David,—the Messiah of whom prophets had prophecied long ago. He had witnessed none of our Lord's mighty miracles. He had not had the opportunity of beholding dead people raised with a word, and lepers healed by a touch. Of all these privileges, his blindness totally deprived him. But he had heard the report of our Lord's mighty works, and hearing had believed. He was satisfied from mere hear-say, that He of whom such wonderful things were reported, must be the promised Saviour, and must be able to heal him. And so when our Lord drew

convey. All other expressions would either weaken the sense of the inspired writers, or convey a false impression to the mind of the reader. To take one solitary instance, what could be more meagre or unsatisfactory than to render the passage now before us in the following way, "Can ye be sprinkled with the sprinkling, or dipped with the dipping, that I am sprinkled or dipped with?"— The firmness of the British and Foreign Bible Society on this point, ought to be cause of thankfulness to all the Protestant churches. In resolving to use the Greek words "baptize" and "baptism," in all their versions, they have exercised a wise discretion.

near, he cried, "Jesus, thou Son of David, have mercy on me."

Let us strive and pray that we may have like precious faith. We too are not allowed to see Jesus with our bodily eyes. But we have the report of His power, and grace, and willingness to save, in the Gospel. We have exceeding great promises from His own lips, written down for our encouragement. Let us trust those promises implicitly, and commit our souls to Christ unhesitatingly. Let us not be afraid to repose all our confidence on His own gracious words, and to believe that what He has engaged to do for sinners, He will surely perform. What is the beginning of all saving faith, but a soul's venture on Christ? What is the life of saving faith, when once begun, but a continual leaning on an unseen Saviour's word? What is the first step of a Christian, but a crying, like Bartimæus, "Jesus have mercy on me?" What is the daily course of a Christian, but keeping up the same spirit of faith? "Though now we see Him not, yet believing we rejoice with joy unspeakable, and full of glory." (1 Peter i. 8.)

We have, in the second place, in these verses, *an example of determined perseverance in the face of difficulties.* We are told that when Bartimæus begun to cry out, "Jesus, thou Son of David, have mercy on me," he met with little encouragement from those who were near him. On the contrary, "many charged him that he should hold his peace." But he was not to be stopped. If others did not know the misery of blindness, he did. If others did not think it worthwhile to take such trouble, in order to obtain relief, he, at any rate, knew better. He cared not for the rebukes of unfeeling bystanders. He heeded not the ridicule which his importunity probably brought on him. "He cried the more a great deal," and so crying obtained his heart's desire, and received his sight.

Let all who wish to be saved, mark well this conduct of Bartimæus, and walk diligently in his steps. Like him, we must care nothing what others think and say of us, when we seek the healing of our souls. There never will be wanting people who will tell us that it is "too soon," or "too late,"—that we are going "too fast," or "too far,"—that we need not pray so much, or read our Bibles so much,—or be so anxious about salvation. We must give no heed to such people. Like Bartimæus, we must cry the more, "Jesus, have mercy on me."

What is the reason that men are so half-hearted in seeking Christ? Why are they so soon deterred, and checked, and discouraged in drawing near to God? The answer is short and simple. They do not feel sufficiently their own sins. They are not thoroughly convinced of the plague of their own hearts, and the disease of their own souls. Once let a man see his own guilt, as it really is, and he will never rest till he has found pardon and peace in Christ. It is they who, like Bartimæus, really know their own deplorable condition, who persevere, like Bartimæus, and are finally healed.

In the last place, we have in these verses, *an example of the constraining influence which gratitude to Christ ought to have upon our souls*. Bartimæus did not return home as soon as he was restored to sight. He would not leave Him from whom he had received such mercy. At once he devoted the new powers, which his cure gave him, to the Son of David who had worked the cure. His history concludes with the touching expression, He "followed Jesus in the way."

Let us see in these simple words, a lively emblem of the effect that the grace of Christ ought to have on every one who tastes it. It ought to make him a follower of Jesus in his life, and to draw him with mighty power into the way of holiness. Freely pardoned, he ought to give himself freely and willingly to Christ's service. Bought at so mighty a price as the blood of Christ, he ought to devote himself heartily and thoroughly to Him who redeemed him. Grace really experienced will make a man feel daily, "What shall I render to the Lord for all His benefits." It did so for the apostle Paul : He says, "the love of Christ constraineth us." (2 Cor. v. 14.) It will do so for all true Christians at the present day. The man who boasts of having an interest in Christ, while he does not follow Christ in his life, is a miserable self-deceiver, and is ruining his own soul. "As many as are led by the Spirit of God, they," and they only, "are the sons of God." (Rom. viii. 14.)

Have we had our eyes opened by the Spirit of God ? Have we yet been taught to see sin, and Christ, and holiness, and heaven, in their true light ? Can we say, One thing I know, that whereas I was blind, now I see ? If so, we shall know the things of which we have been reading by experience. If not, we are yet in the broad way that leadeth to destruction, and have everything to learn.

MARK XI. 1—11.

1 And when they came nigh to Jerusalem, unto Bethphage and Bethany, at the mount of Olives, he sendeth forth two of his disciples,

2 And saith unto them, Go your way into the village over against you: and as soon as ye be entered into it, ye shall find a colt tied, whereon never man sat; loose him, and bring *him*.

3 And if any man say unto you, Why do ye this? say ye that the Lord hath need of him; and straightway he will send him hither.

4 And they went their way, and found the colt tied by the door without in a place where two ways met; and they loose him.

5 And certain of them that stood there said unto them, What do ye, loosing the colt?

6 And they said unto them even as Jesus had commanded: and they let them go.

7 And they brought the colt to Jesus, and cast their garments on him; and he sat upon him.

8 And many spread their garments in the way: and others cut down branches off the trees, and strawed *them* in the way.

9 And they that went before, and they that followed, cried, saying, Hosanna; Blessed *is* he that cometh in the name of the Lord.

10 Blessed *be* the kingdom of our father David, that cometh in the name of the Lord : Hosanna in the highest.

11 And Jesus entered into Jerusalem, and into the temple : and when he had looked round about upon all things, and now the eventide was come, he went out unto Bethany with the twelve.

THE event described in these verses, is a singular exception in the history of our Lord's earthly ministry. Generally speaking, we see Jesus withdrawing Himself from public notice,—often passing His time in the remote parts of Galilee,—not unfrequently abiding in the wilderness,—and so fulfilling the prophecy, that He should "not cry, nor strive, nor let His voice be heard in the streets." Here, and here only, our Lord appears to drop His private character, and of his own choice to call public attention to Himself. He deliberately makes a public entry into Jerusalem, at the head of His disciples. He voluntarily rides into the holy city, surrounded by a vast multitude, crying, Hosanna, like king David returning to his palace in triumph. (2 Sam. xix. 40.) All this too was done at a time when myriads of Jews were gathered out of every land to Jerusalem, to keep the Passover. We may well believe that the holy city rang with the tidings of our Lord's arrival. It is probable there was not a house in Jerusalem in which the entry of the prophet of Nazareth was not known and talked of that night.

These things should always be remembered in reading this portion of our Lord's history. It is not for nothing that this entry into Jerusalem is four times related in the New Testament. It is evident that it is a scene in the earthly life of Jesus, which Christians are intended to study with special attention. Let us study it in that spirit, and see what practical lessons we may learn from the passage for our own souls.

Let us observe, in the first place, *how public our Lord purposely made the last act of His life.* He came to Jerusalem to die, and He desired that all Jerusalem should know it. When He taught the deep things of the Spirit, He often spoke to none but His apostles. When He delivered His parables, He often addressed none but a multitude of poor and ignorant Galileans. When He worked His miracles, He was generally at Capernaum, or in the land of Zebulon and Napthali. But when the time came that He should die, He made a public entry into Jerusalem. He drew the attention of rulers, and priests, and elders, and Scribes, and Greeks, and Romans to Himself. He knew that the most wonderful event that ever happened in this world, was about to take place. The eternal Son of God was about to suffer in the stead of sinful men,—the great sacrifice for sin about to be offered up,—the great Passover Lamb about to be slain,—the great atonement for a world's sin about to be made. He therefore ordered it so that His death was eminently a public death. He over-ruled things in such a way that

the eyes of all Jerusalem were fixed upon Him, and
when He died, He died before many witnesses.

Let us see here one more proof of the unspeakable
importance of the death of Christ. Let us treasure up
His gracious sayings. Let us strive to walk in the steps
of His holy life. Let us prize His intercession. Let us
long for His second coming. But never let us forget
that the crowning fact in all we know of Jesus Christ, is
His death upon the cross. From that death flow all our
hopes. Without that death we should have nothing
solid beneath our feet. May we prize that death more
and more every year we live; and in all our thoughts
about Christ, rejoice in nothing so much as the great fact
that He died for us !

Let us observe, in the second place, in this passage,
*the voluntary poverty which our Lord underwent, when He
was upon earth.* How did He enter Jerusalem when He
came to it on this remarkable occasion ? Did He come
in a royal chariot, with horses, soldiers, and a retinue
around Him, like the kings of this world ? We are told
nothing of the kind. We read that He borrowed the colt
of an ass for the occasion, and sat upon the garments of
His disciples for lack of a saddle. This was in perfect
keeping with all the tenor of His ministry. He never had
any of the riches of this world. When He crossed the sea
of Galilee, it was in a borrowed boat. When He rode into
the holy city, it was on a borrowed beast. When He
was buried, it was in a borrowed tomb.

We have in this simple fact, an instance of that
marvellous union of weakness* and power, riches and

* I use the word "weakness" in this passage advisedly. There

poverty, the godhead and the manhood, which may be so often traced in the history of our blessed Lord. Who that reads the Gospels carefully can fail to observe, that He who could feed thousands with a few loaves, was Himself sometimes hungry,—and He who could heal the sick and infirm, was Himself sometimes weary,—that He who could cast out devils with a word, was Himself tempted,—and He who could raise the dead, could Himself submit to die? We see the very same thing in the passage before us. We see the power of our Lord in His bending the wills of a vast multitude to conduct Him into Jerusalem in triumph. We see the poverty of our Lord in his borrowing an ass, to carry Him when He made His triumphal entry. It is all wonderful, but there is a fitness in it all. It is meet and right that we should never forget the union of the divine and human natures in our Lord's person. If we saw His divine acts only, we might forget that He was man. If we saw His

is scriptural warrant for it in the text, "He was crucified through weakness." (2 Cor. xiii. 4.) Nevertheless I wish it to be distinctly understood, that I utterly disclaim the idea of there being any *moral weakness* in the human nature of Christ. The only weakness I mean is that sinless infirmity, which is inseparably connected with flesh and blood, and from which Adam, before the fall, was not exempt. Of all such weakness, I believe, our Lord was partaker to the fullest extent.

Whether or not our Lord's riding upon an ass instead of a horse, was a mark of humiliation, is a point on which opinions differ widely. Some dwell on the fact that the ass in oriental countries was an animal that even kings rode, and refer to Judges v. 10. "Speak, ye that ride on white asses," &c. Others think that the choice of an ass was purposely made as emblematic of our Lord's lowly nature. Gerhard in his Commentary refers to a saying of Tertullian, that the Gentiles called Christians " asinarii," in ridicule, because they believed in Christ who rode on an ass, and even calumniously charged them with worshipping an ass's head!

seasons of poverty and weakness only, we might forget that He was God. But we are intended to see in Jesus, divine strength and human weakness united in one person. We cannot explain the mystery; but we may take comfort in the thought, "this is our Saviour, this is our Christ,—one able to sympathize, because He is man, but one Almighty to save, because He is God."

Finally, let us see in the simple fact, that our Lord rode on a borrowed ass, one more proof that poverty is in itself no sin. The causes which occasion much of the poverty there is around us, are undoubtedly very sinful. Drunkenness, extravagance, profligacy, dishonesty, idleness, which produce so much of the destitution in the world, are unquestionably wrong in the sight of God. But to be born a poor man, and to inherit nothing from our parents,—to work with our own hands for our bread, and to have no land of our own,—all this is not sinful at all. The honest poor man is as honourable in the sight of God as the richest king. The Lord Jesus Christ Himself was poor. Silver and gold He had none. He had often nowhere to lay His head. Though He was rich, yet for our sakes He became poor. To be like Him in circumstances, cannot be in itself wrong. Let us do our duty in that state of life to which God has called us, and if He thinks fit to keep us poor let us not be ashamed. The Saviour of sinners cares for us as well as for others. The Saviour of sinners knows what it is to be poor.

MARK XI. 12—21.

12 And on the morrow, when they were come from Bethany, he was hungry:

13 And seeing a fig tree afar off having leaves, he came, if haply he might find any thing thereon: and when he came to it, he found nothing but leaves; for the time of figs was not *yet*.

14 And Jesus answered and said unto it, No man eat fruit of thee hereafter for ever. And his disciples heard *it*.

15 And they come to Jerusalem: and Jesus went into the temple, and began to cast out them that sold and bought in the temple, and overthrew the tables of the moneychangers, and the seats of them that sold doves;

16 And would not suffer that any man should carry *any* vessel through the temple.

17 And he taught, saying unto them, Is it not written, My house shall be called of all nations the house of prayer? but ye have made it a den of thieves.

18 And the Scribes and Chief Priests heard *it*, and sought how they might destroy him: for they feared him, because all the people was astonished at his doctrine.

19 And when even was come, he went out of the city.

20 And in the morning, as they passed by, they saw the fig tree dried up from the roots.

21 And Peter calling to remembrance saith unto him, Master, behold, the fig tree which thou cursedst is withered away.

WE see in the beginning of this passage, *one of the many proofs that our Lord Jesus Christ was really man.* We read that "He was hungry." He had a nature and bodily constitution, like our own in all things, sin only excepted. He could weep, and rejoice, and suffer pain. He could be weary, and need rest. He could be thirsty, and need drink. He could be hungry, and need food.

Expressions like this should teach us the condescension of Christ. How wonderful they are when we reflect upon them! He who is the eternal God,—He who made the world and all that it contains,—He from whose hand the fruits of the earth, the fish of the sea, the fowls of the air, the beasts of the field, all had their beginning,—He, even He was pleased to suffer hunger, when He came into the world to save sinners. This is a great mystery. Kindness and love like this pass man's understanding. No wonder that St. Paul speaks of the "unsearchable riches of Christ." (Ephes. iii. 8.)

Expressions like this should teach us Christ's power to sympathize with His believing people on earth. He knows their sorrows by experience. He can be touched with the feeling of their infirmities. He has had experience of a body and its daily wants. He has suffered Himself the severe sufferings that the body of man is liable to. He has tasted pain, and weakness, and weariness, and hunger, and thirst. When we tell Him of these things in our prayers, He knows what we mean, and is no stranger to our troubles. Surely this is just the Saviour and Friend that poor aching, groaning, human nature requires!

We learn, in the second place, from these verses, *the great danger of unfruitfulness and formality in religion.* This is a lesson which our Lord teaches in a remarkable typical action. We are told that coming to a fig-tree in search of fruit, and finding on it "nothing but leaves," He pronounced on it the solemn sentence, "No man eat fruit of thee hereafter for ever." And we are told that the next day the fig-tree was found "dried up from the roots." We cannot doubt for a moment that this whole transaction was an emblem of spiritual things. It was a parable in deeds, as full of meaning as any of our Lord's parables in words.*

* There are two difficulties connected with the story of the withered fig tree, which weigh considerably on some minds, and therefore deserve notice.

1. It is a difficulty with some persons that our Lord should have pronounced any curse at all on the fig tree. They say, that it looks like a needless destruction of an innocent and unoffending creature, and out of keeping with the spirit of Deut. xx. 19.

Such objectors appear to forget that the withering of the fig tree was not a mere empty exhibition of power, like the pretended

But who were they to whom this withered fig tree was intended to speak? It was a sermon of three-fold application, a sermon that ought to speak loudly to the consciences of all professing Christians. Though withered and dried up, that fig tree yet speaks.—There was a voice in it for the Jewish Church. Rich in the leaves of a formal religion, but barren of all fruits of the Spirit, that Church was in fearful danger, at the very time when this withering took place. Well would it have been for

miracles of Mahomet and other false prophets. It was a mighty typical act, teaching deep spiritual lessons, lessons of such importance as might well justify the destruction of one of God's unintelligent creatures, in order to convey them. Remembering this, we have no more right to object to it, than to object to the daily offering of a lamb under the Mosaic law. In that offering the life of an innocent and unoffending creature was daily taken away. But the great end of daily setting before the eyes of man the one sacrifice for sin, justified the taking away the life of the lamb. Just in the same way we may justify our Lord's taking away the life of the tree.

2. It is a difficulty with some persons that the account of St. Mark contains the words, "the time of figs was not yet." They ask to be told why our Lord should have gone to the tree seeking fruit, when the season for figs had not yet arrived?

The answers to this difficulty are various. The simplest of them appears to be as follows. "The time of figs, as a general rule, had not yet come. But our Lord seeing a fig tree covered with leaves, *unlike the other fig trees*, had a right to suppose that figs were to be found on it, and therefore came to it."—It is no small recommendation of this view that it supplies an exact illustration of the state of the Jewish Church, when our Lord was upon earth. The time of figs was not yet, that is, the nations of the earth were all in darkness, and bore no fruit to the glory of God.—But among the nations, there was one covered with leaves, that is the Jewish Church, full of light, knowledge, privileges and high profession.— Seeing this fig tree full of leaves, our Lord came to it seeking fruit, that is, He came to the Jews justly expecting them to have fruit according to their outward profession.— But when our Lord came to this leafy Jewish fig tree, He found it utterly destitute of fruit, faithless, and unbelieving.—And the end was that He pronounced sentence on it, gave it over to be destroyed by the Romans, and scattered the Jews over the earth.

the Jewish church if it had had eyes to see its peril!
—There was a voice in the fig-tree for all the branches of
Christ's visible Church in every age, and every part of
the world.   There was a warning against an empty profession of Christianity, unaccompanied by sound doctrine
and holy living, which some of those branches would
have done well to lay to heart.—But above all there was
a voice in that withered fig tree for all carnal, hypocri-
tical, and false-hearted Christians.   Well would it be
for all who are content with a name to live while in
reality they are dead, if they would only see their own
faces in the glass of this passage.

Let us take care that we each individually learn the
lesson that this fig tree conveys.   Let us always remember, that baptism, and church-membership, and reception
of the Lord's Supper, and a diligent use of the outward
forms of Christianity, are not sufficient to save our souls.
They are leaves, nothing but leaves, and without fruit will
add to our condemnation.   Like the fig leaves of which
Adam and Eve made themselves garments, they will not
hide the nakedness of our souls from the eye of an all-
seeing God, or give us boldness when we stand before
Him at the last day.   No! we must bear fruit, or be lost
for ever.   There must be fruit in our hearts and fruit in
our lives, the fruit of repentance toward God, and faith
toward our Lord Jesus Christ, and true holiness in our
conversation.   Without such fruits as these a profession
of Christianity will only sink us lower into hell.

We learn, in the last place, from this passage, *how
reverently we ought to use places which are set apart for
public worship.*   This is a truth which is taught us in a

striking manner by our Lord Jesus Christ's conduct, when He went into the temple. We are told that "he cast out them that sold and bought in the temple, and overthrew the tables of the moneychangers, and the seats of them that sold doves." And we are told that He enforced this action by warrant of Scripture, saying, "Is it not written, My house shall be called of all nations the house of prayer? but ye have made it a den of thieves."

We need not doubt that there was a deep meaning in this action of our Lord on this occasion. Like the cursing of the fig tree, the whole transaction was eminently typical. But in saying this, we must not allow ourselves to lose sight of one simple and obvious lesson which lies on the surface of the passage. That lesson is the sinfulness of careless and irreverent behaviour in the use of buildings set apart for the public service of God. It was not so much as the house of sacrifice, but as the "house of prayer," that our Lord purified the temple. His action clearly indicates the feeling with which every "house of prayer" should be regarded. A Christian place of worship no doubt is in no sense so sacred as the Jewish tabernacle, or temple. Its arrangements have no typical meaning. It is not built after a divine model, and intended to serve as an example of heavenly things. But it does not follow because these things are so, that a Christian place of worship is to be used with no more reverence than a private dwelling, or a shop, or an inn. There is surely a decent reverence, which is due to a place where Christ and His people regularly meet together and public prayer is offered up,—a reverence which it is foolish and unwise to brand as superstitious, and confound with Popery. There is a certain feeling of sanctity and solemnity which ought to belong to all places where Christ is preached, and souls are born again, a feeling which does not depend on any consecration of man, and ought to be encouraged rather than checked. At all events the mind of the Lord Jesus in this passage seems very plain. He takes notice of men's behaviour in places of worship, and all irreverence or profanity is an offence in His sight.

Let us remember these verses whenever we go to the house of God, and take heed that we go in a serious frame, and do not offer the sacrifice of fools. Let us call to mind where we are,—what we are doing,—what business we are about,—and in whose presence we are engaged. Let us beware of giving God a mere formal service, while our hearts are full of the world. Let us leave our business and money at home, and not carry them with us to church. Let us beware of allowing any buying and selling in our hearts, in the midst of our religious assemblies. The Lord still lives, who cast out buyers and sellers from the temple, and when He sees such conduct He is much displeased.

MARK XI. 22—26.

22 And Jesus answering saith unto them, Have faith in God.

23 For verily I say unto you, That whosoever shall say unto this mountain, Be thou removed, and be thou cast into the sea; and shall not doubt in his heart, but shall believe that those things which he saith shall come to pass; he shall have whatsoever he saith.

24 Therefore I say unto you, What things soever ye desire, when ye pray, believe that ye receive *them,* and ye shall have *them.*

25 And when ye stand praying, forgive, if ye have ought against any: that your Father also which is in heaven may forgive you your trespasses.

26 But if ye do not forgive, neither will your Father which is in heaven forgive your trespasses.

LET us learn from these words of our Lord Jesus Christ, *the immense importance of faith.*

This is a lesson which our Lord teaches first by a proverbial saying. Faith shall enable a man to accomplish works, and overcome difficulties, as great and formidable as the "removing of a mountain, and casting it into the sea."* Afterwards the lesson is impressed upon us still further, by a general exhortation to exercise faith when we pray. "What things soever ye desire, when ye pray, believe that ye receive them, and ye shall have them." This promise must of course be taken with a reasonable qualification. It assumes that a believer will ask things which are not sinful, and which are in accordance with the will of God. When He asks such things, he may confidently believe that his prayer will be answered. To use the words of St. James, "Let him ask in faith, nothing wavering." (James i. 6.)

The faith here commended must be distinguished from

---

* It is clear that a promise like this of "removing mountains" must be taken in a figurative sense. It appears to be a proverbial expression, and to be used as such by St. Paul, 2 Cor. xiii. 11. Moreover it is a promise that must be interpreted with sober and reasonable limitations. We have no right to expect that whatever we take it into our heads to ask of God shall at once be done for us, whether it be for His glory and our sanctification or not. We have no warrant for presuming that in every difficulty and trouble, God will at once work a miracle and deliver us from our anxiety, as soon as we make it a subject of prayer. The things about which we pray, must be things having special reference to our own vocation and providential position. Moses at the head of the twelve tribes of Israel,—Elijah on Mount Carmel,—Paul in the Philippian prison, might confidently expect miraculous interpositions in answer to prayer, in a way that private individuals may not expect in our days. Above all, we must not think to prescribe to God the time and way in which He shall "remove mountains" for us.

that faith which is essential to justification. In principle undoubtedly all true faith is one and the same. It is always trust or belief. But in the object and operations of faith there are diversities, which it is useful to understand. Justifying faith is that act of the soul by which a man lays hold on Christ, and has peace with God. Its special object is the atonement for sin which Jesus made on the cross.—The faith spoken of in the passage now before us is a grace of more general signification, the fruit and companion of justifying faith, but still not to be confounded with it. It is rather a general confidence in God's power, wisdom, and goodwill towards believers. And its special objects are the promises, the word, and the character of God in Christ.

Confidence in God's power and will to help every believer in Christ, and in the truth of every word that God has spoken, is the grand secret of success and prosperity in our religion. In fact, it is the very root of saving Christianity. " By it the elders obtained a good report." " He that cometh unto God must believe that He is, and that He is a rewarder of them that diligently seek Him." To know the full worth of it in the sight of God, we should often study the eleventh chapter of the Epistle to the Hebrews.

Do we desire to grow in grace, and in the knowledge of our Lord Jesus Christ ? Do we wish to make progress in our religion, and become strong Christians, and not mere babes in spiritual things ? Then let us pray daily for more faith, and watch our faith with most jealous watchfulness. Here is the corner-stone of our religion. A flaw or weakness here will affect the whole condition of our inner man. According to our faith will be the degree of our peace, our hope, our joy, our decision in Christ's service, our boldness in confession, our strength in work, our patience in trial, our resignation in trouble, our sensible comfort in prayer. All, all will hinge on the proportion of our faith. Happy are they who know how to rest their whole weight continually on a covenant God, and to walk by faith, not by sight. "He that believeth shall not make haste." (Isai. xxviii. 16.)

Let us learn, for another thing, from these verses *the absolute necessity of a forgiving spirit towards others.* This lesson is here taught us in a striking way. There is no immediate connection between the importance of faith, of which our Lord had just been speaking, and the subject of forgiving injuries. But the connecting link is prayer. First we are told that faith is essential to the success of our prayers. But then it is added, no prayers can be heard which do not come from a forgiving heart. "When ye stand praying, forgive, if ye have ought against any, that your Father also which is in heaven may forgive you your trespasses."

The value of our prayers, we can all understand, depends exceedingly on the state of mind in which we offer them. But the point before us is one which receives far less attention than it deserves. Our prayers must not only be earnest, fervent, and sincere, and in the name of Christ. They must contain one more ingredient besides. They must come from a forgiving heart. We have no right to look for mercy, if we are not ready to extend mercy to our brethren. We cannot really feel the sinfulness of the sins we ask to have pardoned if we

cherish malice towards our fellow men. We must have
the heart of a brother toward our neighbour on earth,
if we wish God to be our Father in heaven. We must
not flatter ourselves that we have the Spirit of adoption
if we cannot bear and forbear.

This is a heart-searching subject. The quantity of
malice, bitterness, and party-spirit among Christians is
fearfully great. No wonder that so many prayers seem
to be thrown away and unheard. It is a subject which
ought to come home to all classes of Christians. All have
not equal gifts of knowledge and utterance in their
approaches to God. But all can forgive their fellow-men.
It is a subject which our Lord Jesus Christ has taken
special pains to impress on our minds. He has given it
a prominent place in that pattern of prayers, the Lord's
prayer. We are all familiar from our infancy with the
words, " forgive us our trespasses as we forgive them that
trespass against us." Well would it be for many, if they
would consider what those words mean !

Let us leave the passage with serious self-inquiry.
Do we know what it is to be of a forgiving spirit ?   Can
we look over the injuries that we receive from time to
time in this evil world ? Can we pass over a transgression and pardon an offence ? If not, where is our
Christianity ? If not, why should we wonder that our
souls do not prosper ?—Let us resolve to amend our ways
in this matter. Let us determine by God's grace to
forgive, even as we hope to be forgiven. This is the
nearest approach we can make to the mind of Christ
Jesus. This is the character which is most suitable to a
poor sinful child of Adam. God's free forgiveness of sins

is our highest privilege in this world. God's free forgiveness will be our only title to eternal life in the
world to come. Then let us be forgiving during the
few years that we are here upon earth.*

MARK XI. 27—33.

27 And they come again to Jerusalem: and as he was walking in the
temple, there come to him the Chief
Priests, and the Scribes, and the
elders,

28 And say unto him, By what authority doest thou these things? and
who gave thee this authority to do
these things?

29 And Jesus answered and said
unto them, I will also ask of you one
question, and answer me, and I will
tell you by what authority I do these
things?

30 The baptism of John, was *it*
from heaven, or of men? answer me.

31 And they reasoned with themselves, saying, If we shall say, From
heaven; he will say, Why then did
ye not believe him?

32 But if we shall say of men; they
feared the people: for all *men* counted
John, that he was a prophet indeed.

33 And they answered and said unto
Jesus, We cannot tell. And Jesus
answering saith unto them, Neither
do I tell you by what authority I do
these things.

LET us observe in these verses *how much spiritual blindness may be in the hearts of those who hold high ecclesiastical
office.* We see "the chief priests and scribes and elders"
coming to our Lord Jesus, and raising difficulties and
objections in the way of His work.

These men, we know, were the accredited teachers and

* The expression "when ye stand praying" in this passage
ought not to be overlooked. It is one of those forms of speech in
the Bible, which ought to teach all Christians not to be dogmatical in laying down minute rules about the externals of religion,
and especially about the precise manner, gesture, or posture in
which a believer ought to pray. If a man is fully persuaded that
he can hold closer communion with God, and pour out his heart
more freely and without distraction, in the attitude of standing
than in that of kneeling, I dare not tell him that he is wrong.
The great point to insist on us is the absolute necessity of praying
with the heart. The last words of Sir Walter Raleigh to his
executioner on the scaffold are a beautiful illustration of the right
view of the question: "Friend, it matters little how a man's head
lies, if his heart be right in the sight of God."

rulers of the Jewish church. They were regarded by the Jews as the fountain and spring-head of religious knowledge. They were, most of them, regularly ordained to the position they held, and could trace their orders by regular descent from Aaron. And yet we find these very men, at the time when they ought to have been instructors of others, full of prejudice against the truth, and bitter enemies of the Messiah ! *

These things are written to shew Christians, that they must beware of depending too much on ordained men. They must not look up to ministers as Popes, or regard them as infallible. The orders of no church confer infallibility, whether they be Episcopal, Presbyterian, or Independent. Bishops, priests, and deacons, at their best, are only flesh and blood, and may err both in doctrine and practice, as well as the chief priests and elders of the Jews. Their acts and teaching must always be tested by the word of God. They must be followed so far as they follow Scripture, and no further. There is only one Priest and Bishop of souls, who makes no mistakes. That one is

* The following remarks from Gerhard's commentary are worth reading :—

"The Church is not tied to those teachers who are in the regular succession, for they frequently err from the path of truth. In such cases the Church ought not to follow their errors, but to embrace the truth as set forth in the word. Thus, Aaron setting up the golden calf,—Urijah the high priest in the time of Ahaz, building a new altar,—Pashur and the other priests in Jeremiah's time, all erred most grievously. And in this very passage, the priests sitting in Moses' seat reject the Messiah Himself, and impugn His authority. But if those who succeeded Aaron in the divinely appointed priesthood of the Old Testament, could err, and in fact, did occasionally err, how much more likely to err are the Popes of Rome, who cannot prove from God's word that the Pope's office has been instituted by Christ in the New Testament."

the Lord Jesus Christ. In Him alone is no weakness, no failure, no shadow of infirmity. Let us learn to lean more entirely on Him. Let us "call no man father on earth." (Matt. xxiii. 9.) So doing, we shall never be disappointed.

Let us observe, in the second place, *how envy and unbelief make men throw discredit on the commission of those who work for God.* These chief priests and elders could not deny the reality of our Lord's miracles of mercy. They could not say that His teaching was contrary to Holy Scripture, or that His life was sinful. What then did they do? They attacked His claim to attention, and demanded His authority;—"By what authority doest thou these things? and who gave thee this authority?"*

There can be no doubt whatever that, as a general principle, all who undertake to teach others, should be

* Brentius has some sensible remarks on the unreasonableness of the chief priests and Pharisees, who would neither keep the temple from the encroachment of the buyers and sellers, nor let others do it for them. They would neither exercise the lawful authority which was in their hands, nor allow of our Lord exercising it for them. He shows the similarity of their conduct to that of the Greek and Roman churches, and to that of a foolish head of a family, who neither corrects his children himself, nor likes any one to correct them for him. And he concludes by saying, "Let us learn that every one should do his own duty, or else yield up his place to another. Let us not be like the dog in the manger, who would neither eat the hay himself, nor yet allow the ox to eat it." The history of the church of Christ contains only too much of the dog in the manger! Ministers and teachers have often neglected the souls of their people shamefully, and yet found fault with any one who has tried to do good, and haughtily demanded his authority!

The reflections of the Roman Catholic writer, Quesnel, on this subject are remarkable: "Those who find themselves vanquished by truth, generally endeavour to reject authority. There are no persons more forward to demand of others a reason for their actions, than those who think they may do everything themselves without control."

regularly appointed to the work. St. Paul himself declares that this was the case with our Lord, in the matter of the priestly office : "No man taketh this honour unto himself, but he that is called of God, as was Aaron." (Heb. v. 4.) And even now, when the office of the sacrificing priest no longer exists, the words of the twenty-third Article of the Church of England are wise and scriptural : "It is not lawful for any man to take upon him the office of public preaching, or ministering the sacraments in the congregation, before he be lawfully called and sent to execute the same." But it is one thing to maintain the lawfulness of an outward call to minister in sacred things, and quite another to assert that it is the one thing needful, without which no work for God can be done. This is the point on which the Jews evidently erred in the time of our Lord's earthly ministry, and on which many have unhappily followed them down to the present day.

Let us beware of this narrow spirit, and specially in these last ages of the world. Unquestionably we must not undervalue order and discipline in the church. It is just as valuable there as it is in an army. But we must not suppose that God is absolutely tied to the use of ordained men. We must not forget that there may be an inward call of the Holy Ghost without any outward call of man, no less than an outward call of man without any inward call of the Holy Ghost. The first question after all is this : "Is a man for Christ, or against Him? What does he teach? How does he live? Is he doing good?" If questions like these can be answered satisfactorily, let us thank God and be content. We must remember that a physician is useless, however high his degree and diploma, if he cannot cure diseases, and a soldier useless, however well dressed and drilled, if he will not face the enemy in the day of battle. The best doctor is the man who can cure, and the best soldier the man who can fight.

Let us observe, in the last place, *what dishonesty and equivocation unbelievers may be led into by prejudice against the truth.* The chief priests and elders dared not answer our Lord's question about John's Baptism. They dared not say, it was "of men," because they feared the people. They dared not confess that it was "of heaven," because they saw our Lord would say, "Why did ye not believe him? He testified plainly of me." What then did they do? They told a direct lie. They said, "we cannot tell."

It is a melancholy fact, that dishonesty like this is far from being uncommon among unconverted people. There are thousands who evade appeals to their conscience by answers which are not true. When pressed to attend to their souls, they say things which they know are not correct. They love the world and their own way, and like our Lord's enemies, are determined not to give them up, but like them also are ashamed to say the truth. And so they answer exhortations to repentance and decision by false excuses. One man pretends that he "cannot understand" the doctrines of the Gospel. Another assures us that he really "tries" to serve God, but makes no progress. A third declares that he has every wish to serve Christ, but "has no time." All these are often nothing better than miserable equivocations. As a general rule, they are as worthless as the chief priests' answer, "we cannot tell."

The plain truth is that we ought to be very slow to give credit to the unconverted man's professed reasons for not serving Christ. We may be tolerably sure, that when he says "I cannot," the real meaning of his heart is "I will not." A really honest spirit in religious matters is a mighty blessing. Once let a man be willing to live up to his light, and act up to his knowledge, and he will soon know of the doctrine of Christ, and come out from the world. (John vii. 17.) The ruin of thousands is simply this, that they deal dishonestly with their own souls. They allege pretended difficulties as the cause of their not serving Christ, while in reality they "love darkness rather than light," and have no honest desire to change. (John iii. 19.)

MARK XII. 1—12.

1 And he began to speak unto them by parables. A *certain* man planted a vineyard, and set an hedge about *it*, and digged *a place for* the winefat, and built a tower, and let it out to husbandmen, and went into a far country.

2 And at the season he sent to the husbandmen a servant, that he might receive from the husbandmen of the fruit of the vineyard.

3 And they caught *him*, and beat him, and sent *him* away empty.

4 And again he sent unto them another servant; and at him they cast stones, and wounded *him* in the head, and sent *him* away shamefully handled.

5 And again he sent another; and him they killed, and many others; beating some, and killing some.

6 Having yet therefore one son, his well-beloved, he sent him also last unto them, saying, They will reverence my son.

7 But those husbandmen said among themselves, This is the heir; come, let us kill him, and the inheritance shall be our's.

8 And they took him, and killed *him*, and cast *him* out of the vineyard.

9 What shall therefore the lord of the vineyard do? he will come and destroy the husbandmen, and will give the vineyard unto others.

10 And have ye not read this Scripture; The stone which the builders rejected is become the head of the corner:

11 This was the Lord's doing, and it is marvellous in our eyes?

12 And they sought to lay hold on him, but feared the people: for they knew that he had spoken the parable against them: and they left him, and went their way.

THE verses before us contain an historical parable. The history of the Jewish nation, from the day that Israel left Egypt down to the time of the destruction of Jerusalem, is here set before us as in a glass. Under the figure of the vineyard and the husbandmen, the Lord Jesus tells the story of God's dealings with his people for fifteen hundred years. Let us study it attentively, and apply it to ourselves.

Let us observe, in the first place, *God's special kindness to the Jewish Church and nation.* He gave to them peculiar privileges. He dealt with them as a man deals with a piece of land which he separates and hedges in for "a vineyard." He gave them good laws and ordinances. He planted them in a goodly land, and cast out seven nations before them. He passed by greater and mightier nations to show them favour. He let alone Egypt, and Assyria, and Greece, and Rome, and showered down mercies on a few millions of people in Palestine. The vineyard of the Lord was the house of Israel. No family under heaven ever received so many signal and distinguishing privileges as the family of Abraham.

And we too, who live in Great Britain, can we say that we have received no special mercies from God? We cannot say so. Why are we not a heathen country, like China? Why are we not a land of idolaters, like Hindostan? We owe it all to the distinguishing favour of God. It is not for our goodness and worthiness, but of God's free grace, that England is what England is among the nations of the earth. Let us be thankful for our mercies, and know the hand from which they come. Let us not be high-minded, but humble, lest we provoke

God to take our mercies away. If Israel had peculiar national privileges, so also has England. Let Englishmen mark this well, and take heed, lest that which happened to Israel should happen also to them.

Let us observe, in the second place, *God's patience and longsuffering towards the Jewish nation.* What is their whole history as recorded in the Old Testament, but a long record of repeated provocations and repeated pardons? Over and over again we read of prophets being sent to them, and warnings being delivered, but too often entirely in vain. One servant after another came to the vineyard of Israel, and asked for fruit.—One servant after another was "sent away empty" by the Jewish husbandmen, and no fruit borne by the nation to the glory of God. "They mocked the messengers of God, and despised his words, and misused his prophets." (2 Chron. xxxvi. 16.) Yet hundreds of years passed away before "the wrath of the Lord arose against his people, till there was no remedy." Never was there a people so patiently dealt with as Israel.

And we too, who dwell in Great Britain, have we no longsuffering of God to be thankful for? Beyond doubt, we have abundant cause to say, that our Lord is patient. He does not deal with us according to our sins, or reward us according to our iniquities. We have often provoked Him to take our candlestick away, and to deal with us as He has dealt with Tyre, and Babylon, and Rome. Yet His longsuffering and lovingkindness continue still. Let us beware that we do not presume on His goodness too far. Let us hear in His mercies a loud call to us to bear fruit, and let us strive to abound in that righteous-

ness which alone exalteth a nation. (Prov. xiv. 34.)
Let every family in the land feel its responsibility to
God, and then the whole nation will be seen showing
forth His praise.

Let us observe, in the third place, *the hardness and
wickedness of human nature, as exemplified in the history
of the Jewish people.*

It is difficult to imagine a more striking proof of this
truth, than the summary of Israel's dealings with God's
messengers, which our Lord sketches in this parable.
Prophet after prophet was sent to them in vain.   Miracle
after miracle was wrought among them, without any
lasting effect.   The Son of God Himself, the well-beloved,
at last came down to them, and was not believed.   God
Himself was manifest in the flesh, dwelling among them,
and "they took Him and killed Him."

There is no truth so little realized and believed as the
"desperate wickedness" of the human heart.   Let the
parable before us this day be always reckoned among the
standing proofs of it.   Let us see in it what men and
women can do, in the full blaze of religious privileges,—
in the midst of prophecies and miracles,—in the presence
of the Son of God Himself.   "The carnal mind is enmity
against God." (Rom. viii. 7.)   Men never saw God face to
face but once, when Jesus became a man, and lived upon
earth.   They saw Him holy, harmless, undefiled, going
about doing good.   Yet they would not have Him, rebelled
against Him, and at last killed Him.   Let us dismiss
from our minds the idea that there is any innate goodness,
or natural rectitude, in our hearts.   Let us put away the
common notion that seeing and knowing what is good is

enough to make a man a Christian. The great experiment has been made in the instance of the Jewish nation. We too, like Israel, might have among us miracles, prophets, and the company of Christ Himself in the flesh, and yet, like Israel, have them in vain. Nothing but the Spirit of God can change the heart. "We must be born again." (John iii. 7.)

Let us observe, in the last place, *that men's consciences may be pricked, and yet they may continue impenitent.* The Jews, to whom our Lord addressed the solemn historical parable which we have been reading, saw clearly that it applied to themselves. They felt that they and their forefathers were the husbandmen to whom the vineyard was let, and who ought to have rendered fruit to God. They felt that they and their forefathers were the wicked labourers, who had refused to give the Master of the vineyard His dues, and had "shamefully handled" His servants, "beating some, and killing some." Above all, they felt that they themselves were planning the last crowning act of wickedness, which the parable described. They were about to kill the well-beloved Son, and "cast Him out of the vineyard." All this they knew perfectly well. "They knew that He had spoken the parable against them." Yet though they knew it, they would not repent. Though convicted by their own consciences, they were hardened in sin.

Let us learn from this awful fact, that knowledge and conviction alone save no man's soul. It is quite possible to know that we are wrong, and be unable to deny it, and yet to cleave to our sins obstinately, and perish miserably in hell. The thing that we all need, is a change of heart and will. For this let us pray earnestly. Till we have this, let us never rest. Without this, we shall never be real Christians, and reach heaven. Without it we may live all our lives, like the Jews, knowing inwardly that we are wrong, and yet, like the Jews, persevere in our own way, and die in our sins.

MARK XII. 13—17.

13 And they send unto him certain of the Pharisees and of the Herodians, to catch him in *his* words.

14 And when they were come, they say unto him, Master, we know that thou art true, and carest for no man: for thou regardest not the person of men, but teachest the way of God in truth: Is it lawful to give tribute to Cæsar or not?

15 Shall we give, or shall we not give? But he, knowing their hypoc-risy, said unto them, Why tempt ye me? bring me a penny, that I may see *it*.

16 And they brought *it*. And he saith unto them, Whose *is* this image and superscription? And they said unto him, Cæsar's.

17 And Jesus answering said unto them, Render to Cæsar the things that are Cæsar's, and to God the things that are God's. And they marvelled at him.

LET us observe in the beginning of this passage, *how men of different religious opinions can unite in opposing Christ.* We read of "Pharisees and Herodians" coming together to "catch our Lord in His words," and perplex Him with a hard question. The Pharisee was a superstitious formalist, who cared for nothing but the outward ceremonies of religion. The Herodian was a mere man of the world, who despised all religion, and cared more for pleasing men than God. Yet when there came among them a mighty teacher who assailed the ruling passions of both alike, and spared neither formalist nor worldling, we see them making common cause, and uniting in a common effort to stop His mouth.

It has always been so from the beginning of the world. We may see the same thing going on at the present day.

Worldly men and formalists have little real sympathy with one another. They dislike one another's principles, and despise one another's ways. But there is one thing which they both dislike even more, and that is the pure Gospel of Jesus Christ. And hence, whenever there is a chance of opposing the Gospel, we shall always see the worldly man and the formalist combine and act together. We must expect no mercy from them : they will show none. We must never reckon on their divisions : they will always patch up an alliance to resist Christ.

Let us observe, for another thing, in this passage, *the exceeding subtlety of the question propounded to our Lord.* His enemies asked him, " Is it lawful to give tribute to Cæsar, the Roman emperor, or not ? Shall we give, or shall we not give ? " Here was a question, which it seemed at first sight impossible to answer without peril. If our Lord had replied " give," the Pharisees would have accused him before the priests, as one who regarded the Jewish nation as under subjection to Rome.—If our Lord had replied, " Do not give," the Herodians would have accused him before Pilate, as a seditious person who taught rebellion against the Roman government. The trap was indeed well planned. Surely we may see in it the cunning hand of one greater than man. That old serpent the devil was there.

We shall do well to remember, that of all questions which have perplexed Christians, none have ever proved so intricate and puzzling, as the class of questions, which the Pharisees and Herodians here propounded.*

* " Nothing is more likely to ensnare ministers, than bringing them to meddle with controversies about civil rights, and to settle

What are the dues of Cæsar, and what are the dues of God,—where the rights of the church end, and where the rights of the state begin,—what are lawful civil claims and what are lawful spiritual claims,—all these are hard knots and deep problems which Christians have often found it difficult to untie, and almost impossible to solve. Let us pray to be delivered from them. Never does the cause of Christ suffer so much as when the devil succeeds in bringing churches into collisions and law-suits with the civil power. In such collisions precious time is wasted,—energies are misapplied,—ministers are drawn off from their proper work,—the souls of people suffer, and a church's victory often proves only one degree better than a defeat.—" Give peace in our time, O Lord," is a prayer of wide meaning, and one that should often be on a Christian's lips.

Let us observe, in the last place, *the marvellous wisdom which our Lord showed in His answer to His enemies.*

Their flattering words did not deceive Him. He " knew their hypocrisy." His all-seeing eye detected the "potsherds covered with silver dross" which stood before Him. (Prov. xxvi. 23.) He was not imposed upon, as too many of His people are, by glowing language and fine speeches.

He made the daily practice of His own enemies supply Him with an answer to their cunning question. He tells them to "bring Him a penny," a common coin which they themselves were in the habit of using. He asks them "whose image and superscription" are stamped upon that

landmarks between the prince and the subjects, which it is fit should be done, while it is not at all fit that they should have the doing of it." *Matthew Henry.*

penny? They are obliged to reply, "Cæsar's." They were themselves using a Roman coin, issued and circulated by the Roman government. By their own confession they were in some way under the power of the Romans, or this Roman money would not have been current among them. At once our Lord silences them by the memorable words, "Render unto Cæsar the things that are Cæsar's, and unto God the things that are God's." He bids them pay tribute to the Roman government in temporal things, for by using its money they allowed themselves bound to do so. Yet he bids them give obedience to God in spiritual things, and not to suppose that duty to an earthly sovereign and a heavenly sovereign are incapable of being reconciled one with the other. In short, He bids the proud Pharisee not to refuse his dues to Cæsar, and the worldly Herodian not to refuse his dues to God.

Let us learn from this masterly decision the great principle, that true Christianity was never meant to interfere with a man's obedience to the civil power. So far from this being the case it ought to make him a quiet, loyal, and faithful subject. He ought to regard the powers that be as "ordained of God," and to submit to their rules and regulations, so long as the law is enforced, though he may not thoroughly approve of them. If the law of the land and the law of God come in collision, no doubt his course is clear,—he must obey God rather than man. Like the three children, though he serves a heathen king, he must not bow down to an idol. Like Daniel, though he submits to a tyrannical government, he must not give over praying in order to please the ruling powers.*

* Sibelius quotes a passage from Augustine on the Psalms which

Let us often pray for a larger measure of that spirit of wisdom, which dwelt so abundantly in our blessed Lord. Many are the evils which have arisen in the Church of Christ, from a morbid and distorted view of the relative positions of the civil government and of God. Many are the rents and divisions which have been occasioned by lack of sound judgment as to their comparative claims. Happy is he who remembers our Lord's decision in this passage, understands it rightly, and makes a practical application of it to his own times.

MARK XII. 18—27.

18 Then come unto him the Sadducees, which say there is no resurrection; and they asked him, saying,

19 Master, Moses wrote unto us, If a man's brother die, and leave *his* wife *behind him*, and leave no children, that his brother should take his wife, and raise up seed unto his brother.

20 Now there were seven brethren: and the first took a wife, and dying left no seed.

21 And the second took her, and died, neither left he any seed: and the third likewise.

22 And the seven had her, and left no seed: last of all the woman died also.

23 In the resurrection therefore, when they shall rise, whose wife shall she be of them? for the seven had her to wife.

24 And Jesus answering said unto them, Do ye not therefore err, because ye know not the Scriptures, neither the power of God?

25 For when they shall rise from the dead, they neither marry, nor are given in marriage; but are as the angels which are in heaven.

26 And as touching the dead, that they rise: have ye not read in the book of Moses, how in the bush God spake unto him, saying, I *am* the God of Abraham, and the God of Isaac, and the God of Jacob?

27 He is not the God of the dead, but the God of the living: ye therefore do greatly err.

is worth reading, as an illustration of the subject now before us. "Julian was an unbelieving emperor. He was an apostate, a wicked man, and an idolater. And yet Christian men served as soldiers under this unbelieving emperor. When the cause of Christ was concerned, they acknowledged no commander but Him that was in heaven. When the emperor wished them to worship idols or burn incense to them, they preferred honouring God before him. But when he said, 'draw out in order of battle, march against that nation,' they obeyed him. They drew a distinction between their eternal master, and their temporal master; and yet were submissive to their temporal master for their eternal master's sake."

THESE verses relate a conversation between our Lord
Jesus Christ and the Sadducees. The religion of these
men, we know, was little better than infidelity. They
said there was "no resurrection." They too, like the
Pharisees, thought to entangle and perplex our Lord with
hard questions. The Church of Christ must not expect
to fare better than its Master. Formalism on one side
and infidelity on another, are two enemies for whose
attacks we must always be prepared.

We learn from this passage, *how much unfairness may
often be detected in the arguments of infidels.*

The question propounded by the Sadducees is a striking
illustration of this. They tell him of a woman who
married seven brothers in succession, had no children, and
outlived her seven husbands. They ask "whose wife" of
all the seven the woman would be "in the resurrection?"
It may well be surmised that the case was a supposed and
not a real one. On the face of it, there is the strongest
appearance of improbability. The chances against such
a case occurring in reality, any actuary would tell us, are
almost infinite. But that was nothing to the Sadducees.
All they cared for was to raise a difficulty, and if possible
to put our Lord to silence. The doctrine of the resurrection they had not the face manfully to deny. The
possible consequences of the doctrine were the ground
which they chose to take up.

There are three things which we shall do well to remember, if unhappily we have at any time to argue with
infidels.—For one thing, let us remember that an infidel
will always try to press us with the difficulties and abstruse things of religion, and especially with those which

are connected with the world to come. We must avoid this mode of argument as far as possible. It is leaving the open field to fight in a jungle. We must endeavour, as far as we can, to make our discussion turn on the great plain facts and evidences of Christianity.—For another thing, let us remember, we must be on our guard against unfairness and dishonesty in argument. It may seem hard and uncharitable to say this. But experience proves that it is needful. Thousands of professed infidels have confessed in their latter days, that they had never studied the Bible which they pretended to deny, and though well read in the works of unbelievers and sceptics, had never calmly examined the foundations of Christianity.— Above all, let us remember that every infidel has a conscience. To this we may always appeal confidently. The very men who talk most loudly and disdainfully against religion, are often feeling conscious, even while they talk, that they are wrong. The very arguments which they have sneered at and ridiculed, will often prove at last not to have been thrown away.

We learn, in the second place, from this passage, *how much of religious error may be traced to ignorance of the Bible.* Our Lord's first words in reply to the Sadducees declare this plainly. He says, " Do ye not err, because ye know not the Scriptures ? "

The truth of the principle here laid down, is proved by facts in almost every age of church history. The reformation in Josiah's day was closely connected with the discovery of the book of the law. The false doctrines of the Jews in our Lord's time were the result of neglecting the Scriptures. The dark ages of Christendom were times when the Bible was kept back from the people. The Protestant Reformation was mainly effected by translating and circulating the Bible. The Churches which are most flourishing at this day, are churches which honour the Bible. The nations which enjoy most moral light, are nations in which the Bible is most known. The parishes in our land where there is most true religion, are those in which the Bible is most studied. The godliest families are Bible-reading families. The holiest men and women are Bible-reading people. These are simple facts which cannot be denied.

Let these things sink deeply into our hearts, and bear fruit in our lives. Let us not be ignorant of the Bible, lest we fall into some deadly error. Let us rather read it diligently, and make it our rule of faith and practice. Let us labour to spread the Bible over the world. The more the book is known, the better the world will be. Not least, let us teach our children to value the Bible. The very best portion we can give them, is a knowledge of the Scriptures.

We learn, in the last place, from this passage, *how different will be the state of things after the resurrection, from the state in which we live now.* Our Lord tells us, that "when they shall rise from the dead, they neither marry, nor are given in marriage; but are as the angels which are in heaven."

It would be foolish to deny that there are many difficulties connected with the doctrine of the life to come. It must needs be so. The world beyond the grave is a world unseen by mortal eye, and therefore unknown. The conditions of existence there, are necessarily hidden from us, and if more were told, we should probably not understand it. Let it suffice us to know that the bodies of the saints shall be raised, and, though glorified, shall be like their bodies on earth ;—so like, that those who knew them once shall know them again. But though raised with a real body, the risen saint will be completely freed from everything which is now an evidence of weakness and infirmity. There shall be nothing like Mahomet's gross and sensual Paradise in the Christian's future existence. Hunger and thirst being no more,—there shall be no need of food. Weariness and fatigue being no more,—there shall be no need of sleep. Death being no more,—there shall be no need of births to supply the place of those who are removed. Enjoying the full presence of God and his Christ,—men and women shall no more need the marriage union, in order to help one another. Able to serve God without weariness, and attend on Him without distraction,—doing His will perfectly, and seeing His face continually,—clothed in a glorious body,—they shall be " as the angels which are in heaven."

There is comfort in all this for the true Christian. In the body that he now has he often "groans being burdened," from a daily sense of weakness and imperfection. (2 Cor. v. 4.) He is now tried by many cares about this world,—what to eat, and what to drink, and what to put on,—how to manage his affairs, where to live, and what company to choose. In the world to come, all shall be changed. Nothing shall be lacking to make his happiness complete.

One thing only we must carefully bear in mind. Let us take heed that we rise again in "the resurrection of life," and not in " the resurrection of condemnation." (John

v. 29.)   To the believer in the Lord Jesus, the resurrection will be the greatest of blessings.   To the worldly,
the godless and the profane, the resurrection will be a
misery and a curse.   Let us never rest till we are one
with Christ and Christ in us, and then we may look forward with joy to a life to come.*

* The text by which our Lord silenced the Sadducees, and proved
the resurrection to be a scriptural doctrine, — has been a cause
of surprise to many Bible readers.   Some have wondered that
our Lord should have chosen this text, when others far more plain
might have been adduced.   Some have been unable to see the
force and cogency of the text as any proof at all of the resurrection
of the body.

As to the particular fitness of the text, as a proof, compared to
others we are perhaps very poor judges.   It may well be suspected
that there is a fulness of meaning in some texts of scripture, which
in our hasty and superficial reading we have not yet fathomed.   At
any rate it is clear that to a Jewish hearer of the Lord the argument
was so forcible as to be unanswerable.   This quotation and the
famous one in John x. 34, go far to show that the Jewish mind
saw a depth of meaning in scriptural expressions, which many of
us in modern times have not at all seen yet.   It is a matter in
which we have much to learn.

As to the text, "I am the God of Abraham, &c.," being a convincing proof of the resurrection of the body, there is a passage
in Bishop Pearson, which is worth reading.   He says of this text
as quoted by our Lord, "With the force of this argument the
multitude was astonished, and the Sadducees silenced.   For under
the name of God was understood a great benefactor, a God of
promise, and to be '*their* God' was to bless them and reward
them; as in them to be 'his servants,' and 'his people' was to
believe in him and obey him.   Now Abraham, Isaac, and Jacob
had not received the promise which they expected, and therefore
God after their death desiring still to be called "their God," he
thereby acknowledgeth that he had a blessing and a reward for
them still, and consequently that he will raise them to another
life, in which they may receive it.   So that the argument of our
Saviour is the same which the Jews have drawn from another
place of Moses.   (Exod. vi. 3, 4.) 'I appeared unto Abraham,
unto Isaac and unto Jacob, by the name of God Almighty, but by
my name Jehovah was I not made known to them.   Nevertheless
I have established my covenant with them, to give them the land
of Canaan.'   It is not said 'to give their sons,' but 'to give *them*
the land,' and therefore because while they lived here they enjoyed
it not, they must rise again that they may receive the promise."

MARK XII. 28—34.

28 And one of the Scribes came, and having heard them reasoning together, and perceiving that he had answered them well, asked him, Which is the first commandment of all?

29 And Jesus answered him, The first of all the commandments is, Hear, O Israel; The Lord our God is one Lord:

30 And thou shalt love the Lord thy God with all thy heart, and with all thy soul, and with all thy mind, and with all thy strength: this is the first commandment.

31 And the second is like, namely this, Thou shalt love thy neighbour as thyself. There is none other commandment greater than these.

32 And the Scribe said unto him, Well, Master, thou hast said the truth: for there is one God; and there is none other but he:

33 And to love him with all the heart, and with all the understanding, and with all the soul, and with all the strength, and to love his neighbour as himself, is more than all whole burnt offerings and sacrifices.

34 And when Jesus saw that he answered discreetly, he said unto him, Thou art not far from the kingdom of God. And no man after that durst ask him any question.

THESE verses contain a conversation between our Lord Jesus Christ and "one of the Scribes." For the third time in one day we see our Lord tried by a hard question. Having put to silence the Pharisees and Sadducees, He is asked to decide a point on which much difference of opinion prevailed among the Jews: "Which is the first commandment of all." We have reason to bless God that so many hard questions were propounded to our Lord. Without them the marvellous words of wisdom which His three answers contain, might never have been spoken at all. Here, as in many other cases, we see how God can bring good out of evil. He can make the most malicious assaults of His enemies work round to the good of His church, and redound to His own praise. He can make the enmity of Pharisees and Sadducees and Scribes minister instruction to His people. Little did the three questioners in this chapter think what benefit their crafty questions would confer on all Christendom. "Out of the eater came forth meat." (Judges xiv. 14.)

Let us observe in these verses, *how high is our Lord Jesus Christ's standard of duty to God and man.*

The question that the Scribe propounded was a very wide one : " Which is the first commandment of all ? " The answer he received was probably very unlike what he expected. At any rate, if he thought that our Lord would commend to him the observance of some outward form or ceremony, he was mistaken. He hears these solemn words : " Thou shalt love the Lord thy God with all thy heart, and with all thy soul, and with all thy mind, and with all thy strength : this is the first commandment. And the second is like, namely this, thou shalt love thy neighbour as thyself."

How striking is our Lord's description of the *feeling* with which we ought to regard both God and our neighbour ! We are not merely to obey the one, or to abstain from injuring the other. In both cases we are to give far more than this. We are to give love, the strongest of all affections, and the most comprehensive. A rule like this includes everything. It makes all petty details unnecessary. Nothing will be intentionally lacking where there is love.

How striking again is our Lord's description of the *measure* in which we should love God and our neighbour ! We are to love God better than ourselves, with all the powers of our inward man. We cannot love Him too well. We are to love our neighbour as ourselves, and to deal with him in all respects as we would like him to deal with us. The marvellous wisdom of this distinction is clear and plain. We may easily err in our affections towards others, either by thinking too little or too much of them.

We therefore need the rule to love them as ourselves, neither more nor less. We cannot err in our affections towards God in the matter of excess. He is worthy of all we can give Him. We are therefore to love Him with all our heart.

Let us keep these two grand rules continually before our minds, and use them daily in our journey through life. Let us see in them a summary of all that we ought to aim at in our practice, both as regards God and man. By them let us try every difficulty of conscience that may happen to beset us, as to right and wrong. Happy is that man who strives to frame his life according to these rules.

Let us learn from this brief exposition of the true standard of duty, how great is the need in which we all naturally stand of the atonement and mediation of our Lord Jesus Christ. Where are the men or women who can say with truth, that they have perfectly loved God and perfectly loved man? Where is the person on earth who must not plead "guilty," when tried by such a law as this? No wonder that the Scripture says, "there is none righteous, no! not one." "By the deeds of the law shall no flesh be justified." (Rom. iii. 10, 20.) It is only gross ignorance of the requirements of God's law which makes people undervalue the Gospel. The man who has the clearest view of the moral law, will always be the man who has the highest sense of the value of Christ's atoning blood.

Let us observe, for another thing, in these verses, *how far a man may go in religion, and yet not be a true disciple of Christ.*

The Scribe, in the passage now before us, was evidently a man of more knowledge than most of his equals. He saw things which many Scribes and Pharisees never saw at all. His own words are a strong proof of this. "There is one God : and there is none other but He : and to love Him with all the heart, and with all the understanding, and with all the soul, and with all the strength, and to love his neighbour as himself, is more than all whole burnt offerings and sacrifices." These words are remarkable in themselves, and doubly remarkable when we remember who the speaker was, and the generation amongst whom he lived. No wonder that we read next, that our Lord said, "thou art not far from the kingdom of God."

But we must not shut our eyes to the fact, that we are nowhere told that this man became one of our Lord's disciples. On this point there is a mournful silence. The parallel passage in St. Matthew throws not a gleam of light on his case. The other parts of the New Testament tell us nothing about him. We are left to draw the painful conclusion that, like the rich young man, he could not make up his mind to give up all and follow Christ ; or that, like the chief rulers, elsewhere mentioned, he "loved the praise of men more than the praise of God." (John xii. 43.) In short, though "not far from the kingdom of God," he probably never entered into it, and died outside.

Cases like that of this Scribe, are unhappily far from being uncommon. There are thousands on every side, who, like him, see much and know much of religious truth, and yet live and die undecided. There are few things which are so much overlooked as the length to which people may go in religious attainments, and yet never be converted, and never saved. May we all mark well this man's case, and take care!

Let us beware of resting our hopes of salvation on mere intellectual knowledge. We live in days when there is great danger of doing so. Education makes children acquainted with many things in religion, of which their parents were once utterly ignorant. But education alone will never make a Christian in the sight of God. We must not only know the leading doctrines of the Gospel with our heads, but receive them into our hearts, and be guided by them in our lives. May we never rest till we are inside the kingdom of God, till we have truly repented, really believed, and have been made new creatures in Christ Jesus. If we rest satisfied with being "not far from the kingdom," we shall find at last that we are shut out for evermore.

MARK XII. 35—44.

35 And Jesus answered and said, while he taught in the temple, How say the Scribes that Christ is the Son of David?

36 For David himself said by the Holy Ghost, The LORD said to my Lord, Sit thou on my right hand, till I make thine enemies thy footstool.

37 David therefore himself calleth him Lord; and whence is he *then* his son? And the common people heard him gladly.

38 And he said unto them in his doctrine, Beware of the Scribes, which love to go in long clothing, and *love* salutations in the marketplaces,

39 And the chief seats in the synagogues, and the uppermost rooms at feasts:

40 Which devour widows' houses, and for a pretence make long prayers: these shall receive greater damnation.

41 And Jesus sat over against the treasury, and beheld how the people cast money into the treasury: and many that were rich cast in much.

42 And there came a certain poor widow, and she threw in two mites, which make a farthing.

43 And he called *unto him* his disciples, and saith unto them, Verily I say unto you, That this poor widow hath cast more in, than all they which have cast into the treasury:

44 For all *they* did cast in of their abundance; but she of her want did cast in all that she had, *even* all her living

WE have seen in the former part of this chapter, how the enemies of our Lord endeavoured to " catch Him in His words." We have seen how the Pharisees, the Sadducees, and the Scribes successively propounded to Him hard questions,—questions, we can hardly fail to observe, more likely to minister strife than edification. The passage before us begins with a question of a very different character. Our Lord Himself propounds it. He asks His enemies about Christ and the meaning of Holy Scripture. Such questions are always truly profitable. Well would it be for the church if theological discussions were less about trifles, and more about weighty matters, and things necessary to salvation.

Let us learn, in the first place, from these verses, *how much there is about Christ in the Old Testament Scriptures.* Our Lord desires to expose the ignorance of the Jewish teachers about the true nature of the Messiah. He does it by referring to a passage in the book of Psalms, and showing that the Scribes did not rightly understand it. And in so doing He shows us that one subject, about which David was inspired by the Holy Ghost to write, was Christ.

We know from our Lord's own words in another place, that the Old Testament Scriptures " testify of Christ." (John v. 39.) They were intended to teach men about Christ, by types, and figures, and prophecy, till He Himself should appear on earth. We should always keep this in mind, in reading the Old Testament, but never so much as in reading the Psalms. Christ is undoubtedly to be found in every part of the Law and the Prophets, but nowhere is He so much to be found, as in the book of Psalms. His experience and sufferings at His first coming into the world,—His future glory, and His final triumph at His second coming,—are the chief subjects of many a passage in that wonderful part of God's word. It is a true saying, that we should look for Christ quite as much as David, in reading the Psalms.

Let us beware of undervaluing, or despising the Old Testament. In its place and proportion, the Old Testament is just as valuable as the New. There are probably many rich passages in that part of the Bible, which have never yet been fully explored. There are deep things about Jesus in it, which many walk over like hidden gold mines, and know not the treasures beneath their feet. Let us reverence *all* the Bible. All is given by inspiration, and all is profitable. One part throws light upon another, and no part can ever be neglected without loss and damage to our souls. A boastful contempt for the Old Testament Scriptures has often proved the first step towards infidelity.

Let us learn, in the second place, from these verses, *how odious is the sin of hypocrisy in the sight of Christ.* This is a lesson which is taught us by our Lord's warning against the Scribes. He exposes some of their notorious practices,—their ostentatious manner of dressing,—their love of the honour and praise of man rather than God, —their love of money, disguised under a pretended concern for widows,—their long-protracted public devotions, intended to make men think them eminently godly. And He winds up all by the solemn declaration, "these shall receive greater damnation."

Of all the sins into which men can fall, none seem so

exceedingly sinful as false profession and hypocrisy. At all events, none have drawn from our Lord's mouth such strong language, and such heavy denunciations. It is bad enough to be led' away captive by open sin, and to serve divers lusts and pleasures. But it is even worse to pretend to have a religion, while in reality we serve the world. Let us beware of falling into this abominable sin. Whatever we do in religion, let us never wear a cloak. Let us be real, honest, thorough, and sincere in our Christianity. We cannot deceive an all-seeing God. We may take in poor short-sighted man by a little talk and profession, and a few cant phrases, and an affectation of devoutness. But God is not mocked. He is a discerner of the thoughts and intents of the heart. His all-seeing eye pierces through the paint, and varnish, and tinsel, which cover the unsound heart. The day of judgment will soon be here. The "joy of the hypocrite is but for a moment." (Job xx. 5.) His end will be shame and everlasting contempt.

One thing, however, must never be forgotten in connection with the subject of hypocrisy. Let us not flatter ourselves, because some make a false profession of religion, that others need not make any profession at all. This is a common delusion, and one against which we must carefully guard. It does not follow, because some bring Christianity into contempt by professing what they do not really believe and feel, that we should run into the other extreme, and bring it into contempt by a cowardly silence and by keeping our religion out of sight. Let us rather be doubly careful to adorn our doctrine by our lives. Let us prove our sincerity by the consistency of our conversation. Let us show the world that there is true coin, as well as counterfeit coin, and that the visible church contains Christians who can witness a good confession, as well as Pharisees and Scribes. Let us confess our Master modestly and humbly, but firmly and decidedly, and show the world that although some men may be hypocrites, there are others who are honest and true.

Let us learn, in the last place, from these verses, *how pleasing to Christ is self-denying liberality in giving.* This is a lesson which is taught us in a striking manner, by our Lord's commendation of a certain poor widow. We are told that He "beheld how the people cast in" their voluntary contributions for God's service into the public collecting box or "treasury." He saw "many that were rich casting in much." At last he saw this poor widow cast in all that she had for her daily maintenance. And then we hear Him pronounce the solemn words, "This poor woman hath cast more in than they all,"—more in the sight of Him who looks not merely at the amount given, but at the ability of the giver,—not merely at the quantity contributed, but at the motive and heart of the contributor.

There are few of our Lord's sayings so much overlooked as this. There are thousands who remember all His doctrinal discourses, and yet contrive to forget this little incident in His earthly ministry. The proof of this is to be seen in the meagre and sparing contributions which are yearly made by Christ's church to do good in the world. The proof is to be seen in the miserably small incomes of all the missionary societies, in proportion to the wealth of the churches. The proof is to be

seen in the long annual lists of self-complacent guinea
subscribers, of whom many could easily give hundreds
of pounds. The stinginess of professing Christians in all
matters which concern God and religion, is one of
the crying sins of the day, and one of the worst signs of
the times. The givers to Christ's cause are but a small
section of the visible church. Not one baptized person
in twenty, probably, knows anything of being "rich
towards God." (Luke xii. 21.) The vast majority spend
pounds on themselves, and give not even pence to Christ.

Let us mourn over this state of things, and pray God
to amend it. Let us pray Him to open men's eyes, and
awake men's hearts, and stir up a spirit of liberality.
Above all, let us each do our own duty, and give liberally
and gladly to every Christian object, while we can.
There will be no giving when we are dead. Let us give
as those who remember that the eyes of Christ are upon
us. He still sees exactly what each gives, and knows
exactly how much is left behind. Above all, let us give
as the disciples of a crucified Saviour, who gave Himself,
for us, body and soul, on the cross. Freely we have
received. Let us freely give.*

* It is probable, according to Arias Montanus and Brenius, that
the words "all her living," mean "all her daily income," and not all
her property.

It may be well to remark in this connection, that nothing can
be more absurd than to say, as some do, that they contribute
"their mite" to an object, when they probably contribute some
trifling sum which they do not miss, and which bears not the most
remote proportion to the widow's scale of liberality.—A man contributes "his mite" when he contributes half his daily income, and
not till then.

MARK XIII. 1—8.

1 And as he went out of the temple, one of his disciples saith unto him, Master, see what manner of stones and what buildings *are here!*

2 And Jesus answering said unto him, Seest thou these great buildings? there shall not be left one stone upon another, that shall not be thrown down.

3 And as he sat upon the mount of Olives over against the temple, Peter and James and John and Andrew asked him privately;

4 Tell us, when shall these things be? and what *shall be* the sign when all these things shall be fulfilled?

5 And Jesus answering them began to say, Take heed lest any *man* deceive you:

6 For many shall come in my name, saying, I am *Christ;* and shall deceive many.

7 And when ye shall hear of wars and rumours of wars, be ye not troubled: for *such things* must needs be; but the end *shall* not *be* yet.

8 For nation shall rise against nation, and kingdom against kingdom: and there shall be earthquakes in divers places, and there shall be famines and troubles: these *are* the beginnings of sorrows.

THE chapter we have now begun is full of prophecy,— prophecy of which part has been fulfilled, and part remains to be accomplished. Two great events form the subject of this prophecy. One is the destruction of Jerusalem, and the consequent end of the Jewish dispensation. The other is the second coming of our Lord Jesus Christ, and the winding up of the state of things under which we now live. The destruction of Jerusalem was an event which happened only forty years after our Lord was crucified. The second coming of Christ is an event which is yet to come, and we may yet live to see it with our own eyes.*

* I think it right to repeat here what I said in commenting on the report of our Lord's prophecy given by St. Matthew, respecting the destruction of Jerusalem. I believe that in the prophecy now under consideration, our Lord had in view a *second* siege of Jerusalem and a *second* tribulation accompanying that siege, as well as the first siege and tribulation when the city was taken by Titus. That such a siege is to be expected, the fourteenth chapter of Zechariah appears to me to be unanswerable proof.

I see no other way of explaining the close connection which appears in the prophecy, between the "affliction" here foretold, and the "coming of the Son of Man in the clouds with power and great

Chapters like this ought to be deeply interesting to every true Christian. No history ought to receive so much of our attention as the past and future history of the Church of Christ. The rise and fall of worldly empires are events of comparatively small importance in the sight of God. Babylon, and Greece, and Rome, and France, and England, are as nothing in His eyes by the side of the mystical body of Christ. The march of armies and the victories of conquerors are mere trifles in comparison with the progress of the Gospel and the final triumph of the Prince of Peace. May we remember this in reading prophetical Scripture! "Blessed is he that readeth." (Rev. i. 3.)

The first thing that demands our attention in the verses before us, is *the prediction of our Lord concerning the temple at Jerusalem.*

The disciples, with the natural pride of Jews, had called their Master's attention to the architectural splendour of the temple. "See," they said, "what manner of stones and what buildings are here!" * They re-

glory." To interpret that "coming of the Son of Man," as the coming of the Roman army in judgment on the Jews, appears to me positive trifling with Scripture.

The view that our Lord is prophesying of *two* sieges of Jerusalem, and *two* tremendous tribulations which would fall especially on the Jews, and of His own second coming as an event which would immediately follow the second siege, makes the whole chapter plain and intelligible.

All these events ought to be deeply interesting to believers; and would be especially so to Jewish believers, like the apostles, in whose time the temple was yet standing, the Jewish dispensation not yet put aside, and Jerusalem not yet destroyed.

*It may be well to remark that the temple here spoken of, was, in a certain sense, the third temple in order which had been built at Jerusalem. The first was built by Solomon, and destroyed by ceived an answer from the Lord very different from what they expected, a heart-saddening answer, and one well calculated to stir up inquisitive thoughts in their minds. No word of admiration falls from His lips. He expresses no commendation of the design or workmanship of the gorgeous structure before Him. He appears to lose sight of the form and comeliness of the material building, in His concern for the wickedness of the nation to which it belonged. "Seest thou," He replies, "these great buildings? There shall not be left one stone upon another, that shall not be cast down."

Let us learn from this solemn saying, that the true glory of a Church does not consist in its buildings for public worship, but in the faith and godliness of its members. The eyes of our Lord Jesus Christ could find no pleasure in looking at the very temple which contained the holy of holies, and the golden candlestick, and the altar of burnt offering. Much less, may we suppose, can He find pleasure in the most splendid place of worship among professing Christians, if His word and His Spirit are not honoured in it.

We shall all do well to remember this. We are naturally inclined to judge things by the outward appearance, like children who value poppies more than corn. We are too apt to suppose that where there is a stately ecclesiastical building and a magnificent ceremonial,—carved stone and painted glass,—fine music and gorgeously-dressed ministers, there must be some real religion. And

Nebuchadnezzar. The second was built by Ezra and Nehemiah. The third, if it may be so called, was enlarged and almost re-built, about the time of our Lord Jesus Christ's birth, by Herod. The enormous size of the stones used in building it, and the general magnificence of the whole fabric, are attested not only by Josephus, but by heathen writers.

yet there may be no religion at all. It may be all form, and show, and appeal to the senses. There may be nothing to satisfy the conscience,—nothing to cure the heart. It may prove on inquiry that Christ is not preached in that stately building, and the word of God not expounded. The ministers may perhaps be utterly ignorant of the Gospel, and the worshippers may be dead in trespasses and sins. We need not doubt that God sees no beauty in such a building as this. We need not doubt the Parthenon had no glory in God's sight compared to the dens and caves where the early Christians worshipped, or that the meanest room where Christ is preached at this day, is more honourable in His eyes than the cathedral of St. Peter's at Rome.

Let us however not run into the absurd extreme of supposing that it matters not what kind of building we set apart for God's service. There is no Popery in making a church handsome. There is no true religion in having a dirty, mean, shabby, and disorderly place of worship. "Let all things be done decently and in order." (1 Cor. xiv. 40.) But let it be a settled principle in our religion, however beautiful we make our churches, to regard pure doctrine and holy practice as their principal ornaments. *Without* these two things, the noblest ecclesiastical edifice is radically defective. It has no glory if God is not there. *With* these two things, the humblest brick cottage where the Gospel is preached, is lovely and beautiful. It is consecrated by Christ's own presence, and the Holy Spirit's own blessing.

The second thing that demands our attention in these verses, is *the remarkable manner in which our Lord commences the great prophecy of this chapter.*

We are told that four of His disciples, aroused no doubt by His warning prediction about the temple, applied to Him for further information. "Tell us," they said, "when shall these things be? and what shall be the sign when all these things shall be fulfilled?"

The answer which our Lord gives to these questions, begins at once with a prediction of coming false doctrine and coming wars. If His disciples thought He would promise them immediate success and temporal prosperity in this world, they were soon undeceived. So far from bidding them expect a speedy victory of truth, He tells them to look out for the rise of error. "Take heed lest any man deceive you.—Many shall come in my name, saying, I am Christ." So far from bidding them expect a general reign of peace and quietness, He tells them to prepare for wars and troubles. "Nation shall rise against nation, and kingdom against kingdom.—There shall be earthquakes in divers places, and there shall be famines and troubles: these are the beginnings of sorrows."

There is something deeply instructive in this opening of our Lord's prophetical discourse. It seems like the key note of what His Church is to expect between His first and second advents. It looks as if it were specially intended to correct the mistaken views, not only of His apostles, but of the vast body of professing Christians in every age. It looks as if our Lord knew well that man is always catching at the idea of a "good time coming," and as if He would give us plain notice that there will be no "good time" till He returns. It may not be pleasant to us to hear such tidings. But it is in strict accordance with what we read in the prophet Jeremiah:

" The prophets that have been before, prophesied of war, and of evil, and of pestilence. The prophet which prophesieth of peace, when the word of the prophet shall come to pass, then shall the prophet be known, that the Lord hath truly sent him." (Jer. xxviii. 8, 9.)

Let us learn from our Lord's opening prediction to be moderate in our expectations. Nothing has created so much disappointment in the Church of Christ, as the extravagant expectations in which many of its members have indulged. Let us not be carried away by the common idea, that the world will be converted before the Lord Jesus returns, and the earth filled with the knowledge of the Lord. It will not be so. There is nothing in Scripture to justify such expectations. Let us cease to expect a reign of peace. Let us rather look for wars. Let us cease to expect all men to be made holy by any existing instrumentality,—schools, missions, preaching, or anything of the kind. Let us rather look for the rise of Antichrist Himself. Let us understand that we live in a day of election, and not of universal conversion. There will be no universal peace till the Prince of Peace appears. There will be no universal holiness till Satan is bound. It may cost us much to hold such opinions as these. But there is not a church or congregation on earth, whose state does not show that these opinions are true, and that while " Many are called, few are chosen." It may bring on us the unkind remarks and the unfavourable judgment of many. But the end will prove who is right and who is wrong. For that end let us wait patiently. Let us labour, and teach, and work, and pray. But let it not surprise us if we find our

Lord's word strictly true: "Narrow is the way which leadeth unto life, and few there be that find it." (Matt. v. 14.)

MARK XIII. 9—13.

9 But take heed to yourselves: for they shall deliver you up to councils; and in the synagogues ye shall be beaten: and ye shall be brought before rulers and kings for my sake, for a testimony against them.

10 And the Gospel must first be published among all nations.

11 But when they shall lead *you*, and deliver you up, take no thought beforehand what ye shall speak, neither do ye premeditate: but whatsoever shall be given you in that hour, that speak ye: for it is not ye that speak, but the Holy Ghost.

12 Now the brother shall betray the brother to death, and the father the son; and children shall rise up against *their* parents, and shall cause them to be put to death.

13 And ye shall be hated of all *men* for my name's sake: but he that shall endure unto the end, the same shall be saved.

IN reading the prophecies of the Bible concerning Christ's Church, we shall generally find judgment and mercy blended together. They are seldom all bitter without any sweet,—seldom all darkness without any light. The Lord knows our weakness and readiness to faint, and has taken care to mingle consolations with threatenings,— kind words with hard words, like warp and woof in a garment. We may remark this throughout the book of Revelation. We may see it all through the prophecy we are now considering. We may note it in the few verses which we have just read.

Let us observe, in the first place, *what troubles our Lord bids His people expect between the time of His first and second comings.* Trouble, no doubt, is the portion of all men, since the day that Adam fell. It came in with the thorns and thistles. " Man is born to trouble as the sparks fly upwards." (Job v. 7.) But there are special

troubles to which believers in Jesus Christ are liable,
and of these our Lord gives them plain warning.

They must expect trouble *from the world.* They
must not look for the help of "rulers and kings." They
will find their ways and their doctrines bring them no
favour in high places. On the contrary, they will often
be imprisoned, beaten, and brought before judgment seats
as malefactors, for no other reason than their adherence
to the Gospel of Christ.

They must expect trouble from *their own relations.*
" Brother shall betray brother to death, and the father the
son." Their own flesh and blood will often forget to love
them, from hatred to their religion. They will find sometimes that the enmity of the carnal mind against God,
is stronger than even the ties of family and blood.

We shall do well to lay these things to heart, and to
"count the cost " of being a Christian. We must think it
no strange thing if our religion brings with it some bitter
things. Our lot, no doubt, is cast in favourable times.
The lines of a British Christian are fallen in pleasant
places. We have no reason to be afraid of death or
imprisonment, if we serve Christ. But, for all that, we
must make up our minds to endure a certain proportion of
hardship, if we are real, thorough, and decided Christians.
We must be content to put up with laughter, ridicule,
mockery, slander, and petty persecution. We must even
bear hard words and unkindness from our nearest and
dearest relations. The "offence of the cross" is not ceased.
" The natural man receiveth not the things of the Spirit of
God." They that are " born after the flesh " will persecute those that are " born after the Spirit." (1 Cor. ii.

14. Gal. iv. 29.) The utmost consistency of life will not prevent it. If we are converted, we must never be surprised to find that we are hated for Christ's sake.

Let us observe, in the second place, *what rich encouragement the Lord Jesus holds out to His persecuted people.* He sets before them three rich cordials to cheer their souls.

For one thing, He tells us that "the Gospel must first be preached among all nations." It must be, and it shall be. In spite of men and devils, the story of the cross of Christ shall be told in every part of the world. The gates of hell shall not prevail against it. Notwithstanding persecution, imprisonment, and death, there never shall be wanting a succession of faithful men, who shall proclaim the glad tidings of salvation by grace. Few may believe them. Many of their hearers may continue hardened in sin. But nothing shall prevent the Gospel being preached. The word shall never be bound, though those who preach it may be imprisoned and slain. (2 Tim. ii. 9.)

For another thing, our Lord tells us, that those who are placed in special trial for the Gospel's sake, shall have special help in their time of need. The Holy Ghost shall assist them in making their defence. They shall have a mouth and wisdom which their adversaries shall not be able to gainsay or resist. As it was with Peter and John and Paul, when brought before Jewish and Roman councils, so shall it be with all true-hearted disciples. How thoroughly this promise has been fulfilled, the histories of Huss, and Luther, and Latimer, and Ridley, and Baxter, abundantly prove. Christ has been faithful to His word.

For another thing, our Lord tells us that patient perseverance shall result in final salvation. " He that shall endure unto the end, the same shall be saved." Not one of those who endure tribulation shall miss his reward. All shall at length reap a rich harvest. Though they sow in tears, they shall reap in joy. Their light affliction, which is but for a moment, shall lead to an eternal weight of glory.

Let us gather comfort from these comfortable promises for all true-hearted servants of Christ. Persecuted, vexed, and mocked as they are now, they shall find at length they are on the victorious side. Beset, perplexed, tried, as they sometimes are, they shall never find themselves entirely forsaken. Though cast down, they shall not be destroyed. Let them possess their souls in patience. The end of all that they see going on around them is certain, fixed, and sure. The kingdoms of this world shall yet become the kingdoms of their God and of his Christ. And when the scoffers and ungodly, who so often insulted them, are put to shame, believers shall receive a crown of glory that fadeth not away.*

---

* There is a promise in the passage now expounded which is often much perverted. I allude to the implied promise contained in the words,—" Take no thought beforehand what ye shall speak, neither do ye premeditate : but whatsoever shall be given you in that time, that speak ye."

The perversion I mean, consists in supposing that this passage warrants ministers in getting up to preach unprepared every Sunday, and in expecting special help of the Holy Ghost in addressing regular congregations, when they have neither meditated, read, nor taken pains about their subject.

A moment's reflection must show any reader, that such an application of the passage before us is utterly unjustifiable. The passage has no reference whatever to the regular Sabbath sermon

MARK XIII. 14—23.

14 But when ye shall see the abomination of desolation, spoken of by Daniel the prophet, standing where it ought not, (let him that readeth understand,) then let them that be in Judæa flee to the mountains:

15 And let him that is on the housetop not go down into the house, neither enter *therein*, to take any thing out of his house:

16 And let him that is in the field not turn back again for to take up his garment.

17 But woe to them that are with child, and to them that give suck in those days!

18 And pray ye that your flight be not in the winter.

19 For *in* those days shall be affliction, such as was not from the beginning of the creation which God created unto this time, neither shall be.

20 And except that the Lord had shortened those days, no flesh should be saved: but for the elect's sake, whom he hath chosen, he hath shortened the days.

21 And then if any man shall say to you, Lo, here *is* Christ; or, lo, *he is* there; believe *him* not:

22 For false Christs and false prophets shall rise, and shall shew signs and wonders, to seduce, if *it were* possible, even the elect.

23 But take ye heed: behold, I have foretold you all things.

WE are taught in these verses *the lawfulness of using means to provide for our own personal safety.* The language of our Lord Jesus Christ on the subject is clear and unmistakeable: "Let them that be in Judæa flee to the mountains:—let him that is on the house-top not go down into the house:—let him that is in the field not turn back again:—pray ye that your flight be not in the winter." Not a word is said to make us suppose that flight from danger, in certain circumstances, is unworthy of a Christian. As to the time prophesied of in the passage before us, men may differ widely. But as to the lawfulness of taking measures to avoid peril, the teaching of the passage is plain.

of a minister, and only holds out the promise of special help in special times of need.

It would be well for the Church if this was more remembered than it is. At present it may be feared this promise is not unfrequently made an excuse for ministerial idleness, and undigested sermons. Men seem to forget, when they enter the pulpit, that what costs nothing is worth nothing, and that the " foolishness of preaching" and foolish preaching, are widely different things.

The lesson is one of wide application, and of much usefulness. A Christian is not to neglect the use of means, because he is a Christian, in the things of this life, any more than in the things of the life to come. A believer is not to suppose that God will take care of him, and provide for his wants, if he does not make use of means and the common sense which God has given him, as well as other people. Beyond doubt he may expect the special help of his Father in heaven, in every time of need. But he must expect it in the diligent use of lawful means. To profess to trust God, while we idly sit still and do nothing, is nothing better than enthusiasm and fanaticism, and brings religion into contempt.

The word of God contains several instructive examples on this subject, to which we shall do well to take heed. The conduct of Jacob, when he went to meet his brother Esau, is a striking case in point. He first prays a most touching prayer, and then sends his brother a carefully arranged present. (Gen. xxxii. 9—13.) The conduct of Hezekiah, when Sennacherib came against Jerusalem, is another case. "With us," he tells the people, "is the Lord our God, to fight our battles." And yet, at the same time, he built up the walls of the city, and made darts and shields. (2 Chron. xxxii. 5.)—The conduct of St. Paul is another case. Frequently we read of his fleeing from one place to another, to preserve life. Once we see him let down from the walls of Damascus by a basket. Once we hear him telling the soldiers on board the Alexandrian corn ship, "Except the shipmen abide in the ship, ye cannot be saved." (Acts xxvii. 31.) We know the great apostle's faith and confidence. We

know his courage and reliance on his Master. And yet
we see that even he never despised the use of means.
Let us not be ashamed to do likewise.

One thing only let us bear in mind. Let us not rest
upon means while we use them. Let us look far beyond
them to the blessing of God. It is a great sin to be like
Asa, and seek not to the Lord but to the physicians. To
use all means diligently, and then leave the whole event
in the hand of God, is the mark at which a true believer
ought to aim.

We are taught, for another thing, in these verses, *the
great privileges of God's elect.* Twice in the passage our
Lord uses a remarkable expression about them. He says
of the great tribulation, "Except that the Lord had
shortened those days, no flesh should be saved ; but for
the elect's sake, whom He hath chosen, He hath shortened
the days." He says again of the false Christs and false
prophets, that they "shall show signs and wonders, to
deceive, if it were possible, the elect."

It is plain from this, and other passages in the Bible,
that God has an elect people in the world. They are
those, according to the seventeenth article of our church,
whom " He has constantly decreed by His counsel, secret
to us, to deliver from curse and damnation ; those whom
He hath chosen in Christ out of mankind, and decreed
to bring by Christ to everlasting salvation, as vessels
made to honour." To them, and them only, belong
the great privileges of justification, sanctification, and
final glory. They, and they only, are "called by the
Spirit in due season." They, and they only, "obey the
calling. They are made sons of God by adoption.

They are made like the image of God's only begotten
Son, Jesus Christ. They walk religiously in good works,
and at length, by God's mercy, attain to everlasting
felicity." To them belong the precious promises of the
Gospel. They are the bride, the Lamb's wife. They
are the Holy Catholic Church, which is Christ's body.
They are those whom God especially cares for in the
world. Kings, princes, noblemen, rich men, are all
nothing in God's eyes, compared to His elect. These
things are plainly revealed in Scripture. The pride of
man may not like them. But they cannot be gainsaid.

The subject of election is, no doubt, deep and mysterious. Unquestionably it has been often sadly perverted
and abused. But the misuse of truths must not prevent
us from using them. Rightly used, and fenced with
proper cautions, election is a doctrine "full of sweet,
pleasant, and unspeakable comfort." Before we leave the
subject, let us see what these cautions are.

For one thing, we must never forget that God's election does not destroy man's responsibility and accounta-
bleness for his own soul. The same Bible which speaks
of election, always addresses men as free agents, and
calls on them to repent, to believe, to seek, to pray, to
strive, to labour. "In our doings," most wisely says the
seventeenth article, "that will of God is to be followed,
which we have expressly declared unto us in the word
of God."

For another thing, let us never forget that the great
thing we have to do, is to repent and believe the Gospel.
We have no right to take any comfort from God's election, unless we can show plain evidence of repentance

and faith. We are not to stand still, troubling ourselves with anxious speculations whether we are elect or not, when God commands us plainly to repent and believe. (Acts xvii. 30. 1 John iii. 23.) Let us cease to do evil. Let us learn to do well. Let us break off from sin. Let us lay hold on Christ. Let us draw near to God in prayer. So doing, we shall soon know and feel whether we are God's elect. To use the words of an old divine, we must begin at the *grammar school* of repentance and faith, before we go to the *university* of election. It was when Paul remembered the faith, and hope, and love of the Thessalonians, that he said, "I know your election of God."* (1 Thess. i. 4.)

MARK XIII. 24—31.

24 But in those days, after that tribulation, the sun shall be darkened, and the moon shall not give her light,

25 And the stars of heaven shall fall, and the powers that are in heaven shall be shaken.

26 And then shall they see the Son of man coming in the clouds with great power and glory.

27 And then shall he send his angels, and shall gather together his elect from the four winds, from the uttermost part of the earth to the uttermost part of heaven.

28 Now learn a parable of the fig tree; When her branch is yet tender, and putteth forth leaves, ye know that summer is near:

29 So ye in like manner, when ye shall see these things come to pass, know that it is nigh, *even* at the doors.

30 Verily I say unto you, that this generation shall not pass, till all these things be done.

31 Heaven and earth shall pass away: but my words shall not pass away.

* The meaning of the "abomination of desolation," in this passage, has always perplexed the commentators. The most common view undoubtedly is, that it signifies the Roman armies, who executed God's judgment on the Jewish nation.

It may be questioned whether this interpretation completely fulfils the prophecy. I venture, though with much diffidence, to suggest that a more complete and literal accomplishment yet remains to come. The remarkable words of St. Paul to the Thessalonians, appear to me scarcely to have received yet a complete fulfilment: "He, as God, sitteth in the temple of God, shewing himself that he is God." (2 Thess. ii. 4.) I own that it seems to me by no means improbable that a personal anti-christ, yet to

THIS part of our Lord's prophecy on the Mount of Olives is entirely unfulfilled. The events described in it are all yet to take place. They may possibly take place in our own day. The passage therefore is one which we ought always to read with peculiar interest.

Let us observe, in the first place, *what solemn majesty will attend our Lord Jesus Christ's second coming to this world.* The language that is used about the sun, moon, and stars, conveys the idea of some universal convulsion of the universe at the close of the present dispensation. It reminds us of the apostle Peter's words, "the heavens shall pass away with a great noise, and the elements shall melt with fervent heat." (2 Pet. iii. 10.) At such a time as this, amidst terror and confusion, exceeding all that even earthquakes or hurricanes are known to produce, men "shall see the Son of Man coming in the clouds with great power and glory."

The second coming of Christ shall be utterly unlike the first. He came the first time in weakness, a tender infant, born of a poor woman in the manger at Bethlehem, unnoticed, unhonoured, and scarcely known. He shall come the second time in royal dignity, with the armies of heaven around Him, to be known, recognized, and feared, by all the tribes of the earth. He came the first time to suffer,—to bear our sins,—to be reckoned a curse,—to be despised, rejected, unjustly condemned, and slain. He shall come the second time to reign,—to put down every enemy beneath his feet,—to take the king-

be revealed at Jerusalem, may prove the final accomplishment of these words. I desire to avoid dogmatism on the subject. I only suggest it as a possible and probable thing.

doms of this world for His inheritance,—to rule them with righteousness,—to judge all men, and to live for evermore.

How vast the difference! How mighty the contrast! How startling the comparison between the second advent and the first! How solemn the thoughts that the subject ought to stir up in our minds! Here are *comfortable* thoughts for Christ's friends. Their own King will soon be here. They shall reap according as they have sown. They shall receive a rich reward for all that they have endured for Christ's sake. They shall exchange their cross for a crown.—Here are *confounding* thoughts for Christ's foes. That same Jesus of Nazareth, whom they have so long despised and rejected, shall at length have the preeminence. That very Christ, whose Gospel they have refused to believe, shall appear as their Judge, and helpless, hopeless, and speechless, they will have to stand before His bar. May we all lay these things to heart, and learn wisdom!

Let us observe, in the next place, that *the first event after the Lord's second coming, shall be the gathering of His elect.* "He shall send His angels and gather together His elect from the four winds."

The safety of the Lord's people shall be provided for, when judgment falls upon the earth. He will do nothing till He has placed them beyond the reach of harm. The flood did not begin till Noah was safe in the ark. The fire did not fall on Sodom till Lot was safe within the walls of Zoar. The wrath of God on unbelievers shall not be let loose till believers are hidden and secure.

The true Christian may look forward to the advent of

Christ without fear. However terrible the things that shall come upon the earth, his Master will take care that no harm comes to him.—He may well bear patiently the partings and separations of this present time. He shall have a joyful meeting, by and bye, with all his brethren in the faith, of every age, and country, and people, and tongue. Those who meet in that day, shall meet to part no more.—The great gathering is yet to come. (2 Thess. ii. 1.)

Let us observe, in the next place, *how important it is to note the signs of our own times.* Our Lord bids His disciples "learn a parable of the fig-tree." Just as its budding leaves tell men that summer is near, so the fulfilment of events in the world around us, should teach us that the Lord's coming "is nigh, even at the doors."

It becomes all true Christians to observe carefully the public events of their own day. It is not only a duty to do this, but a sin to neglect it. Our Lord reproved the Jews for "not discerning the signs of the times." (Matt. xvi. 3.) They did not see that the sceptre was passing away from Judah, and the weeks of Daniel running out. Let us beware of falling into their error. Let us rather open our eyes, and look at the world around us. Let us mark the drying up of the Turkish power, and the increase of missionary work in the world. Let us mark the revival of Popery, and the rise of new and subtle forms of infidelity. Let us mark the rapid spread of lawlessness and contempt for authority. What are these things but the budding of the fig-tree ? They show us that this world is wearing out, and needs a new and better dynasty. It needs its rightful king, even Jesus. May we watch, and keep our garments, and live ready to meet our Lord! (Rev. xvi. 15.)

Let us observe, lastly, in these verses, *how carefully our Lord asserts the certainty of His predictions being fulfilled.* He speaks as though He foresaw the incredulity and scepticism of these latter days. He warns us emphatically against it :—" Heaven and earth shall pass away, but my words shall not pass away."

We ought never to allow ourselves to suppose that any prophecy is improbable or unlikely to be fulfilled, merely because it is contrary to past experience. Let us not say, " Where is the likelihood of Christ coming again ? Where is the likelihood of the world being burned up?" We have nothing to do with "likely or unlikely" in such matters. The only question is, "what is written in God's word?" The words of St. Peter should never be forgotten : " There shall come in the last days scoffers, walking after their own lusts, saying, where is the promise of His coming ? " (2 Pet. iii. 3, 4.)

We shall do well to ask ourselves, what we should have thought, if we had lived on earth two thousand years ago. Should we have thought it more probable that the Son of God would come on earth as a poor man and die, or that He would come on earth as a King and reign ? Should we not have said at once, that if He came at all, He would come to reign and not to die ? Yet we know that He did come as "a man of sorrows," and died on the cross. Then let us not doubt that He will come the second time in glory, and reign as a King for evermore.

Let us leave the passage with a thorough conviction of

the truth of every jot of its predictions. Let us believe that every word of it shall prove at last to have been fully accomplished. Above all, let us strive to live under an abiding sense of its truth, like good servants ready to meet their master. Then, whatever be the fulfilment of it, or however soon, we shall be safe.*

MARK XIII. 32—37.

32 But of that day and *that* hour knoweth no man, no, not the angels which are in heaven, neither the Son, but the Father.

33 Take ye heed, watch and pray: for ye know not when the time is.

34 *For the Son of man is* as a man taking a far journey, who left his house, and gave authority to his servants, and to every man his work, and commanded the porter to watch.

35 Watch ye therefore : for ye know not when the master of the house cometh, at even, or at midnight, or at the cockcrowing, or in the morning:

36 Lest coming suddenly he find you sleeping.

37 And what I say unto you I say unto all, Watch.

THESE verses conclude St. Mark's report of our Lord's prophecy on the Mount of Olives. They ought to form

* I am aware that some interpreters of the passage now expounded, explain its language very differently from myself. Many regard the "sun, moon, and stars" as emblems of kings and rulers, —the "coming of the Son of Man," as a general expression signifying any great exhibition of divine power,—and the "sending forth of His angels," as nothing more than the sending of ministers and messengers of the Gospel to gather together the people of God.

I will only say that I can see no ground or warrant for such interpretations. They appear to me to be a dangerous tampering with the plain literal meaning of Scripture, and to give a great handle to the Arian, and Socinian, and the Jew, in the arguments that they respectively bring forward in support of their own peculiar views.

I take this opportunity of expressing my decided opinion, that the word "generation" in the verse, "this generation shall not pass away," can only mean "this nation or people,—the Jewish nation, —shall not pass away."

The view that it means "the generation of men which is alive now while I am speaking," would make our Lord to say that which a personal application of the whole discourse to our consciences.

We learn from these verses, that *the exact time of our Lord Jesus Christ's second advent is purposely withheld from His church.* The event is certain. The precise day and hour are not revealed. "Of that day and hour knoweth no man, no, not the angels which are in heaven." *

was not true. His words were in no sense completely fulfilled when the generation to which He spoke had passed away.

The view that it means "the same generation which is alive when these things begin, shall also see them accomplished," appears to me untenable for one simple reason. It is not the natural meaning of the Greek words, from which our translation is made.

* There is undoubtedly some difficulty in the words of our Lord, "Of that day and hour knoweth no man, no, not the angels are in heaven, neither the Son." The question has often been raised, "How can the Lord Jesus be ignorant of anything, since He is very God, and says Himself, "I and my Father are one?" How can the expression be reconciled with the saying, 'In Him are hid all the treasures of wisdom and knowledge?' " (Col. 2, 3.)

The answer to these questions is to be found in our deep ignorance of the great mystery of the union of two natures in one Person. That our Lord Jesus Christ was at the same time perfect God, and perfect man we know. That these two distinct natures were both found together in His Person, we also know. But how, and in what way, and to what extent the divine nature did not always operate in Him so as to overshadow the human nature, I believe it to be impossible for mortal man to explain.—Enough for us to know that we sometimes see in our Lord's words and actions, the "man Christ Jesus," and sometimes see the "God over all blessed for ever." But though we see clearly, and admire, we cannot explain. We can only say, in the present instance, that our Lord spake as a man, and not as God.

Bullinger, in an able note on the subject, gives an interesting quotation from Cyril, of which the following passage is a portion:

"Just as the Saviour was willing to endure hunger, and thirst, and other sufferings of this kind, so also, as man, He is ignorant of "that great day." For He sometimes speaks as God, and sometimes as man, in order that He may show Himself to be both very

There is deep wisdom and mercy in this intentional
silence. We have reason to thank God that the thing has
been hidden from us. Uncertainty about the date of the
Lord's return is calculated to keep believers in an attitude of constant expectation, and to preserve them from
despondency. What a dreary prospect the early church
would have had before it, if it had known for certain
that Christ would not return to earth for at least fifteen
hundred years! The hearts of men like Athanasius,
Chrysostom, and Augustine, might well have sunk within
them, if they had been aware of the centuries of darkness through which the world would pass, before their
Master came back to take the kingdom.—What a quickening motive, on the other hand, true Christians have
perpetually had, for a close walk with God! They have
never known, in any age, that their Master might not
come suddenly to take account of His servants. This
very uncertainty has supplied them with a reason for
living always ready to meet Him.

There is one caution connected with the subject, which

God and very man. As God He said to His disciples, "Our friend
Lazarus sleepeth," when no one had told Him. As man He
asked the sister of Lazarus, when He came to them at the end of
His journey, "Where have ye laid him?" He who, when far off,
knew that Lazarus was dead, how could He be ignorant, when
present, of the place where the body of Lazarus was? It is
utterly improbable that He should have known the one thing, and
been ignorant of the other. But the truth is, that He knew both
as God, while He was ignorant of both as man. Therefore, in the
same way, He both knew not and yet knew "that day and that
hour." As man He knew not. As God He knew."

It is a sensible remark of Gualter, that pressing an excessively
literal interpretation of texts like this, is the sure way to revive
old heresies, and to bring into doubt, sometimes the divine, and
sometimes the human nature of Christ.

must not be overlooked. We must not allow the uncertainty of the time of our Lord's second advent to prevent our giving attention to the unfulfilled prophecies of Scripture. This is a great delusion, but one into which, unhappily, many Christians fall. There is a wide distinction to be drawn between dogmatical and positive assertions about dates, and a humble, prayerful searching into the good things yet to come. Against dogmatism about times and seasons, our Lord's words in this place are a standing caution. But as to the general profitableness of studying prophecy, we can have no plainer authority than the apostle Peter's words : "Ye do well that ye take heed to prophecy ;" and the apostle John's words in Revelation : "Blessed is he that readeth." (2 Peter i. 19. Rev. i. 3.)

We learn, in the second place, from these verses, *what are the practical duties of all true believers in the prospect of the second coming of Jesus Christ.* Our Lord mentions three things, to which His people should attend. He tells them plainly that He is coming again one day, in power and great glory. He tells them at the same time, that the precise hour and date of that coming are not known. What then are His people to do ? In what position of mind are they to live ? They are to watch. They are to pray. They are to work.

We are to *watch.* We are to live always on our guard. We are to keep our souls in a wakeful, lively state, prepared at any time to meet our Master. We are to beware of anything like spiritual lethargy, dulness, deadness, and torpor. The company, the employment of time, the society which induces us to forget Christ and

His second advent, should be marked, noted, and avoided. "Let us not sleep as do others," says the apostle, "but let us watch and be sober." (1 Thess. v. 6.)

We are to *pray.* We are to keep up habits of regular communion and intercourse with God. We are to allow no strangeness to come in between us and our Father in heaven, but to speak with Him daily; that so we may be ready at any moment to see Him face to face. Moreover, we are to make special prayer about the Lord's coming, that we may be "found in peace, without spot and blameless," and that our hearts may at no time be "overcharged" with the cares of this life, and so the day come upon us unawares. (2 Peter iii. 14. Luke xxi. 34.)

Finally, we are to *work.* We are to realize that we are all servants of a great Master, who has given to every man his work, and expects that work to be done. We are to labour to glorify God, each in our particular sphere and relation. There is always something for every one to do. We are to strive each of us to shine as a light,—to be the salt of our own times,—to be faithful witnesses for our Master, and to honour Him by conscientiousness and consistency in our daily conversation. Our great desire must be to be found not idle and sleeping, but working and doing.*

Such are the simple injunctions to which our Lord would have us attend. They ought to stir up in the hearts of all professing Christians great self-examination.

---

* "Be doing something," says Jerome, "that the devil may always find you engaged."—It was a common saying of Calvin, towards the end of his life, when his friends would have had him do less work, for his health's sake, "would you have my Master find me idle?"

Are we looking for our Saviour's return ? Do we long for His appearing ? Can we say with sincerity, Come, Lord Jesus ? Do we live as if we expected Christ to come again ? These are questions which demand serious consideration. May we give them the attention which they deserve !

Does our Lord require us to neglect any of the duties of life, in the expectation of His return ? He requires nothing of the kind. He does not bid the farmer neglect his land, or the labourer his work, the merchant his business, or the lawyer his calling. All He asks is that baptized people should live up to the faith into which they were baptized,—should live as penitent people,— live as believing people,—live as people who know that "without holiness no man can see the Lord."—So living, we are ready to meet our Master. Not living in this way, we are neither fit for death, judgment, nor eternity. To live in this way is to be truly happy, because it is to be truly prepared for anything that may come upon the earth. Let us never be content with a lower standard of practical Christianity than this. The last words of the prophecy are peculiarly solemn : "What I say unto you, I say unto all, Watch ! "

MARK XIV. 1—9.

1 After two days was *the feast of* the Passover, and of unleavened bread : and the Chief Priests and the Scribes sought how they might take him by craft, and put *him* to death.

2 But they said, Not on the feast *day*, lest there be an uproar of the people.

3 And being in Bethany, in the house of Simon the leper, as he sat at meat, there came a woman having an alabaster box of ointment of spike-nard very precious; and she brake the box, and poured *it* on his head.

4 And there were some that had indignation within themselves, and said, Why was this waste of the ointment made ?

5 For it might have been sold for more than three hundred pence, and have been given to the poor. And they murmured against her.

6 And Jesus said, Let her alone; why trouble ye her? she hath wrought a good work on me.

7 For ye have the poor with you always, and whensoever ye will ye may do them good: but me ye have not always.

8 She hath done what she could: she is come aforehand to anoint my body to the burying.

9 Verily I say unto you, Wheresoever this Gospel shall be preached thoughout the whole world, *this* also that she hath done shall be spoken of for a memorial of her.

THIS chapter begins that part of St. Mark's Gospel, which describes our Lord's sufferings and death. Hitherto we have chiefly seen our Saviour as our prophet and teacher. We have now to see Him as our High Priest. Hitherto we have had to consider His miracles and sayings. We have now to consider His vicarious sacrifice on the cross.

Let us first observe in these verses, *how God can disappoint the designs of wicked men, and over-rule them to His own glory.*

It is plain from St. Mark's words, and the parallel passage in St. Matthew, that our Lord's enemies did not intend to make His death a public transaction. "They sought to take Him by craft." "They said, not on the feast day, lest there be an uproar of the people." In short, it would appear that their original plan was to do nothing till the feast of the passover was over, and the passover-worshippers had returned to their own homes.

The overruling providence of God completely defeated this politic design. The betrayal of our Lord took place at an earlier time than the chief priests had expected. The death of our Lord took place on the very day when Jerusalem was most full of people, and the passover feast was at its height. In every way the counsel of these wicked men was turned to foolishness. They thought they were going to put an end for ever to Christ's spiritual kingdom; and in reality they were helping to establish it. They thought to have made Him vile and contemptible by the crucifixion; and in reality they made Him glorious. They thought to have put Him to death privily, and without observation; and instead, they were compelled to crucify Him publicly, and before the whole nation of the Jews. They thought to have silenced His disciples, and stopped their teaching; and instead, they supplied them with a text and a subject for evermore. So easy is it for God to cause the wrath of man to praise Him. (Psalm lxxvi. 10.)

There is comfort in all this for true Christians. They live in a troubled world, and are often tossed to and fro by anxiety about public events. Let them rest themselves in the thought that everything is ordered for good by an all-wise God. Let them not doubt that all things in the world around them are working together for their Father's glory. Let them call to mind the words of the second Psalm: "The kings of the earth set themselves, and the rulers take counsel together against the Lord." And yet it goes on, "He that sitteth in the heavens shall laugh: the Lord shall have them in derision." It has been so in time past. It will be so in time to come.

Let us observe, secondly, in these verses, *how good works are sometimes undervalued and misunderstood.* We are told of the good work of a certain woman, in pouring ointment on our Lord's head, in a house at Bethany.*

* The question has often been raised, whether there were one, two, or three women who anointed our Lord during His earthly

She did it, no doubt, as a mark of honour and respect, and in token of her own gratitude and love towards Him. Yet this act of her's was blamed by some. Their cold hearts could not understand such costly liberality. They called it "waste." "They had indignation within themselves." They "murmured against her."

The spirit of these narrow-minded fault-finders is unhappily only too common. Their followers and successors are to be found in every part of Christ's visible church.

ministry. Theophylact is of opinion that there were three. For this opinion much may be said.

1. The woman spoken of in the seventh chapter of St. Luke appears first in order. The city in which this anointing took place does not appear to be Bethany. The woman is spoken of as having been "a sinner." The house is described as that of a Pharisee. The anointing was of our Lord's "feet," and not of His "head." There is strong internal evidence that the whole transaction took place at a comparatively early period of our Lord's ministry. All these points should be noticed.

2. The anointing described by St. John appears next in order. This, we are distinctly told, was "six days" before the passover. The person who anointed our Lord was Mary, the sister of Lazarus. The part of Him anointed was again His "feet," and not His "head." These points ought also to be noticed.

3. The anointing described by St. Matthew and St. Mark comes third in order. This, we are told, was only "two days" before the feast of the passover. In this case we are not told the name of the woman who anointed our Lord. But we are told that the ointment was poured on His "head."

The question of course occurs to our minds : "Is it likely and probable that this event would take place no less than three times?" In reply to that it may be fairly said, that to anoint a person as a mark of honour and respect, was far more common in our Lord's time than we in England suppose ; and that anointing was a far more frequent practice than we in this climate can imagine. And it seems perfectly possible that the same thing may have happened three times.

The main difficulty, of course, is the close similarity of the language used at the anointing described by John, and at that described by Matthew and Mark. This can only be explained by supposing that our Lord twice said the same things.

There is never wanting a generation of people who decry what they call "extremes" in religion, and are incessantly recommending what they term "moderation" in the service of Christ. If a man devotes his time, money, and affections to the pursuit of worldly things, they do not blame him. If he gives himself up to the service of money, pleasure, or politics, they find no fault. But if the same man devotes himself, and all he has, to Christ, they can scarcely find words to express their sense of his folly.—"He is beside himself." "He is out of his mind." "He is a fanatic." "He is an enthusiast." "He is righteous over-much." "He is an extreme man."—In short, they regard it as "waste."

Let charges like these not disturb us, if we hear them made against us, because we strive to serve Christ. Let us bear them patiently, and remember that they are as old as Christianity itself. Let us pity those who make such charges against believers. They show plainly that they have no sense of obligation to Christ. A cold heart makes a slow hand. If a man once understands the sinfulness of sin, and the mercy of Christ in dying for him, he will never think anything too good or too costly to give to Christ. He will rather feel, "what shall I render to the Lord for all His benefits." (Psalm cxvi. 12.) He will fear wasting time, talents, money, affections on the things of this world. He will not be afraid of wasting them on his Saviour. He will fear going into extremes about business, money, politics, or pleasure ; but he will not be afraid of doing too much for Christ.

Let us observe, in the last place, how *highly our Lord*

Jesus Christ esteems any service done to Himself. No-where, perhaps, in the Gospels, do we find such strong praises bestowed on any person, as this woman here receives. Three points, in particular, stand out promi-nently in our Lord's words, to which many who now ridicule and blame others for their religion's sake, would do well to take heed.

For one thing, our Lord says, "Why trouble ye her?" —A heart-searching question that, and one which all who persecute others because of their religion would find it hard to answer!—What cause can they show? What reason can they assign for their conduct? None! none at all. They trouble others out of envy, malice, igno-rance, and dislike of the true Gospel.

For another thing, our Lord says, "She hath done a good work."—How great and marvellous is that praise, from the lips of the King of kings ! Money is often given to the Church, or bestowed on charitable institutions, from ostentation, or other false motives. But it is the person who loves and honours Jesus Himself, who really "does good works."

For another thing, our Lord says, "She hath done what she could."—No stronger word of commendation than that could possibly have been used. Thousands live and die without grace, and are lost eternally, who are always saying, "I try all I can. I do all I can." And yet in saying so, they tell as great a lie as Ananias and Sapphira. Few, it may be feared, are to be found like this woman, and really deserve to have it said of them, that they "do what they can."

Let us leave the passage with practical self-application.

Let us, like this holy woman, whose conduct we have just heard described, devote ourselves, and all we have, to Christ's glory. Our position in the world may be lowly, and our means of usefulness few. But let us, like her, "do what we can."

Finally, let us see in this passage a sweet foretaste of things yet to come in the day of judgment. Let us believe that the same Jesus who here pleaded the cause of His loving servant, when she was blamed, will one day plead for all who have been His servants in this world. Let us work on, remembering that His eye is upon us, and that all we do is noted in His book.—Let us not heed what men say or think of us, because of our religion. The praise of Christ, at the last day, will more than compensate for all we suffer in this world from unkind tongues.

MARK XIV. 10—16.

10 And Judas Iscariot, one of the twelve, went unto the Chief Priests, to betray him unto them.

11 And when they heard *it*, they were glad, and promised to give him money. And he sought how he might conveniently betray him.

12 And the first day of unleavened bread, when they killed the Passover, his disciples said unto him, Where wilt thou that we go and prepare that thou mayest eat the Passover?

13 And he sendeth forth two of his disciples, and saith unto them, Go ye into the city, and there shall meet you a man bearing a pitcher of water: follow him.

14 And wheresoever he shall go in, say ye to the goodman of the house, The Master saith, Where is the guest-chamber, where I shall eat the Passover with my disciples?

15 And he will shew you a large upper room furnished *and* prepared: there make ready for us.

16 And his disciples went forth, and came into the city, and found as he had said unto them: and they made ready the Passover.

In these verses, St. Mark tells us how our Lord was delivered into the hands of His enemies. It came to pass through the treachery of one of His own twelve disciples. The false apostle, Judas Iscariot, betrayed Him.

We ought to mark, firstly, in this passage, *to what lengths a man may go in a false profession of religion.*

It is impossible to conceive a more striking proof of this painful truth, than the history of Judas Iscariot. If ever there was a man who at one time looked like a true disciple of Christ, and bade fair to reach heaven, that man was Judas. He was chosen by the Lord Jesus Himself to be an apostle. He was privileged to be a companion of the Messiah, and an eye-witness of His mighty works, throughout His earthly ministry. He was an associate of Peter, James, and John. He was sent forth to preach the kingdom of God, and to work miracles in Christ's name. He was regarded by all the eleven apostles as one of themselves. He was so like his fellow disciples, that they did not suspect him of being a traitor. And yet this very man turns out at last a false-hearted child of the devil,—departs entirely from the faith,— assists our Lord's deadliest enemies, and leaves the world with a worse reputation than any one since the days of Cain. Never was there such a fall, such an apostacy, such a miserable end to a fair beginning,—such a total eclipse of a soul!

And how can this amazing conduct of Judas be accounted for? There is only one answer to that question. "The love of money" was the cause of this unhappy man's ruin. That same grovelling covetousness, which enslaved the heart of Balaam, and brought on Gehazi a leprosy, was the destruction of Iscariot's soul. No other explanation of his behaviour will satisfy the plain statements of Scripture. His act was an act of mean covetousness, without a redeeming feature about it. The Holy Ghost declares plainly "he was a thief." (John xii. 6.) And his case stands before the world as an eternal comment on the solemn words, "the love of money is the root of all evil." (1 Tim. vi. 10.)

Let us learn from this melancholy history of Judas, to be " clothed with humility," and to be content with nothing short of the grace of the Holy Ghost in our hearts. Knowledge, gifts, profession, privileges, church-member-ship, power of preaching, praying, and talking about religion, are all useless things, if our hearts are not converted. They are all no better than sounding brass, and a tinkling cymbal, if we have not put off the old man, and put on the new. They will not deliver us from hell.—Above all, let us remember our Lord's caution, to "beware of covetousness." (Luke xii. 15.) It is a sin that eats like a canker, and once admitted into our hearts, may lead us finally into every wickedness. Let us pray to be "content with such things as we have." (Heb. xiii. 6.) The possession of money is not the one thing needful. Riches entail great peril on the souls of those who have them. The true Christian ought to be far more afraid of being rich than of being poor.

We ought to mark, secondly, in this passage, the *intentional connection between the time of the Jewish pass-over and the time of Christ's death.* We cannot doubt for a moment that it was not by chance, but by God's providential appointment, that our Lord was crucified in the passover week, and on the very day that the passover lamb was slain. It was meant to draw the attention of the Jewish nation to Him as the true Lamb of God. It was meant to bring to their minds the true object and purpose of His death. Every sacrifice, no doubt, was intended to point the Jew onward to the one great sacrifice for sin which Christ offered. But none, certainly, was so striking a figure and type of our Lord's sacrifice, as the slaying of the passover lamb. It was preeminently an ordinance which was a "schoolmaster unto Christ." (Gal. iii. 24.) Never was there a type so full of meaning in the whole circle of Jewish ceremonies, as the passover was at its original institution.

Did the passover remind the Jew of the marvellous deliverance of his forefathers out of the land of Egypt, when God slew the first-born? No doubt it did. But it was also meant to be a sign to him of the far greater redemption and deliverance from the bondage of sin, which was to be brought in by our Lord Jesus Christ.

Did the passover remind the Jew, that by the death of an innocent lamb, the families of his forefathers were once exempted from the death of their first-born? No doubt it did. But it was also meant to teach him the far higher truth, that the death of Christ on the cross was to be the life of the world.

Did the passover remind the Jew that the sprinkling of blood on the door-posts of his forefathers' houses, preserved them from the sword of the destroying angel? No doubt it did. But it was also meant to show him the far more important doctrine that Christ's blood sprinkled on man's conscience, cleanses it from all stain of guilt, and makes him safe from the wrath to come.

Did the passover remind the Jew that none of his forefathers were safe from the destroying angel, in the night when he slew the first-born, unless he actually ate of the slain lamb? No doubt it did. But it was meant to guide his mind to the far higher lesson, that all who would receive benefit from Christ's atonement, must actually feed upon Him by faith, and receive Him into their hearts.

Let us call these things to mind, and weigh them well. We shall then see a peculiar fitness and beauty in the time appointed by God for our Lord Jesus Christ's death on the cross. It happened at the very season when the mind of all Israel was being directed to the deliverance from Egypt, and to the events of that wondrous night, when it took place. The lamb slain and eaten by every member of the family,—the destroying angel,—the safety within the blood-sprinkled door, would have been talked over and considered in every Jewish household, the very week that our blessed Lord was slain. It would be strange indeed if such a remarkable death as His, at such a time, did not set many minds thinking, and open many eyes. To what extent we shall never know till the last day.

Let it be a rule with us, in the reading of our Bibles, to study the types and ordinances of the Mosaic law with prayerful attention. They are all full of Christ. The altar,—the scape-goat,—the daily burnt-offering,—the day of atonement, are all so many finger-posts pointing to the great sacrifice offered by our Lord on Calvary. Those who neglect to study the Jewish ordinances, as dark, dull, and uninteresting parts of the Bible, only show their own ignorance, and miss great advantages.

Those who examine them with Christ as the key to their meaning, will find them full of Gospel light and comfortable truth.*

MARK XIV. 17—25.

17 And in the evening he cometh with the twelve.

18 And as they sat and did eat, Jesus said, Verily I say unto you, One of you which eateth with me shall betray me.

19 And they began to be sorrowful, and to say unto him one by one, *Is* it I? and another *said, Is* it I?

20 And he answered and said unto them, *It is* one of the twelve that dippeth with me in the dish.

21 The Son of man indeed goeth, as it is written of him: but woe to that man by whom the Son of man is betrayed! good were it for that man if he had never been born.

22 And as they did eat, Jesus took bread, and blessed, and brake *it*, and gave to them, and said, Take, eat: this is my body.

23 And he took the cup, and when he had given thanks, he gave *it* to them: and they all drank of it.

24 And he said unto them, This is my blood of the new testament, which is shed for many.

25 Verily I say unto you, I will drink no more of the fruit of the vine, until that day that I drink it new in the kingdom of God.

---

* It may be well to observe in this connection, that it admits of much question, whether the common view of the word "passover" is the correct one. At any rate, the following passage from Bishop Lowth on Isaiah xxxi. 5. deserves careful consideration. He says:

"The common notion of God's passing over the houses of the Israelites is, that in going through the land of Egypt to smite the first-born, seeing the blood on the door of the houses of the Israelites, He passed over, or skipped those houses, and forbore to smite them. But that this is not the true notion of the thing, will be plain from considering the words of the sacred historian, where he describes very explicitly the action: 'For Jehovah will pass through to smite the Egyptians; and when He seeth the blood on the lintels and on the two side posts, Jehovah *will spring forward over or before the door*, and will not suffer the destroyer to come into your houses to smite you.' Exod. xii. 23.—Here are manifestly two distinct agents, with which the notion of passing over is not consistent; for that supposes but one agent. The two agents are, the destroying angel passing through to smite every house, and Jehovah the protector, keeping pace with him, who seeing the door of the Israelites marked with blood, leaps forward, throws Himself with a sudden motion in the way, opposes the destroying angel, and protects and saves that house against him, nor suffers him to smite it." The words of Isaiah xxxi. 5. ought to be studied attentively, in order to understand the fitness and propriety of this interpretation.

THESE verses contain St. Mark's account of the institution of the Lord's Supper. The simplicity of the description deserves special observation. Well would it have been for the Church, if men had not departed from the simple statements of Scripture about this blessed sacrament! It is a mournful fact that it has been corrupted by false explanations and superstitious additions, until its real meaning, in many parts of Christendom, is utterly unknown. Let us however, at present, dismiss from our minds all matters of controversy, and study the words of St. Mark with a view to our own personal edification.

Let us learn from the passage before us, that *self-examination should precede the reception of the Lord's Supper*. We cannot doubt that this was one object of our Lord's solemn warning, "One of you which eateth with me shall betray me." He meant to stir up in the minds of His disciples, those very searchings of heart which are here so touchingly recorded : "They began to be sorrowful, and to say unto Him one by one, Is it I ? and another said, Is it I ?" He meant to teach His whole Church throughout the world, that the time of drawing near to the Lord's table should be a time for diligent self-inquiry.

The benefit of the Lord's Supper depends entirely on the spirit and frame of mind in which we receive it. The bread which we there eat, and the wine which we there drink, have no power to do good to our souls, as medicine does good to our bodies, without the cooperation of our hearts and wills. They will not convey any blessing to us, by virtue of the minister's consecration, if we do not receive them rightly, worthily, and with faith. **To** assert, as some do, that the Lord's supper must do good to all communicants, whatever be the state of mind in which they receive it, is a monstrous and unscriptural figment, and has given rise to gross and wicked superstition.

The state of mind which we should look for in ourselves, before going to the Lord's table, is well described in the Catechism of the Church of England. We ought to "examine ourselves whether we repent truly of our former sins,—whether we stedfastly purpose to lead a new life,—whether we have a lively faith in God's mercy through Christ,—and a thankful remembrance of His death,—and whether we are in charity with all men." If our conscience can answer these questions satisfactorily, we may receive the Lord's supper without fear. More than this God does not require of any communicant. Less than this ought never to content us.

Let us take heed to ourselves in the matter of the Lord's supper. It is easy to err about it on either side.—On the one hand, we are not to be content with staying away from the Lord's table under the vague plea of unfitness. As long as we so stay away, we are disobeying a plain command of Christ, and are living in sin.—But, on the other hand, we are not to go to the Lord's table as a mere form, and without thought. As long as we receive the sacrament in that state of mind, we derive no good from it, and are guilty of a great transgression.—It is an awful thing to be unfit for the sacrament, for this is to be unfit to die. It is a no less awful thing to receive it unworthily, for this is most provoking to God. The only safe course is to be a decided servant of Christ, and to live the life of faith in Him.—Then we may draw near with boldness, and take the sacrament to our comfort.

Let us learn, in the second place, from these verses, that *the principal object of the Lord's Supper, is to remind us of Christ's sacrifice for us on the cross.* The bread is intended to bring to our recollection the "body" of Christ, which was wounded for our transgressions. The wine is intended to bring to our recollection the "blood" of Christ, which was shed to cleanse us from all sin. The atonement and propitiation which our Lord effected by His death as our Surety and Substitute, stand out prominently in the whole ordinance. The false doctrine which some teach, that His death was nothing more than the death of a very holy man, who left us an example how to die, turns the Lord's supper into an unmeaning ordinance, and cannot possibly be reconciled with our Lord's words at its institution.

A clear understanding of this point is of great importance. It will place us in the right position of mind, and teach us how we ought to feel in drawing near to the Lord's table.—It will produce in us true *humility* of spirit. The bread and wine will remind us how sinful sin must be, when nothing but Christ's death could atone for it.—It will produce in us *hopefulness* about our souls. The bread and wine will remind us that though our sins are great, a great price has been paid for our redemption. —Not least, it will produce in us *gratitude*. The bread and wine will remind us how great is our debt to Christ, and how deeply bound we are to glorify Him in our lives. May these be the feelings that we experience, whenever we receive the Lord's supper !

Finally, we learn from these verses, *the nature of the spiritual benefits, which the Lord's Supper is intended to convey, and the persons who have a right to expect them.* We may gather this lesson from the significant actions which are used in receiving this sacrament. Our Lord commands us to "eat" bread and to "drink" wine. Now eating and drinking are the acts of a living person. The object of eating and drinking is to be strengthened and refreshed. The conclusion we are meant to draw, is manifestly this, that the Lord's supper is appointed for "the strengthening and refreshing of our souls," and that those who ought to partake of it are those who are lively, real Christians. All such will find this sacrament a means of grace. It will assist them to rest in Christ more simply, and to trust in Him more entirely. The visible symbols of bread and wine will aid, quicken, and confirm their faith.

A right view of this point is of the utmost moment in these latter days. We must always beware of thinking that there is any way of eating Christ's body, and drinking Christ's blood, but by faith,—or that receiving the Lord's supper will give any man a different interest in Christ's sacrifice on the cross from that which faith gives. Faith is the one grand mean of communication between the soul and Christ. The Lord's supper can aid, quicken, and confirm faith, but can never supersede it, or supply its absence. Let this never be forgotten. Error on this point is a most fatal delusion, and leads to many superstitions.

Let it be a settled principle in our Christianity, that no unbeliever ought to go to the Lord's table, and that the sacrament will not do our souls the slightest good, if we do not receive it with repentance and faith. The Lord's supper is not a converting or justifying ordinance, and those who come to it unconverted and unjustified, will go away no better than they came, but rather worse. It is an ordinance for believers, and not for unbelievers,—for the living, and not for the dead. It is meant to sustain life, but not to impart it,—to strengthen and increase grace, but not to give it,—to help faith to grow, but not to sow or plant it. Let these things sink down into our hearts, and never be forgotten.

Are we alive unto God? This is the great question. If we are, let us go to the Lord's supper, and receive it thankfully, and never turn our backs on the Lord's table. If we do not go, we commit a great sin.

Are we yet dead in sin and worldliness? If we are, we have no business at the communion. We are on the broad way that leadeth to destruction. We must repent. We must be born again. We must be joined to Christ by faith. Then, and not till then, we are fit to be communicants.*

* There are two expressions in the passage now expounded, which deserve a special notice. One is, the "fruit of the vine." The other is "the kingdom of God."

1. The words, "fruit of the vine," applied by our Lord to the cup of wine which He had just been giving to His disciples, in the institution of the Lord's supper, appear entirely to overthrow the Romish doctrine of transubstantiation. The wine, it appears, did not really and literally become Christ's blood, as the Roman Catholics say. Our Lord Himself speaks of it as the juice of grapes, "the fruit of the vine." It is clear therefore, that when He said of that cup of wine before, "this is my blood," He meant nothing more than this, "this represents—is an emblem of—my blood."

2. The words, "kingdom of God," applied by our Lord to a time

26 And when they had sung an hymn, they went out into the mount of Olives.

27 And Jesus saith unto them, All ye shall be offended because of me this night : for it is written, I will smite the shepherd, and the sheep shall be scattered.

28 But after that I am risen, I will go before you into Galilee.

29 But Peter said unto him, Although all shall be offended, yet *will* not I.

30 And Jesus saith unto him, Verily I say unto thee, That this day, *even* in this night, before the cock crow twice, thou shalt deny me thrice.

31 But he spake the more vehemently, If I should die with thee, I will not deny thee in any wise. Likewise also said they all.

WE see in these verses, *how well our Lord foreknew the weakness and infirmity of His disciples.* He tells them plainly what they were going to do. "All ye shall be offended because of me this night." He tells Peter in particular of the astounding sin which he was about to commit: "This night, before the cock crow, thou shalt deny me thrice."

Yet our Lord's fore-knowledge did not prevent His choosing these twelve disciples to be His apostles. He allowed them to be His intimate friends and companions, knowing perfectly well what they would one day do. He granted them the mighty privilege of being continually with Him, and hearing His voice, with a clear foresight of the melancholy weakness and want of faith which they would exhibit at the end of His ministry. This is a remarkable fact, and deserves to be had in continual remembrance.

and state of things yet future, appear to show plainly that He did not consider God's kingdom to have come, when He spoke. Moreover the words have not yet received a fulfilment, as it is not known that our Lord administered the Lord's supper to His disciples after His resurrection. The words therefore are meant to turn our minds towards the time of our Lord's second advent. Then, and not till then, "the kingdom of God" will be fully set up. Then, and not till then, we shall sit down at the marriage supper of the Lamb, and drink the new wine in the kingdom.

Let us take comfort in the thought that the Lord Jesus does not cast off His believing people because of failures and imperfections. He knows what they are. He takes them, as the husband takes the wife, with all their blemishes and defects, and, once joined to Him by faith, will never put them away. He is a merciful and compassionate High-priest. It is His glory to pass over the transgressions of His people, and to cover their many sins. He knew what they were before conversion,—wicked, guilty, and defiled; yet He loved them. He knows what they will be after conversion,—weak, erring, and frail; yet He loves them. He has undertaken to save them, notwithstanding all their shortcomings, and what He has undertaken He will perform.

Let us learn to pass a charitable judgment on the conduct of professing believers. Let us not set them down in a low place, and say they have no grace, because we see in them much weakness and corruption. Let us remember that our Master in heaven bears with their infirmities, and let us try to bear with them too. The Church of Christ is little better than a great hospital. We ourselves are all, more or less, weak, and all daily need the skilful treatment of the heavenly Physician. There will be no complete cures till the resurrection day.

We see, in the second place, in these verses, *how much comfort professing Christians may miss by carelessness and inattention.* Our Lord spoke plainly of His resurrection: "After that I am risen, I will go before you into Galilee." Yet His words appear to have been thrown away, and spoken in vain. Not one of His disciples seems to have noticed them, or treasured them up in his heart. When

He was betrayed, they forsook Him. When He was crucified, they were almost in despair. And when He rose again on the third day, they would not believe that it was true. They had heard of it frequently with the hearing of the ear, but it had never made any impression on their hearts.

What an exact picture we have here of human nature! How often we see the very same thing among professing Christians in the present day! How many truths we read yearly in the Bible, and yet remember them no more than if we had never read them at all! How many words of wisdom we hear in sermons heedlessly and thoughtlessly, and live on as if we had never heard them! The days of darkness and affliction come upon us by and bye, and then we prove unarmed and unprepared. On sick-beds, and in mourning, we see a meaning in texts and passages which we at one time heard listlessly and unconcerned. Things flash across our minds at such seasons, and make us feel ashamed that we had not noticed them before. We then remember to have read them, and heard them, and seen them, but they made no impression upon us. Like Hagar's well in the wilderness, they were close at hand, but, like Hagar, we never saw them. (Gen. xxi. 19.)

Let us pray for a quick understanding in hearing and reading God's word. Let us search into every part of it, and not lose any precious truth in it for want of care. So doing, we shall lay up a good foundation against the time to come, and in sorrow and sickness be found armed.

Let us mark how little reason ministers have to be surprised, if the words that they preach in sermons are often unnoticed and unheeded. They only drink of the same cup with their Master. Even He said many things which were not noticed when first spoken. And yet we know that "never man spake like this man." "The disciple is not greater than His Master, nor the servant than his Lord." We have need of patience. Truths that seem neglected at first, often bear fruit after many days.

We see in the last place, in these verses, *how much ignorant self-confidence may sometimes be found in the hearts of professing Christians.* The apostle Peter could not think it possible that he could ever deny his Lord. "If I should die with thee," he says, "I will not deny thee in any wise." And he did not stand alone in his confidence. The other disciples were of the same opinion. "Likewise also said they all."

Yet what did all this confident boasting come to? Twelve hours did not pass away before all the disciples forsook our Lord and fled. Their loud professions were all forgotten. The present danger swept all their promises of fidelity clean away. So little do we know how we shall act in any particular position until we are placed in it! So much do present circumstances alter our feelings!

Let us learn to pray for humility. "Pride goeth before destruction, and a haughty spirit before a fall." (Prov. xvi. 18.) There is far more wickedness in all our hearts than we know. We never can tell how far we might fall, if once placed in temptation. There is no degree of sin into which the greatest saint may not run, if he is not held up by the grace of God, and if he does not watch and pray. The seeds of every wickedness lie hidden in our hearts. They only need the convenient season to spring forth into a mischievous vitality. "Let him that thinketh he standeth take heed lest he fall." "He that trusteth his own heart is a fool." (1 Cor. x. 12. Prov. xxviii. 26.) Let our daily prayer be, "Hold thou me up and I shall be safe."

MARK XIV. 32—42.

32 And they came to a place which was named Gethsemane: and he saith to his disciples, Sit ye here, while I shall pray.
33 And he taketh with him Peter and James and John, and began to be sore amazed, and to be very heavy;
34 And saith unto them, My soul is exceeding sorrowful unto death: tarry ye here, and watch.
35 And he went forward a little, and fell on the ground, and prayed that, if it were possible, the hour might pass from him.
36 And he said, Abba, Father, all things are possible unto thee; take away this cup from me: nevertheless not what I will, but what thou wilt.
37 And he cometh, and findeth them sleeping, and saith unto Peter, Simon, sleepest thou? couldest not thou watch one hour?
38 Watch ye and pray, lest ye enter into temptation. The spirit truly is ready, but the flesh is weak.
39 And again he went away, and prayed, and spake the same words.
40 And when he returned, he found them asleep again, (for their eyes were heavy,) neither wist they what to answer him.
41 And he cometh the third time, and saith unto them, Sleep on now, and take your rest: it is enough, the hour is come; behold, the Son of man is betrayed into the hands of sinners.
42 Rise up, let us go; lo, he that betrayeth me is at hand.

THE history of our Lord's agony in the garden of Gethsemane is a deep and mysterious passage of Scripture. It contains things which the wisest divines cannot fully explain. Yet it has upon its surface plain truths of most momentous importance.

Let us mark, in the first place, *how keenly our Lord felt the burden of a world's sin*. It is written that He "began to be sore amazed, and to be very heavy; and saith unto them, My soul is exceeding sorrowful unto death,"—and that "he fell on the ground, and prayed, that, if it were possible, the hour might pass from him."

There is only one reasonable explanation of these expressions. It was no mere fear of the physical suffering of death, which drew them from our Lord's lips. It was a sense of the enormous load of human guilt, which began at that time to press upon Him in a peculiar way. It was a sense of the unutterable weight of our sins and transgressions which were then specially laid upon Him. He was being "made a curse for us." He was bearing our griefs and carrying our sorrows, according to the covenant He came on earth to fulfil. He was being "made sin for us who Himself knew no sin." His holy nature felt acutely the hideous burden laid upon Him. These were the reasons of His extraordinary sorrow.

We ought to see in our Lord's agony in Gethsemane the exceeding sinfulness of sin. It is a subject on which the thoughts of professing Christians are far below what they should be. The careless, light way in which such sins as swearing, sabbath-breaking, lying and the like, are often spoken of, is a painful evidence of the low condition of men's moral feelings. Let the recollection of Gethsemane have a sanctifying effect upon us. Whatever others do, let us never "make a mock at sin."

Let us mark, in the second place, *what an example our Lord gives us of the importance of prayer in time of trouble.* In the hour of His distress we find Him employing this great remedy. Twice we are told that when His soul was exceeding sorrowful, "He prayed."

We shall never find a better receipt than this for the patient bearing of affliction. The first person to whom we should turn in our trouble is God. The first complaint we should make should be in the form of a prayer. The reply may not be given immediately. The relief we want may not be granted at once. The thing that tries us may never be removed and taken away. But the mere act of pouring out our hearts, and unbosoming ourselves at a throne of grace will do us good. The advice of St. James is wise and weighty: "Is any afflicted? Let him pray." (James v. 13.)

Let us mark, in the third place, *what a striking example our Lord gives us of submission of will to the will of God.* Deeply as His human nature felt the pressure of a world's guilt, He still prays that, " if it were possible," the hour might pass from him. " Take away this cup from me : nevertheless not what I will, but what thou wilt." *

---

* Men are so apt to run into error on the subject of the divine and human natures in Christ, that the following quotation may be worth reading.

" There are two distinct wills in Christ. But although they be truly distinct and different one from the other, yet they are not contrary one to the other, but they are subordinate each to other ; the human will of Christ being always subject to His divine will, and most ready to be ordered and ruled by it. Therefore here we see that He doth submit His will, as He was man, to the divine will of God the Father, which divine will of the Father was also Christ's own will. This truth we are to hold and maintain against those old heretics, which were called Monothelites, because they held there was but one kind of will in Christ, namely His divine will.—This heresy sprung up in the Eastern church about 600 years after Christ ; and it did very much molest and trouble the church for many years.—It was a branch of the gross heresy of Eutyches which sprung up 200 years before. This Eutyches confounded the two natures in Christ, holding that as there was but one Person after the personal union, so there was but one nature in Christ,—viz. the divine nature, the human nature being swallowed up. To maintain this the better, his followers maintained that Christ had but one kind of will. This heresy was condemned by the 6th general council at Constantinople, as well as by other ancient councils. And the fathers of the church in those times, did confute it by these very words of our Saviour which we have now in hand."—*Petter on Mark.*

We can imagine no higher degree of perfection than that which is here set before us. To take patiently whatever God sends,—to like nothing but what God likes,—to wish nothing but what God approves,—to prefer pain, if it please God to send it, to ease, if God does not think fit to bestow it,—to lie passive under God's hand, and know no will but His,—this is the highest standard at which we can aim, and of this our Lord's conduct in Gethsemane is a perfect pattern.

Let us strive and labour to have "the mind that was in Christ" in this matter. Let us daily pray and endeavour to be enabled to mortify our self-will.—It is for our happiness to do so. Nothing brings us so much misery on earth as having our own way.—It is the best proof of real grace to do so. Knowledge, and gifts, and convictions, and feelings, and wishes, are all very uncertain evidences. They are often to be found in unconverted persons. But a continually increasing disposition to submit our own wills to the will of God, is a far more healthy symptom. It is a sign that we are really "growing in grace, and in the knowledge of Jesus Christ."

Let us mark, lastly, in these verses, *how much infirmity may be found even in the best Christians.* We have a painful illustration of this truth in the conduct of Peter, James, and John. They slept when they ought to have watched and prayed. Though invited by our Lord to watch with Him, they slept. Though warned a short time before that danger was at hand, and their faith likely to fail, they slept. Though fresh from the Lord's table, with all its touching solemnities, they slept. Never was there a more striking proof that the best of men are but men, and that, so long as saints are in the body, they are compassed with infirmity.

These things are written for our learning. Let us take heed that they are not written in vain. Let us ever be on our guard against the slothful, indolent, lazy spirit in religion, which is natural to us all, and specially in the matter of our private prayers. When we feel that spirit creeping over us, let us remember Peter, James, and John in the garden, and take care.

The solemn counsel which our Lord addresses to His disciples should often ring in our ears: "Watch and pray lest ye enter into temptation. The spirit truly is ready, but the flesh is weak." It should be the Christian's daily motto from the time of his conversion to the hour of his death.

Are we true Christians? and would we keep our souls awake? Let us not forget that we have within us a double nature,—a ready "spirit" and weak "flesh,"—a carnal nature inclined to evil, and a spiritual nature inclined to good. These two are contrary one to the other. (Gal. v. 17.) Sin and the devil will always find helpers in our hearts. If we do not crucify and rule over the flesh, it will often rule over us and bring us to shame.

Are we true Christians, and would we keep our souls awake? Then let us never forget to "watch and pray." We must watch like soldiers,—we are upon enemy's ground. We must always be on our guard. We must fight a daily fight and war a daily warfare. The Christian's rest is yet to come.—We must pray without ceasing, regularly, habitually, carefully, and at stated times. We must pray as well as watch, and watch as well as pray.

Watching without praying is self-confidence and self-conceit. Praying without watching is enthusiasm and fanaticism. The man who knows his own weakness, and knowing it both watches and prays, is the man that will be held up and not allowed to fall.

MARK XIV. 43—52.

43 And immediately, while he yet spake, cometh Judas, one of the twelve, and with him a great multitude with swords and staves, from the Chief Priests and the Scribes and the elders.

44 And he that betrayed him had given them a token, saying, Whomsoever I shall kiss, that same is he; take him, and lead *him* away safely.

45 And as soon as he was come, he goeth straightway to him, and saith, Master, master; and kissed him.

46 And they laid their hands on him, and took him.

47 And one of them that stood by drew a sword, and smote a servant of the High Priest, and cut off his ear.

48 And Jesus answered and said unto them, Are ye come out, as against a thief, with swords and *with* staves to take me?

49 I was daily with you in the temple teaching, and ye took me not. but the Scriptures must be fulfilled.

50 And they all forsook him, and fled.

51 And there followed him a certain young man, having a linen cloth cast about *his* naked *body;* and the young men laid hold on him:

52 And he left the linen cloth, and fled from them naked.

LET us notice in these verses, *how little our Lord's enemies understood the nature of His kingdom.* We read that Judas came to take Him "with a great multitude, with swords and staves." It was evidently expected that our Lord would be vigorously defended by His disciples, and that He would not be taken prisoner without fighting. The chief priests and scribes clung obstinately to the idea, that our Lord's kingdom was a worldly kingdom, and therefore supposed that it would be upheld by worldly means. They had yet to learn the solemn lesson contained in our Lord's words to Pilate, "My kingdom is not of this world:—now is my kingdom not from hence." (John xviii. 36.)

We shall do well to remember this in all our endeavours to extend the kingdom of true religion. It is not
to be propagated by violence, or by an arm of flesh.
"The weapons of our warfare are not carnal." "Not by
might, nor by power, but by my Spirit, saith the Lord of
hosts." (2 Cor. x. 4. Zech. iv. 6.) The cause of truth
does not need force to maintain it. False religions, like
Mahometanism, have often been spread by the sword.
False Christianity, like that of the Roman church, has
often been enforced on men by bloody persecutions. But
the real Gospel of Christ requires no such aids as these.
It stands by the power of the Holy Ghost. It grows by
the hidden influence of the Holy Ghost on men's hearts
and consciences. There is no clearer sign of a bad cause
in religion than a readiness to appeal to the sword.

Let us notice, secondly, in these verses, *how all things
in our Lord's passion happened according to God's word.*
His own address to those who took Him, exhibits this in
a striking manner : "the Scriptures must be fulfilled."

There was no accident or chance in any part of the close of
our Lord's earthly ministry. The steps in which He walked
from Gethsemane to Calvary, were all marked out hundreds of years before. The twenty-second Psalm, and
the fifty-third chapter of Isaiah, were literally fulfilled.
The wrath of His enemies,—His rejection by His own
people,—His being dealt with as a malefactor,—His
being condemned by the assembly of the wicked,—all had
been foreknown, and all foretold. All that took place
was only the working out of God's great design to provide an atonement for a world's sin. The armed men
whom Judas brought to lay hands on Jesus, were, like

Nebuchadnezzar and Sennacherib, unconscious instruments in carrying God's purposes into effect.

Let us rest our souls on the thought, that all around us is ordered and overruled by God's almighty wisdom. The course of this world may often be contrary to our wishes. The position of the Church may often be very unlike what we desire. The wickedness of worldly men, and the inconsistencies of believers, may often afflict our souls. But there is a hand above us, moving the vast machine of this universe, and making all things work together for His glory. The Scriptures are being yearly fulfilled. Not one jot or tittle in them shall ever fail to be accomplished. The kings of the earth may take counsel together, and the rulers of the nations may set themselves against Christ. (Psal. ii. 2.) But the resurrection morning shall prove that, even at the darkest time, all things were being done according to the will of God.

Let us notice, lastly, in these verses, *how much the faith of true believers may give way*. We are told that when Judas and his company laid hands on our Lord, and He quietly submitted to be taken prisoner, the eleven disciples "all forsook Him and fled." Perhaps up to that moment they were buoyed up by the hope that our Lord would work a miracle, and set Himself free. But when they saw no miracle worked, their courage failed them entirely. Their former protestations were all forgotten. Their promises to die with their Master, rather than deny Him, were all cast to the winds. The fear of present danger got the better of faith. The sense of immediate peril drove every other feeling out of their minds. They "all forsook him and fled."

There is something deeply instructive in this incident. It deserves the attentive study of all professing Christians. Happy is he who marks the conduct of our Lord's disciples, and gathers from it wisdom !

Let us learn from the flight of these eleven disciples, not to be over confident in our own strength. The fear of man does indeed bring a snare. We never know what we may do, if we are tempted, or to what extent our faith may give way. Let us be clothed with humility.

Let us learn to be charitable in our judgment of other Christians. Let us not expect too much from them, or set them down as having no grace at all, if we see them overtaken in a fault. Let us not forget that even our Lord's chosen apostles forsook Him in His time of need. Yet they rose again by repentance, and became pillars of the Church of Christ.

Finally, let us leave the passage with a deep sense of our Lord's ability to sympathize with His believing people. If there is one trial greater than another, it is the trial of being disappointed in those we love. It is a bitter cup, which all true Christians have frequently to drink. Ministers fail them. Relations fail them. Friends fail them. One cistern after another proves to be broken, and to hold no water. But let them take comfort in the thought, that there is one unfailing Friend, even Jesus, who can be touched with the feeling of their infirmities, and has tasted of all their sorrows. Jesus knows what it is to see friends and disciples failing Him in the hour of need. Yet He bore it patiently, and loved them notwithstanding all. He is never weary of forgiving. Let us strive to do likewise. Jesus, at any rate, will never fail us. It is written, " His compassions fail not." (Lam. iii. 22.*

* The question has often been asked, "Who was the 'certain young man,' mentioned at the end of this passage, on whom the young men laid hold, and who fled away naked?" St. Mark is the only evangelist who relates this circumstance ; and he has given us no clue to further knowledge as to who it was, or why the event is mentioned.

No satisfactory answer to these questions has yet been given. The utmost that can be said of any of the explanations attempted, is, that they are conjectures and speculations.

"Some," says Petter in his commentary on Mark, "have thought that it was one of the twelve disciples, viz., James the son of Alpheus, the Lord's brother, or kinsman of our Saviour, (whose appearance was perhaps like our Lord's.) " This is the view of Epiphanius and Jerome. Others have thought that it was John, the beloved disciple. This is the view of Ambrose, Chrysostom, and Gregory. But it could be neither of them, nor any other of the twelve, because it is said immediately before, that they " all fled " upon the taking of our Saviour, whereas this young man followed our Saviour at this time. It is more likely that it was some good young man, who dwelt near the garden of Gethsemane, who hearing the noise and stir that was made about the taking and binding of our Saviour, did arise suddenly out of his bed to see what was the matter, and perceiving that they had cruelly taken and bound our Saviour, and were leading Him away, did follow after Him to see what would be done with Him, whereby it appears that he was a well-wisher to our Saviour."

Theophylact and Euthymius think it probable that it was some young man who followed our Lord from the house where He ate the passover with His disciples. Some think that it was the Evangelist Mark himself.

Some have thought that St. Mark's purpose in relating the event, is to show the cruelty, rage, and ferocity of those who took our Lord. They were ready to lay hands on any one who was any where near Him, and to make prisoners indiscriminately of all who even appeared to be connected with Him.

Some have thought that the whole transaction exhibits the utter desertion of our Lord. " This young man," says Clarius, " would rather escape naked than be taken as one of the followers of Christ."

Some have thought that it is related to show the real peril in

MARK XIV. 53—65.

53 And they led Jesus away to the High Priest: and with him were assembled all the Chief Priests and the elders and the Scribes.

54 And Peter followed him afar off, even into the palace of the High Priest: and he sat with the servants, and warmed himself at the fire.

55 And the Chief Priests and all the council sought for witness against Jesus to put him to death; and found none.

56 For many bare false witness against him, but their witness agreed not together.

57 And there arose certain, and bare false witness against him, saying,

58 We heard him say, I will destroy this temple that is made with hands, and within three days I will build another made without hands.

59 But neither so did their witness agree together.

60 And the High Priest stood up in the midst, and asked Jesus, saying, Answerest thou nothing? what *is it which* these witness against thee?

61 But he held his peace, and answered nothing. Again the High Priest asked him, and said unto him, Art thou the Christ, the Son of the Blessed?

62 And Jesus said, I am: and ye shall see the Son of man sitting on the right hand of power, and coming in the clouds of heaven.

63 Then the High Priest rent his clothes, and saith, What need we any further witnesses?

64 Ye have heard the blasphemy: what think ye? And they all condemned him to be guilty of death.

65 And some began to spit on him, and to cover his face, and to buffet him, and to say unto him, Prophesy. and the servants did strike him with the palms of their hands.

SOLOMON tells us in the book of Ecclesiastes, that one evil he has seen under the sun, is when "folly is set in great dignity, and the rich sit in low place." (Eccles. x. 6.) We can imagine no more complete illustration of his words than the state of things we have recorded in the

which the disciples were, and to make it plain that they saved their lives only by their flight.

One eminent divine regards the whole event as strongly figurative. He sees in it an antitype of what took place on the day of atonement, and at the cleansing of a leper. He considers the young man escaping to represent the goat let go free, and the bird let loose; while our Lord represents the goat offered up, and the bird slain. See Lev. xiv. 7, and xvi. 22.

I offer no opinion on any of the above explanations, excepting that I look on the last as eminently fanciful and unsatisfactory. Bullinger remarks sensibly, "It does not interest us much to know who this young man was, and it would not bring any very great fruit to us, if we did know. If it had been useful and wholesome for us to know, the Spirit of God would not have been silent, seeing that He is often marvellously diligent in relating very minute things."

passage before us. We see the Son of God, "in whom are hid all the treasures of wisdom and knowledge," arraigned as a malefactor before " the chief priests, and elders, and scribes." We see the heads of the Jewish nation combining together to kill their own Messiah, and judging Him who will one day come in glory to judge them and all mankind. These things sound marvellous, but they are true.

Let us observe in these verses, *how foolishly Christians sometimes thrust themselves into temptation.* We are told that when our Lord was led away prisoner, "Peter followed Him afar off, even into the palace of the high priest : and he sat with the servants, and warmed himself at the fire." * There was no wisdom in this act. Having once forsaken his Master and fled, he ought to have remembered his own weakness, and not to have ventured into danger again. It was an act of rashness and presumption. It brought on him fresh trials of faith, for which he was utterly unprepared. It threw him into bad company, where he was not likely to get good but harm. It paved the way for his last and greatest transgression,—his thrice-repeated denial of his Master.

But it is an experimental truth that ought never to be overlooked, that when a believer has once begun to back-

---

* In the expression " warmed himself at the fire," it is worthy of remark, that the Greek word which we translate "fire," is not the same as that translated "fire of coals," in John xviii. 18.   It would rather bear the meaning of "light," or a fire so blazing as to give light.

The remark is not without interest, as it explains how easily Peter was recognized and discovered by those who sat around him, as one of Christ's disciples. The bright light of the fire shining upon him made concealment impossible.

slide and leave his first faith, he seldom stops short at his first mistake. He seldom makes only one stumble. He seldom commits only one fault. A blindness seems to come over the eyes of his understanding. He appears to cast over-board his common sense and discretion. Like a stone rolling down-hill, the further he goes on in sinning, the faster and more decided is his course. Like David, he may begin with idleness, and end with committing every possible crime. Like Peter, he may begin with cowardice,—go on to foolish trifling with temptation, and then end with denying Christ.

If we know anything of true saving religion, let us ever beware of the beginnings of backsliding. It is like the letting out of water, first a drop and then a torrent. Once out of the way of holiness, there is no saying to what we may come. Once giving way to petty incon- sistencies, we may find ourselves one day committing every sort of wickedness. Let us keep far from the brink of evil. Let us not play with fire. Let us never fear being too particular, too strict, and too precise. No petition in the Lord's prayer is more important than the last but one, "Lead us not into temptation."

Let us observe, in the second place, in these verses, *how much our Lord Jesus Christ had to endure from lying lips, when tried before the chief priests.* We are told that "many bare false witness against Him ; but their witness agreed not together."

We can easily conceive that this was not the least heavy part of our blessed Saviour's passion. To be seized unjustly as a malefactor, and put on trial as a criminal when innocent, is a severe affliction. But to hear men

inventing false charges against us and coining slanders,—
to listen to all the malignant virulence of unscrupulous
tongues let loose against our character, and know that it
is all untrue,—this is a cross indeed !   " The words of a
talebearer," says Solomon, " are as wounds." (Prov.
xviii. 8.)   " Deliver my soul," says David, "from lying lips
and a deceitful tongue." (Psalm cxx. 2.)   All this was a
part of the cup which Jesus drank for our sakes.   Great
indeed was the price at which our souls were redeemed !

Let it never surprise true Christians if they are
slandered and misrepresented in this world.   They must
not expect to fare better than their Lord.   Let them
rather look forward to it, as a matter of course, and see in
it a part of the cross which all must bear after conversion.
Lies and false reports are among Satan's choicest weapons.
When he cannot deter men from serving Christ, he
labours to harass them and make Christ's service un-
comfortable.   Let us bear it patiently, and not count it
a strange thing.   The words of the Lord Jesus should
often come to our minds : " Woe unto you, when all men
shall speak well of you."   " Blessed are ye, when men
shall revile you, and persecute you, and say all manner
of evil against you falsely for my sake." (Luke vi. 26.
Matt. v. 11.)

Let us observe, lastly, in these verses, *what distinct
testimony our Lord bore to His own Messiahship, and second
advent in glory.*   The high priest asks Him the solemn
question, " Art thou the Christ, the Son of the blessed ?"
He receives at once the emphatic reply, " I am : and ye
shall see the Son of Man sitting on the right hand of
power, and coming in the clouds of heaven."

These words of our Lord ought always to be had in remembrance. The Jews could never say after these words, that they were not clearly told that Jesus of Nazareth was the Christ of God. Before the great council of their priests and elders, He declared, " I am the Christ." The Jews could never say after these words, that He was so lowly and poor a person, that He was not worthy to be believed. He warned them plainly that His glory and greatness was all yet to come. They were only deferred and postponed till His second advent. They would yet see Him in royal power and majesty, " sitting on the right hand of power," coming in the clouds of heaven, a Judge, a Conqueror, and a King. If Israel was unbelieving, it was not because Israel was not told what to believe.

Let us leave the passage with a deep sense of the reality and certainty of our Lord Jesus Christ's second coming. Once more at the very end of His ministry, and in the face of His deadly enemies, we find Him asserting the mighty truth that He will come again to judge the world. Let it be one of the leading truths in our own personal Christianity. Let us live in the daily recollection, that our Saviour is one day coming back to this world. Let the Christ in whom we believe, be not only the Christ who died for us and rose again,—the Christ who lives for us and intercedes,—but the Christ who will one day return in glory, to gather together and reward His people, and to punish fearfully all His enemies.

MARK XIV. 66—72.

66 And as Peter was beneath in the palace, there cometh one of the maids of the High Priest:

67 And when she saw Peter warming himself, she looked upon him, and said, And thou also wast with Jesus of Nazareth.

68 But he denied, saying, I know not, neither understand I what thou sayest. And he went out into the porch; and the cock crew.

69 And a maid saw him again, and began to say to them that stood by, This is one of them.

70 And he denied it again. And a little after, they that stood by said again to Peter, Surely thou art one of them: for thou art a Galilæan, and thy speech agreeth thereto.

71 And he began to curse and to swear, saying, I know not this man of whom ye speak.

72 And the second time the cock crew. And Peter called to mind the word that Jesus said unto him, Before the cock crow twice, thou shalt deny me thrice. And when he thought thereon, he wept.

A SHIPWRECK is a melancholy sight, even when no lives are lost. It is sad to think of the destruction of property, and disappointment of hopes which generally attend it. It is painful to see the suffering and hardship, which the ship's crew often have to undergo in their struggle to escape from drowning. Yet no shipwreck is half so melancholy a sight as the backsliding and fall of a true Christian. Though raised again by God's mercy, and finally saved from hell, he loses much by his fall. Such a sight we have brought before our minds in the verses we have now read. We are there told that most painful and instructive story, how Peter denied his Lord.

Let us learn, in the first place, from these verses, *how far and how shamefully a great saint may fall.* We know that Simon Peter was an eminent apostle of Jesus Christ. He was one who had received special commendation from our Lord's lips, after a noble confession of His Messiahship: "Blessed art thou Simon Barjona:"—"I will give unto thee the keys of the kingdom of heaven." He was one who had enjoyed special privileges, and had special mercies shown to him. Yet here we see this same Simon Peter so entirely overcome by fear that he actually denies his Lord. He declares that he knows not Him whom he had accompanied and lived with for three years! He declares that he knows not Him who had healed his own wife's mother, taken him up into the mount of transfiguration, and saved him from drowning in the sea of Galilee! And he not only denies his Master once, but does it three times! And he not only denies Him simply, but does it " cursing and swearing! " And above all, he does all this in the face of the plainest warnings, and in spite of his own loud protestation that he would do nothing of the kind, but rather die!

These things are written to show the Church of Christ what human nature is, even in the best of men. They are intended to teach us that, even after conversion and renewal of the Holy Ghost, believers are compassed with infirmity and liable to fall. They are meant to impress upon us the immense importance of daily watchfulness, prayerfulness, and humility, so long as we are in the body. " Let him that thinketh he standeth, take heed lest he fall."

Let us carefully remember that Simon Peter's case does not stand alone. The word of God contains many other examples of the infirmity of true believers, which we shall do well to observe. The histories of Noah, Abraham, David, Hezekiah, will supply us with mournful proof, that " the infection of sin remains even in the regenerate," and that no man is so strong as to be beyond the danger of falling. Let us not forget this. Let us walk humbly with our God. " Happy is the man that feareth alway." (Prov. xxviii. 14.)

Let us learn, in the second place, from these verses,

how small a temptation may cause a saint to have a great fall. The beginning of Peter's trial was nothing more than the simple remark of " a maid of the High Priest." " Thou also wert with Jesus of Nazareth." There is nothing to show that these words were spoken with any hostile purpose. For anything we can see, they might fairly mean that this maid remembered that Peter used to be a companion of our Lord. But this simple remark was enough to overthrow the faith of an eminent apostle, and to make him begin to deny his Master. The chiefest and foremost of our Lord's chosen disciples is cast down, not by the threats of armed men, but by the saying of one weak woman !

There is something deeply instructive in this fact. It ought to teach us that no temptation is too small and trifling to overcome us, except we watch and pray to be held up. If God be for us we may remove mountains and get the victory over a host of foes. " I can do all things," says Paul, " through Christ that strengtheneth me." (Phil. iv. 22.) If God withdraw His grace, and leave us to ourselves, we are like a city without gates and walls, a prey to the first enemy, however weak and contemptible.

Let us beware of making light of temptations because they seem little and insignificant. There is nothing little that concerns our souls. A little leaven leaveneth the whole lump. A little spark may kindle a great fire. A little leak may sink a great ship. A little provocation may bring out from our hearts great corruption, and end in bringing our souls into great trouble.

Finally, let us learn from these verses *that backsliding*

brings saints into great sorrow. The conclusion of the passage is very affecting. " Peter called to mind the words that Jesus said unto him. Before the cock crow thou shalt deny me thrice." Who can pretend to describe the feelings that must have flashed across the apostle's mind ? Who can conceive the shame and confusion, and self-reproach, and bitter remorse which must have overwhelmed his soul ? To have fallen so foully ! To have fallen so repeatedly ! To have fallen in the face of such plain warnings ! All these must have been cutting thoughts. The iron must indeed have entered into his soul. There is deep and solemn meaning in the one single expression used about him,—"when he thought thereon he wept."

The experience of Peter is only the experience of all God's servants who have yielded to temptation. Lot, and Samson, and David, and Jehoshaphat in Bible history,— Cranmer and Jewell in the records of our own English Church,—have all left evidence, like Peter, that " the backslider in heart shall be filled with his own ways." (Prov. xiv. 14.) Like Peter, they erred grievously. Like Peter, they repented truly. But, like Peter, they found that they reaped a bitter harvest in this world. Like Peter, they were freely pardoned and forgiven. But, like Peter, they shed many tears.

Let us leave the passage with the settled conviction that sin is sure to lead to sorrow, and that the way of most holiness is always the way of most happiness. The Lord Jesus has mercifully provided that it shall never profit His servants to walk carelessly and to give way to temptation. If we will turn our backs on Him we shall be sure to smart for it. Though He forgives us, He will make us feel the folly of our own ways. Those that follow the Lord most fully, shall always follow Him most comfortably. "Their sorrows shall be multiplied who hasten after other gods." (Psalm xvi. 4.)

MARK XV. 1—15.

1 And straightway in the morning the Chief Priests held a consultation with the elders and Scribes and the whole council, and bound Jesus, and carried *him* away, and delivered *him* to Pilate.

2 And Pilate asked him, Art thou the king of the Jews? And he answering said unto him, Thou sayest *it*.

3 And the Chief Priests accused him of many things: but he answered nothing.

4 And Pilate asked him again, saying, Answerest thou nothing? behold how many things they witness against thee.

5 But Jesus yet answered nothing; so that Pilate marvelled.

6 Now at *that* feast he released unto them one prisoner, whomsoever they desired.

7 And there was *one* named Barabbas, *which lay* bound with them that had made insurrection with him, who had committed murder in the insurrection.

8 And the multitude crying aloud began to desire *him to do* as he had ever done unto them.

9 But Pilate answered them, saying, Will ye that I release unto you the King of the Jews?

10 For he knew that the Chief Priests had delivered him for envy.

11 But the Chief Priests moved the people, that he should rather release Barabbas unto them.

12 And Pilate answered and said again unto them, What will ye then that I shall do *unto him* whom ye call the King of the Jews?

13 And they cried out again, Crucify him.

14 Then Pilate said unto them, Why, what evil hath he done? And they cried out the more exceedingly, Crucify him.

15 And *so* Pilate, willing to content the people, released Barabbas unto them, and delivered Jesus, when he had scourged *him*, to be crucified.

THESE verses begin the chapter in which St. Mark describes the slaying of "the Lamb of God, which taketh away the sin of the world." It is a part of the Gospel history which should always be read with peculiar reverence. We should call to mind, that Christ was cut off, not for Himself, but for us. (Dan. ix. 26.) We should remember that His death is the life of our souls, and that unless His blood had been shed, we must have perished miserably in our sins.

Let us mark in these verses, *what a striking proof the Jewish rulers gave to their own nation that the times of Messiah had come.*

The chapter opens with the fact, that the chief priests bound Jesus and "delivered Him to Pilate," the Roman Governor. Why did they do so? Because they had no longer the power of putting any one to death, and were under the dominion of the Romans. By this one act and deed they declared that the prophecy of Jacob was fulfilled. "The sceptre had departed from Judah, and the lawgiver from between his feet," and Shiloh the Messiah, whom God had promised to send, must have come. (Gen. xlix. 10.) Yet there is nothing whatever to show that they remembered this prophecy. Their eyes were blinded. They either could not, or would not, see what they were doing.

Let us never forget that wicked men are often fulfilling God's predictions to their own ruin, and yet know it not. In the very height of their madness, folly, and unbelief, they are often unconsciously supplying fresh evidence that the Bible is true. The unhappy scoffers who make a jest of all serious religion, and can scarcely talk of Christianity without ridicule and scorn, would do well to remember that their conduct was long ago foreseen and foretold. "There shall come in the last days scoffers, walking after their own lusts." (2 Peter iii.)

Let us mark, secondly, in these verses, *the meekness and lowliness of our Lord Jesus Christ.* When He stood before Pilate's bar, and was "accused of many things," He answered nothing. Though the charges against Him were false, and He knew no sin, He was content to endure the contradiction of sinners against Himself, not answering again. (Heb. xii. 3.) Though He was innocent of any transgression, He submitted to hear groundless accusations made against Him without a murmur. Great is the contrast between the second Adam and the first! Our first father Adam was guilty, and yet tried to excuse himself. The second Adam was guiltless, and yet made no defence at all. "As a sheep before her shearers is dumb, so openeth he not his mouth." (Isai. liii. 7.)

Let us learn a practical lesson from our Saviour's example. Let us learn to suffer patiently, and not to complain, whatever God may think fit to lay upon us. Let us take heed to our ways, that we offend not in our tongues, in the hour of temptation. (Psal. xxxix. 1.) Let us beware of giving way to irritation and ill-temper, however provoking and undeserved our trials may seem to be. Nothing in the Christian character glorifies God so much as patient suffering. "If when ye do well and suffer for it, ye take it patiently, this is acceptable with God. For even hereunto were ye called, because Christ also suffered for us, leaving us an example that ye should follow His steps." (1 Peter ii. 20, 21.)

Let us mark, thirdly, in these verses, *the wavering and undecided conduct of Pilate.*

It is clear from the passage before us that Pilate was convinced of our Lord's innocence. "He knew that the chief priests had delivered him for envy." We see him feebly struggling for a time to obtain our Lord's acquittal, and so to satisfy his own conscience. At last he yields to the importunity of the Jews, and "willing to content the people," delivers Jesus to be crucified, —to the eternal disgrace and ruin of his own soul.

A man in high place without religious principles, is one of the most pitiable sights in the world. He is like a large ship tossed to and fro on the sea without compass or rudder. His very greatness surrounds him with temptations and snares. It gives him power for good or evil, which, if he knows not how to use it aright, is sure to bring him into difficulties, and to make him unhappy.—Let us pray much for great men. They need great grace to keep them from the devil. High places are slippery places. No wonder that St. Paul recommends intercession " for kings and for all that are in authority." —(1 Tim. ii. 1.) Let us not envy great men. They have many and peculiar temptations. How hardly shall a rich man enter the kingdom of God. "Seekest thou great things for thyself ? seek them not." (Jerem. xl. 5.)

Let us mark, fourthly, in these verses, *the exceeding guilt of the Jews in the matter of the death of Christ.* At the eleventh hour the chief priests had an opportunity of repenting, if they would have taken it. They had the choice given them whether Jesus or Barabbas should be let go free. Coolly and deliberately they persevered in their bloody work. They chose to have a murderer let go free. They chose to have the Prince of Life put to death. The *power* of putting our Lord to death was no longer theirs. The *responsibility* of His death they publicly took upon themselves.—"What will ye that I shall do unto him ?" was Pilate's question. "Crucify him, crucify him," was the awful answer.—The agents in our Lord's death were undoubtedly Gentiles. But the guilt of our Lord's death must always rest chiefly upon the Jews.

We marvel at the wickedness of the Jews at this part

of our Lord's history,—and no wonder. To reject Christ and choose Barabbas was indeed an astounding act! It seems as if blindness, madness, and folly could go no further. But let us take heed that we do not unwittingly follow their example. Let us beware that we are not found at last to have chosen Barabbas and rejected Christ. The service of sin and the service of God are continually before us. The friendship of the world and the friendship of Christ are continually pressed upon our notice. Are we making the right choice? Are we cleaving to the right Friend? These are solemn questions. Happy is he who can give them a satisfactory answer.

Let us mark, finally, in these verses, *what a striking type the release of Barabbas affords of the Gospel plan of salvation.* The guilty is set free and the innocent is put to death. The great sinner is delivered, and the sinless one remains bound. Barabbas is spared, and Christ is crucified.

We have in this striking fact a vivid emblem of the manner in which God pardons and justifies the ungodly. He does it, because Christ hath suffered in their stead, the just for the unjust. They deserve punishment, but a mighty Substitute has suffered for them. They deserve eternal death, but a glorious Surety has died for them. We are all by nature in the position of Barabbas. We are guilty, wicked, and worthy of condemnation. But " when we were without hope," Christ the innocent died for the ungodly. And now God for Christ's sake can be just, and yet "the justifier of him which believeth in Jesus."

Let us bless God that we have such a glorious salvation

set before us. Our plea must ever be, not that we are
deserving of acquittal, but that Christ has died for us.
Let us take heed, that having so great a salvation we
really make use of it for our own souls. May we never
rest till we can say by faith, " Christ is mine.—I deserve
hell.—But Christ has died for me, and believing in Him
I have a hope of heaven."

MARK XV. 16—32.

16 And the soldiers led him away
into the hall, called Prætorium ; and
they call together the whole band.
17 And they clothed him with purple, and platted a crown of thorns,
and put it about his *head*,
18 And began to salute him, Hail,
King of the Jews !
19 And they smote him on the head
with a reed, and did spit upon him,
and bowing *their* knees worshipped
him.
20 And when they had mocked him,
they took off the purple from him,
and put his own clothes on him, and
led him out to crucify him.
21 And they compel one Simon a
Cyrenian, who passed by, coming out
of the country, the Father of Alexander and Rufus, to bear his cross.
22 And they bring him unto the
place Golgotha, which is, being interpreted, The place of a skull.
23 And they gave him to drink wine
mingled with myrrh : but he received
it not.
24 And when they had crucified
him, they parted his garments, cast-

ing lots upon them, what every man
should take.
25 And it was the third hour, and
they crucified him.
26 And the superscription of his
accusation was written over, THE
KING OF THE JEWS.
27 And with him they crucify two
thieves; the one on his right hand,
and the other on his left.
28 And the Scripture was fulfilled,
which saith, And he was numbered
with the transgressors.
29 And they that passed by railed
on him, wagging their heads, and
saying, Ah, thou that destroyest the
temple, and buildest *it* in three days,
30 Save thyself, and come down
from the cross.
31 Likewise also the Chief Priests
mocking said among themselves with
the Scribes, He saved others ; himself
he cannot save.
32 Let Christ the King of Israel
descend now from the cross, that we
may see and believe. And they that
were crucified with him reviled him.

THE passage we have now read, is one of those which
show us the infinite love of Christ towards sinners. The
sufferings described in it would fill our minds with mingled
horror and compassion, if they had been inflicted on one
who was only a man like ourselves. But when we reflect

that the sufferer was the eternal Son of God, we are lost in wonder and amazement. And when we reflect further that these sufferings were voluntarily endured to deliver sinful men and women like ourselves from hell, we may see something of St. Paul's meaning when he says, "The love of Christ passeth knowledge." "God commendeth His love toward us in that while we were yet sinners, Christ died for us." (Ephes. iii. 19 ; Rom. v. 8.)

We shall find it useful to examine separately the several parts of our Lord's passion. Let us follow Him step by step from the moment of His condemnation by Pilate to His last hour upon the cross. There is a deep meaning in every jot and tittle of His sorrows. All were striking emblems of spiritual truths. And let us not forget, as we dwell on the wondrous story, that we and our sins were the cause of all these sufferings. "Christ suffered for sins, the just for the unjust, that He might bring us to God." (1. Peter iii. 18.) It is the death of our own Surety and Substitute that we are reading.

First of all we see Jesus delivered into the hands of the Roman soldiers, as a criminal condemned to death. He, before whom the whole world will one day stand and be judged, allowed Himself to be sentenced unjustly, and given over into the hands of wicked men.

And why was this ? It was that we, the poor sinful children of men, believing on Him, might be delivered from the pit of destruction, and the torment of the prison of hell. It was that we might be set free from every charge in the day of judgment, and be presented faultless before God the Father with exceeding joy.

Secondly, we see Jesus insulted and made a laughing-

stock by the Roman soldiers. They "clothed Him with
purple" in derision, and put "a crown of thorns" on His
head, in mockery of His kingdom. "They smote Him
on the head with a reed, and did spit upon Him,"
as one utterly contemptible, and no better than "the
filth of the world." (1 Cor. iv. 13.)

And why was this? It was that we, vile as we are,
might have glory, honour, and eternal life through faith
in Christ's atonement. It was done that we might be
received into God's kingdom with triumph at the last day,
and receive the crown of glory that fadeth not away.

Thirdly, we see Jesus stripped of His garments and
crucified naked before His enemies. The soldiers who
led Him away "parted His garments, casting lots upon
them."

And why was this? It was that we, who have no
righteousness of our own, might be clothed in the perfect
righteousness that Christ has wrought out for us, and not
stand naked before God at the last day. It was done
that we, who are all defiled with sin, might have a wedding-
garment, wherein we may sit down by the side of angels,
and not be ashamed.

Fourthly, we see Jesus suffering the most ignominious
and humiliating of all deaths, even the death of the cross.
It was the punishment reserved for the worst of malefactors. The man on whom it was inflicted was counted
accursed. It is written, "Cursed is every one that
hangeth on a tree." (Gal. iii. 13)

And why was this? It was that we, who are born
in sin and children of wrath, might be counted blessed for
Christ's sake. It was done to remove the curse which

we all deserve because of sin, by laying it on Christ. "Christ hath redeemed us from the curse of the law, being made a curse for us." (Gal. iii. 13.)

Fifthly, we see Jesus reckoned a transgressor and a sinner. "With Him they crucify two thieves." He who had done no sin, and in whom there was no guile, "was numbered with the transgressors."

And why was this? It was that we, who are miserable transgressors, both by nature and practice, may be reckoned innocent for Christ's sake. It was done that we, who are worthy of nothing but condemnation, may be counted worthy to escape God's judgment, and be pronounced not guilty before the assembled world.

Lastly, we see Jesus mocked when dying, as one who was an impostor, and unable to save Himself.

And why was this? It was that we, in our last hours, through faith in Christ may have strong consolation. It all came to pass that we may enjoy strong assurance,—may know whom we have believed, and may go down the valley of the shadow of death fearing no evil.

Let us leave the passage with a deep sense of the enormous debt which all believers owe to Christ. All that they have, and are, and hope for, may be traced up to the doing and dying of the Son of God. Through His condemnation, they have acquittal,—through His sufferings, peace,—through His shame, glory,—through His death, life. Their sins were imputed to Him. His righteousness is imputed to them. No wonder that St. Paul says, "Thanks be unto God for His unspeakable gift." (2. Cor. ix. 15.)

Finally, let us leave the passage with the deepest sense

of Christ's unutterable love to our souls. Let us remember what we are, corrupt, evil, and miserable sinners. Let us remember who the Lord Jesus is, the eternal Son of God, the maker of all things. And then let us remember, that for our sakes Jesus voluntarily endured the most painful, horrible, and disgraceful death. Surely the thought of this love should constrain us daily to live not unto ourselves but unto Christ. It should make us ready and willing to present our bodies a living sacrifice to Him who lived and died for us. (2 Cor. v. 4. Rom. xii. 1.) Let the cross of Christ be often before our minds. Rightly understood, no object in all Christianity is so likely to have a sanctifying as well as a comforting effect on our souls.

MARK XV. 33—38.

33 And when the sixth hour was come, there was darkness over the whole land until the ninth hour.

34 And at the ninth hour Jesus cried with a loud voice, saying, Eloi, Eloi, lama sabachthani? which is, being interpreted, My God, my God, why hast thou forsaken me?

35 And some of them that stood by, when they heard *it*, said, Behold, he calleth Elias.

36 And one ran and filled a spunge full of vinegar, and put *it* on a reed, and gave him to drink, saying, Let alone; let us see whether Elias will come to take him down.

37 And Jesus cried with a loud voice, and gave up the ghost.

38 And the veil of the temple was rent in twain from the top to the bottom.

WE have in these verses the death of our Lord Jesus Christ. All deaths are solemn events. Nothing in the whole history of a man is so important as his end. But never was there a death of such solemn moment as that which is now before us. In the instant that our Lord drew His last breath, the work of atonement for a world's sin was accomplished. The ransom for sinners was at length paid. The kingdom of heaven was thrown fully open to all believers.—All the solid hope that mortal men enjoy about their souls, may be traced to the giving up the ghost on the cross.

Let us observe, in these verses, *the visible signs and wonders which accompanied our Lord's death.* St. Mark mentions two in particular, which demand our attention. One is the darkening of the sun for the space of three hours. The other is the rending of the veil which divided the holy of holies from the holy place in the temple. Both were miraculous events. Both had, no doubt, a deep meaning about them. Both were calculated to arrest the attention of the whole multitude assembled at Jerusalem. The darkness would strike even thoughtless Gentiles, like Pilate and the Roman soldiers. The rent veil would strike even Annas and Caiaphas and their unbelieving companions. There were probably few houses in Jerusalem that evening in which men would not say, " we have heard and seen strange things to-day."

What did the miraculous darkness teach? It taught the exceeding wickedness of the Jewish nation. They were actually crucifying their own Messiah, and slaying their own King. The sun himself hid his face at the sight.—It taught the exceeding sinfulness of sin in the eyes of God. The Son of God himself must needs be left without the cheering light of day, when He became sin for us and carried our transgressions.*

---

* It is almost unnecessary to remark, that the darkness which covered the heaven on the day of the crucifixion, could not possibly have been occasioned by an eclipse of the sun, because the passover was always held at full moon. It is evident that the darkness was miraculous, and caused by some special interference with the course of nature.

What did the miraculous rending of the veil mean? It taught the abolition and termination of the whole Jewish law of ceremonies. It taught that the way into the holiest of all was now thrown open to all mankind by Christ's death. (Heb. ix. 8.) It taught that Gentiles as well as Jews might now draw nigh to God with boldness, through Jesus the one High Priest, and that all barriers between man and God were for ever cast down.

May we never forget the practical lesson of the rent veil! To attempt to revive the Jewish ceremonial in the Church of Christ, by returning to altars, sacrifices, and a priesthood, is nothing better than closing up again the rent veil, and lighting a candle at noon day.

May we never forget the practical lesson of the miraculous darkness! It should lead our minds on to that blackness of darkness which is reserved for all obstinate unbelievers. (Jude 13.) The darkness endured by our blessed Surety on the cross was only for three hours. The chains of darkness which shall bind all who reject His atonement and die in sin, shall be for evermore.

Let us observe, secondly, in these verses, *how truly and really our Lord Jesus Christ was made a curse for us, and bore our sins.* We see it strikingly brought out in those marvellous words which He used at the ninth hour, " My God, my God, why hast thou forsaken me."

It would be useless to pretend to fathom all the depth of meaning which these words contain. They imply an amount of mental suffering, such as we are unable to conceive. The agony of some of God's holiest servants has been occasionally very great, under an impression of God's favour being withdrawn from them. What then

may we suppose was the agony of the holy Son of God,—
when all the sin of all the world was laid upon His head,
—when He felt Himself reckoned guilty, though without
sin,—when He felt His Father's countenance turned away
from Him ? The agony of that season must have been
something past understanding. It is a high thing. We
cannot attain to a comprehension of it. We may believe
it, but we cannot explain and find it out to perfection.

One thing, however, is very plain, and that is the impossibility of explaining these words at all, except we
receive the doctrine of Christ's atonement and substitution
for sinners. To suppose, as some dare to do, that Jesus
was nothing more than a man, or that His death was
only a great example of self-sacrifice, makes this dying
cry of His utterly unintelligible. It makes Him appear
less patient and calm in a dying hour than many a
martyr, or even than some heathen philosophers. One
explanation alone is satisfactory. That explanation is
the mighty scriptural doctrine of Christ's vicarious sacrifice and substitution for us on the cross. He uttered
His dying cry, under the heavy pressure of a world's
sin laid upon Him, and imputed to Him.

Let us observe, lastly, in these verses, *that it is possible
to be forsaken of God for a time, and yet to be loved by
Him.* We need not doubt this, when we read our
Lord's dying words on the cross. We hear Him saying
to His Father, " Why hast thou forsaken me ? " and yet
addressing Him as " my God." We know too that our
Lord was only forsaken for a season, and that even when
forsaken He was the beloved Son in whom, both in His
suffering and doing, the Father was " well pleased."

There is deep experimental instruction in this, which deserves the notice of all true Christians. No doubt there is a sense in which our Lord's feeling of being "forsaken" was peculiar to Himself, since He was suffering for our sins and not for His own. But still after making this allowance, there remains the great fact that Jesus was for a time "forsaken of the Father," and yet for all that was the Father's "Beloved Son." As it was with the Great Head of the Church, so it may be in a modified sense with His members. They too, though chosen and beloved of the Father, may sometimes feel God's face turned away from them. They too, sometimes from illness of body, sometimes from peculiar affliction, sometimes from carelessness of walk, sometimes from God's sovereign will to draw them nearer to Himself, may be constrained to cry, "My God, My God, why hast thou forsaken me?"

It becomes believers who feel "forsaken," to learn from our Lord's experience not to give way to despair. No doubt they ought not to be content with their position. They ought to search their own hearts, and see whether there is not some secret thing there which causes their consolations to be small. (Job xv. 11) But let them not write bitter things against themselves, and hastily conclude that they are cast off for ever, or are self-deceivers, and have no grace at all. Let them still wait on the Lord, and say with Job, "Though he slay me yet will I trust in him." (Job xiii. 15) Let them remember the words of Isaiah and David, "Who is among you that feareth the Lord,—that walketh in darkness, and hath no light? let him trust in the name of the Lord, and stay upon his God." "Why art thou cast down, O my soul, and why art thou disquieted within me? Hope thou in God, for I shall yet praise him." (Isaiah l. 10. Psalm xlii. 11.)

MARK XV. 39—47.

39 And when the centurion, which stood over against him, saw that he so cried out, and gave up the ghost, he said, Truly this man was the Son of God.

40 There were also women looking on afar off: among whom was Mary Magdalene, and Mary the mother of James the less and of Joses, and Salome;

41 (Who also, when he was in Galilee, followed him, and ministered unto him;) and many other women which came up with him unto Jerusalem.

42 And now when the even was come, because it was the preparation, that is, the day before the sabbath,

43 Joseph of Arimathæa, an honourable counsellor, which also waited for the kingdom of God, came, and went in boldly unto Pilate, and craved the body of Jesus.

44 And Pilate marvelled if he were already dead: and calling *unto him* the centurion, he asked him whether he had been any while dead.

45 And when he knew *it* of the centurion, he gave the body to Joseph.

46 And he bought fine linen, and took him down, and wrapped him in the linen, and laid him in a sepulchre which was hewn out of a rock, and rolled a stone unto the door of the sepulchre.

47 And Mary Magdalene and Mary *the mother* of Joses beheld where he was laid.

THE death of our Lord Jesus Christ is the most important fact in Christianity. On it depend the hopes of all saved sinners both for time and eternity. We need not therefore be surprised to find the reality of His death carefully placed beyond dispute. Three kinds of witnesses to the fact are brought before us in the verses we have now read. The Roman centurion, who stood near the cross,—the women who followed our Lord from Galilee to Jerusalem,—the disciples, who buried Him, were all witnesses that Jesus really died. Their united evidence is above suspicion. They could not be deceived. What they saw was no swoon, or trance, or temporary insensibility. They saw that same Jesus, who was crucified, lay down His life, and become obedient even unto death. Let this be established in our minds. Our Saviour really and truly died.

Let us notice, for one thing, in this passage, *what honourable mention is here made of women.* We are specially told that, when our Lord gave up the ghost, "there were women looking on afar off." The names of some of them are recorded. We are also told that they were the same who had followed our Lord in Galilee and ministered unto Him, and that there were "many other women which came up with him to Jerusalem."

We should hardly have expected to have read such things. We might well have supposed that, when all the disciples ~~but one~~ had forsaken our Lord and fled, the weaker and more timid sex would not have dared to show themselves His friends. It only shows us what grace can do. God sometimes chooses the weak things of the world to confound the things that are mighty. The last are sometimes first, and the first last. The faith of women sometimes stands upright, when the faith of men fails and gives way.

But it is interesting to remark throughout the New Testament how often we find the grace of God glorified in women, and how much benefit God has been pleased to confer through them on the Church, and on the world. In the Old Testament, we see sin and death brought in by the woman's transgression. In the New, we see Jesus born of a woman, and life and immortality brought to light by that miraculous birth. In the Old Testament, we often see woman proving a hindrance and a snare to man. The women before the flood, the histories of Sarah, Rebecca, Rachel, Delilah, Bath-sheba, Jezebel, are all painful examples. In the New Testament, we generally see women mentioned as a help and assistance to the cause of true religion. Elizabeth, Mary, Martha, Dorcas, Lydia, and the women named by St. Paul to the Romans, are all cases in point. The contrast is striking, and we need not doubt intentional. It is one of the many proofs, that grace is more abundant under the Gospel than under the law. It seems meant to teach us that women have an important place in the Church of Christ, one that ought to be assigned to them, and one that they ought to fill. There is a great work that women can do for God's glory, without being public teachers. Happy is that congregation in which women know this, and act upon it!

Let us notice, for another thing, in this passage, *that Jesus has friends of whom little is known.* We cannot conceive a more remarkable proof of this than the person who is here mentioned for the first time, Joseph of Arimathæa. We know nothing of this man's former history. We know not how he had learned to love Christ, and to desire to do Him honour. We know nothing of his subsequent history after our Lord left the world. All we know is the touching collection of facts before us. We are told that he "waited for the kingdom of God," and that at a time when our Lord's disciples had all forsaken Him, He "went in boldly unto Pilate, and craved the body of Jesus," and buried it honourably in his own tomb. Others had honoured and confessed our Lord when they saw Him working miracles, but Joseph honoured Him and confessed himself a disciple, when he

saw Him a cold, blood-sprinkled corpse.   Others had
shown love to Jesus while He was speaking and living,
but Joseph showed love when He was silent and dead.

Let us take comfort in the thought that there are true
Christians on earth, of whom we know nothing, and in
places where we should not expect to find them.   No
doubt the faithful are always few.   But we must not
hastily conclude that there is no grace in a family or
in a parish, because our eyes may not see it.   We know in
part and see only in part, outside the circle in which our
own lot is cast.   The Lord has many "hidden ones" in
the Church, who, unless brought forward by special
circumstances, will never be known till the last day.
The words of God to Elijah should not be forgotten,
"Yet I have left me seven thousand in Israel." (1 Kings
xix. 18.)

Let us notice, lastly, in this passage, *what honour our
Lord Jesus Christ has placed on the grave, by allowing
Himself to be laid in it.*   We read that he was "laid in
a sepulchre hewn out of a rock," and a "stone rolled
unto the door."

This is a fact that in a dying world we should always
remember.   It is appointed unto men once to die.   We
are all going to one place, and we naturally shrink from
it.   The coffin and the funeral, the worm and corruption, are all painful subjects.   They chill us, sadden us,
and fill our minds with heaviness.   It is not in flesh and
blood to regard them without solemn feelings.   One
thing, however, ought to comfort believers, and that is
the thought, that the grave is "the place where the
Lord once lay."   As surely as He rose again victorious

from the tomb, so surely shall all who believe in Him rise gloriously in the day of His appearing. Remembering this, they may look down with calmness into the "house appointed for all living." They may recollect that Jesus Himself was once there on their behalf, and has robbed death of his sting. They maysay to themselves, " the sting of death is sin, and the strength of sin is the law: but thanks be to God who giveth us the victory through our Lord Jesus Christ." (1 Cor. xv. 56, 57.)

The great matter that concerns us all, is to make sure that we are spiritually buried with Christ, while we are yet alive. We must be joined to Him by faith, and conformed to His image. With Him we must die to sin, and be buried by baptism into His death. (Rom. vi. 4.) With Him we must rise again, and be quickened by His Spirit. Except we know these things, Christ's death and burial will profit us nothing at all.

MARK XVI. 1—8.

1 And when the sabbath was past, Mary Magdalene, and Mary the *mother* of James, and Salome, had bought sweet spices, that they might come and anoint him.

2 And very early in the morning the first *day* of the week, they came unto the sepulchre at the rising of the sun.

3 And they said among themselves, Who shall roll us away the stone from the door of the sepulchre?

4 And when they looked, they saw that the stone was rolled away: for it was very great.

5 And entering into the sepulchre, they saw a young man sitting on the right side, clothed in a long white garment; and they were affrighted.

6 And he saith unto them, Be not affrighted: Ye seek Jesus of Nazareth, which was crucified: he is risen; he is not here: behold the place where they laid him.

7 But go your way, tell his disciples and Peter that he goeth before you into Galilee: there shall ye see him, as he said unto you.

8 And they went out quickly, and fled from the sepulchre ; for they trembled and were amazed: neither said they any thing to any *man;* for they were afraid.

LET us observe, in this passage, *the power of strong love*

to Christ. We have a forcible illustration of this in the conduct of Mary Magdalene, and the other Mary, which St. Mark here records. He tells us that they had "bought sweet spices" to anoint our Lord, and that " very early in the morning, the first day of the week, they came unto the sepulchre, at the rising of the sun."

We may well believe that it required no small courage to do this. To visit a grave in the dim twilight of an eastern day-break, would try most women, under any circumstances. But to visit the grave of one who had been put to death as a common malefactor, and to rise early to show honour to one whom their nation had despised, this was a mighty boldness indeed. Yet these are the kind of acts which show the difference between weak faith and strong faith,—between weak feeling and strong feeling towards Christ. These holy women had tasted of our Lord's pardoning mercies. Their hearts were full of gratitude to Him for light, and hope, and comfort, and peace. They were willing to risk all consequences in testifying their affection to their Saviour. So true are the words of Canticles : "Love is strong as death,—many waters cannot quench love, neither can the floods drown it." (Cant. viii. 6, 7.)

Why is it that we see so little of this strong love to Jesus among Christians of the present day ? How is it that we so seldom meet with saints who will face any danger, and go through fire and water for Christ's sake ? There is only one answer. It is the weak faith, and the low sense of obligation to Christ, which so widely prevail. A low and feeble sense of sin will always produce a low and feeble sense of the value of salvation. A slight

sense of our debt to God will always be attended by a
slight sense of what we owe for our redemption. It is the
man who feels much forgiven who loves much. "To whom
little is forgiven, the same loveth little." (Luke vii. 47.)

Let us observe, secondly, in this passage, how *the
difficulties which Christians fear, will sometimes disappear
as they approach them.* These holy women, as they
walked to our Lord's grave, were full of fears about the
stone at the door. "They said among themselves, Who
shall roll us away the stone from the door of the
sepulchre?" But their fears were needless. Their
expected trouble was found not to exist. "When they
looked, they saw that the stone was rolled away."

What a striking emblem we have in this simple narrative, of the experience of many Christians! How often
believers are oppressed and cast down by anticipation of
evils, and yet, in the time of need, find the thing they
feared removed, and the "stone rolled away." A large
proportion of a saint's anxieties arise from things which
never really happen. We look forward to all the possi-
bilities of the journey towards heaven. We conjure up
in our imagination all kinds of crosses and obstacles.
We carry mentally to-morrow's troubles, as well as
to-day's. And often, very often, we find at the end,
that our doubts and alarms were groundless, and that
the thing we dreaded most has never come to pass at all.
Let us pray for more practical faith. Let us believe
that in the path of duty, we shall never be entirely
forsaken. Let us go forward boldly, and we shall often
find that the lion in the way is chained, and the seeming hedge of thorns is only a shadow.

Let us observe, thirdly, in this passage, *that the friends of Christ have no cause to be afraid of angels.* We are told, that when Mary Magdalene and her companion saw an angel sitting in the sepulchre, "they were affrighted." But they were at once reassured by his words: "Be not affrighted: ye seek Jesus of Nazareth, which was crucified."

The lesson, at first sight, may seem of little importance. We see no visions of angels in the present day. We do not expect to see them. But the lesson is one which we may find useful at some future time. The day is drawing near when the Lord Jesus shall come again to judge the world, with all the angels round Him. The angels in that day shall gather together His elect from the four winds. The angels shall gather the tares into bundles to burn them. The angels shall gather the wheat of God into His barn. Those whom the angels take they shall carry to glory, honour and immortality. Those whom they leave behind shall be left to shame and everlasting contempt.

Let us strive so to live, that when we die we may be carried by angels into Abraham's bosom. Let us endeavour to be known of angels as those who seek Jesus, and love Him in this world, and so are heirs of salvation. Let us give diligence to make our repentance sure, and so to cause joy in the presence of the angels of God. Then, whether we wake or sleep, when the archangel's voice is heard, we shall have no cause to be afraid. We shall rise from our grave, and see in the angels our friends and fellow-servants, in whose company we shall spend a blessed eternity.

Let us observe, lastly, in this passage, the *exceeding kindness of God towards His backsliding servants.* The message which the angel conveys is a striking illustration of this truth. Mary Magdalene and the other Mary were bid to tell the disciples that " Jesus goeth before them into Galilee," and that " there they shall see Him." But the message is not directed generally to the eleven Apostles. ·This alone, after their late desertion of their master, would have been a most gracious action. Yet Simon Peter, who had denied his Lord three times, is specially mentioned by name. Peter, who had sinned particularly, is singled out and noticed particularly. There were to be no exceptions in the deed of grace. All were to be pardoned. All were to be restored to favour,—and Simon Peter as well as the rest.

We may well say when we read words like these, " This is not the manner of man." On no point perhaps are our views of religion so narrow, low, and contracted, as on the point of God's exceeding willingness to pardon penitent sinners. We think of Him as such an one as ourselves. We forget that " He delighteth in mercy." (Micah vii. 18.)

Let us leave the passage with a determination to open the door of mercy very wide to sinners, in all our speaking and teaching about religion. Not least, let us leave it with a resolution never to be unforgiving towards our fellow-men. If Christ is so ready to forgive us, we ought to be very ready to forgive others.

9 Now when *Jesus* was risen early the first *day* of the week, he appeared first to Mary Magdalene, out of whom he had cast seven devils.

10 *And* she went and told them that had been with him, as they mourned and wept.

11 And they, when they had heard that he was alive, and had been seen of her, believed not.

12 After that he appeared in another form unto two of them, as they walked, and went into the country.

13 And they went and told *it* unto the residue: neither believed they them.

14 Afterward he appeared unto the eleven as they sat at meat, and upbraided them with their unbelief and hardness of heart, because they believed not them which had seen him after he was risen.

LET us mark, in these verses, *what abundant proof we have that our Lord Jesus Christ really rose again from the dead.* In this one passage St. Mark records no less than three distinct occasions on which He was seen after His resurrection. First, he tells us, our Lord appeared to one witness, Mary Magdalene,—then to two witnesses, two disciples walking into the country,—and lastly to eleven witnesses, the eleven apostles all assembled together. Let us remember, in addition to this, that other appearances of our Lord are described by other writers in the New Testament, beside those mentioned by St. Mark. And then let us not hesitate to believe, that of all the facts of our Lord's history, there is none more thoroughly established than the fact, that He rose from the dead.

There is great mercy in this. The resurrection of Christ is one of the foundation-stones of Christianity. It was the seal of the great work that He came on earth to do. It was the crowning proof that the ransom He paid for sinners was accepted, the atonement for sin accomplished, the head of him who had the power of death bruised, and the victory won. It is well to remark how often the resurrection of Christ is referred to by

the apostles. " He was delivered for our offences," says
Paul, " and was raised again for our justification." (Rom.
iv. 25.) " He hath begotten us again to a lively hope,"
says Peter, " by the resurrection of Jesus Christ from the
dead." (1 Peter i. 3.)

We ought to thank God that the fact of the resurrection is so clearly established. The Jew, the Gentile,
the priests, the Roman guard, the women who went
to the tomb, the disciples who were so backward to
believe, are all witnesses whose testimony cannot be
gainsaid. Christ has not only died for us, but has also
risen again. To deny it shows far greater credulity than
to believe it. To deny it a man must put credit in
monstrous and ridiculous improbabilities. To believe it
a man has only to appeal to simple undeniable facts.

Let us mark, secondly, in these verses, *our Lord Jesus
Christ's singular kindness to Mary Magdalene.* We are
told that " when he was risen early the first day of the
week, he appeared first to Mary Magdalene, out of whom
he had cast seven devils." To her before all others of
Adam's children, was granted the privilege of being first
to behold a risen Saviour. Mary, the mother of our
Lord, was yet alive. John, the beloved disciple, was yet
upon earth. Yet both were passed over on this occasion
in favour of Mary Magdalene. A woman who at one
time had probably been chief of sinners, a woman who
at one time had been possessed by seven devils, was the
first to whom Jesus showed Himself alive, when He rose
victorious from the tomb. The fact is remarkable, and
full of instruction.*

* There is nothing in the New Testament to justify the common

We need not doubt, for one thing, that, by appearing "first to Mary Magdalene," our Lord meant to show us how much He values love and faithfulness. Last at the cross and first at the grave, last to confess her Master while living, and first to honour Him when dead, this warm-hearted disciple was allowed to be the first to see Him, when the victory was won. It was intended to be a perpetual memorial to the Church, that those who honour Christ, He will honour, and that those who do much for Him upon earth, shall find Him even upon earth doing much for them. May we never forget this. May we ever remember that for those who forsake all for Christ's sake there is "an hundred-fold now in this present time."

We need not doubt, for another thing, that our Lord's appearing "first to Mary Magdalene" was intended to comfort all who have become penitent believers, after having run into great excesses of sin. It was meant to show us that, however far we may have fallen, we are raised to entire peace with God, if we repent and believe the Gospel. Though before far off, we are made nigh. Though before enemies, we are made dear children. Old things are passed away, and all things are become new. (1 Cor. v. 17.)

notion that Mary Magdalene had been a sinner against the seventh commandment more than other commandments. There is no scriptural warrant for calling hospitals and asylums intended for fallen women, "Magdalene Hospitals." No better authority can be discovered for the common idea on the subject than tradition.

At the same time it is only fair to say, that there seems strong probability for supposing that the sins of Mary Magdalene had been very great. There was probably some grave cause for her being possessed by seven devils, though the nature of it has not been revealed to us.

The blood of Christ makes us completely clean in God's sight. We may have begun like Augustine, and John Newton, and been ringleaders in every kind of iniquity. But once brought to Christ, we need not doubt that all is forgiven. We may draw nigh with boldness, and have access with confidence. Our sins and iniquities, like those of Mary Magdalene, are remembered no more.

Let us mark, lastly, in these verses, *how much weakness there is sometimes in the faith of the best Christians.* Three times in this very passage we find St. Mark describing the unbelief of the eleven apostles. Once, when Mary Magdalene told them that our Lord had risen, "they believed not."—Again, when our Lord had appeared to two of them, as they walked, we read of the residue, "neither believed they them."—Finally, when our Lord Himself appeared to them as they sat at meat, we are told that "he upbraided them for their unbelief and hardness of heart." Never perhaps was there so striking an example of man's unwillingness to believe that which runs counter to his early prejudices. Never was there so remarkable a proof of man's forgetfulness of plain teaching. These eleven men had been told repeatedly by our Lord that He would rise again. And yet, when the time came, all was forgotten, and they were found unbelieving.

Let us however see in the doubts of these good men the over-ruling hand of an all-wise God. If they were convinced at last, who were so unbelieving at first, how strong is the proof supplied us that Christ rose indeed. It is the glory of God to bring good out of evil. The very doubts of the eleven apostles are the confirmation of our faith in these latter days.

Let us learn from the unbelief of the apostles, a useful practical lesson for ourselves. Let us cease to feel surprise when we find doubts arising in our own heart. Let us cease to expect perfection of faith in other believers. We are yet in the body. We are men of like passions with the apostles. We must count it no strange thing, if our experience is sometimes like their's, and if our faith, like their's, sometimes gives way. Let us resist unbelief manfully. Let us watch, and pray, and strive to be delivered from its power. But let us not conclude that we have no grace, because we are sometimes harassed with doubts, nor suppose that we have no part or lot with the apostles, because at seasons we feel unbelieving.

Let us not fail to ask ourselves, as we leave this passage, whether we have risen with Christ, and been made partakers spiritually of His resurrection. This, after all, is the one thing needful. To know the facts of Christianity with the head, and to be able to argue for them with the tongue, will not save our souls. We must yield ourselves to God as those alive from the dead. (Rom. vi. 13.) We must be raised from the death of sin, and walk in newness of life. This and this only is saving Christianity.

MARK XVI. 15—18.

15 And he said unto them, Go ye into all the world, and preach the Gospel to every creature.

16 He that believeth and is baptized shall be saved; but he that believeth not shall be damned.

17 And these signs shall follow them that believe; In my name shall they cast out devils; they shall speak with new tongues;

18 They shall take up serpents; and if they drink any deadly thing, it shall not hurt them; they shall lay hands on the sick, and they shall recover.

WE ought to notice, firstly, in these verses, *the parting commission which our Lord gives to His apostles.* He is addressing them for the last time. He marks out their work till He comes again, in words of wide and deep significance, "Go ye into all the world, and preach the gospel to every creature."

The Lord Jesus would have us know that all the world needs the Gospel. In every quarter of the globe man is the same, sinful, corrupt, and alienated from God. Civilized or uncivilized, in China, or in Africa, he is by nature everywhere the same, without knowledge, without holiness, without faith, and without love. Wherever we see a child of Adam, whatever be his colour, we see one whose heart is wicked, and who needs the blood of Christ, the renewing of the Holy Ghost, and reconciliation with God.

The Lord Jesus would have us know that the salvation of the Gospel is to be offered freely to all mankind. The glad tidings that "God so loved the world that he gave his only begotten Son," and that "Christ has died for the ungodly," is to be proclaimed freely "to every creature." We are not justified in making any exception in the proclamation. We have no warrant for limiting the offer to the elect. We come short of the fulness of Christ's words, and take away from the breadth of His sayings, if we shrink from telling any one, "God is full of love to you, Christ is willing to save you." "Whosoever will, let him take the water of life freely." (Rev. xx. 17.)

Let us see in these words of Christ, the strongest argument in favour of missionary work, both at home and abroad. Remembering these words, let us be un-

wearied in trying to do good to the souls of all mankind.
If we cannot go to the heathen in China and Hindostan,
let us seek to enlighten the darkness which we shall
easily find within reach of our own door.   Let us labour
on, unmoved by the sneers and taunts of those who dis-
approve missionary operations, and hold them up to
scorn.   We may well pity such people.   They only
show their ignorance, both of Scripture and of Christ's
will.   They understand neither what they say, nor
whereof they affirm.

We ought to notice, secondly, in these verses, *the
terms which our Lord tells us should be offered to all who
hear the Gospel.* " He that believeth and is baptized
shall be saved ; but he that believeth not shall be damned."
Every word in that sentence is of deep importance.   Every
expression in it deserves to be carefully weighed.

We are taught here the importance of baptism.   It is
an ordinance generally necessary to salvation, where it
can be had.   Not " he that believeth " simply, but
" he that believeth and is baptized shall be saved."
Thousands no doubt receive not the slightest benefit from
their baptism.   Thousands are washed in sacramental
water, who are never washed in the blood of Christ.   But
it does not follow therefore that baptism is to be despised
and neglected.   It is an ordinance appointed by Christ
Himself, and when used reverently, intelligently, and
prayerfully, is doubtless accompanied by a special blessing.
The baptismal water itself conveys no grace.   We must
look far beyond the mere outward element to Him who
commanded it to be used.   But the public confession
of Christ, which is implied in the use of that water, is a

sacramental act, which our Master Himself has commanded; and when the ordinance is rightly used, we may
confidently believe that He seals it by His blessing.

We are taught here, furthermore, the absolute necessity
of faith in Christ to salvation. This is the one thing
needful. "He that believeth not" is the man that shall
be lost for evermore. He may have been baptized, and
made a member of the visible church. He may be a
regular communicant at the Lord's Table. He may
even believe intellectually all the leading articles of the
creed. But all shall profit him nothing if he lacks saving
faith in Christ. Have we this faith? This is the great
question that concerns us all. Except we feel our sins,
and feeling them flee to Christ by faith, and lay hold on
Him, we shall find at length we had better never have
been born.

We are taught here, furthermore, the certainty of
God's judgments on those who die unbelieving. "He
that believeth not shall be damned." How awful the
words sound! How fearful the thought that they came
from the lips of Him who said, "My words shall not pass
away." Let no man deceive us with vain words. There
is an eternal hell for all who will persist in their wickedness, and depart out of this world without faith in Christ.
The greater the mercy offered to us in the Gospel, the
greater will be the guilt of those who obstinately refuse
to believe. "Oh! that men were wise. Oh! that they
would consider their latter end." (Deut. xxxii. 29.) He
that died upon the cross, has given us plain warning that
there is a hell, and that unbelievers shall be damned.
Let us take heed that His warning is not given to us in vain!

We ought to notice, lastly, in these verses, *the gracious promises of special help which our Lord holds out in His parting words to His apostles.* He knew well the enormous difficulties of the work which He had just commissioned them to do. He knew the mighty battle they would have to fight with heathenism, the world, and the devil. He therefore cheers them by telling them that miracles shall help forward their work. " Signs shall follow them that believe. In my name they shall cast out devils; they shall speak with new tongues; they shall take up serpents; and if they shall drink any deadly thing it shall not hurt them; they shall lay hands on the sick, and they shall recover." The fulfilment of most of these promises is to be found in the Acts of the Apostles.

The age of miracles no doubt is long passed. They were never meant to continue beyond the first establishment of the Church. It is only when plants are first planted, that they need daily watering and support. The whole analogy of God's dealings with His church forbids us to expect that miracles would always continue. In fact, miracles would cease to be miracles, if they happened regularly without cessation or intermission. It is well to remember this. The remembrance may save us much perplexity.

But though the age of physical miracles is past, we may take comfort in the thought that the church of Christ shall never want Christ's special aid in its seasons of special need. The great Head in heaven will never forsake His believing members. His eye is continually upon them. He will always time His help wisely, and come to their succour in the day that He is wanted.

" When the enemy shall come in like a flood, the Spirit of the Lord shall lift up a standard against him." (Isai. lix. 19.)

Finally, let us never forget, that Christ's believing Church in the world is of itself a standing miracle. The conversion and perseverance in grace of every member of that Church, is a sign and wonder, as great as the raising of Lazarus from the dead. The renewal of every saint is as great a marvel as the casting out of a devil, or the healing of a sick man, or the speaking with a new tongue. Let us thank God for this and take courage. The age of spiritual miracles is not yet past. Happy are they who have learned this by experience, and can say, " I was dead, but am alive again : I was blind, but I see."

MARK XVI. 19—20.

19 So then after the Lord had spoken unto them, he was received up into heaven, and sat on the right hand of God.

20 And they went forth, and preached every where, the Lord working with *them*, and confirming the word with signs following. Amen.

THESE words form the conclusion of St. Mark's Gospel. Short as the passage is, it is a singularly suitable conclusion to the history of our Lord Jesus Christ's earthly ministry. It tells us where our Lord went, when He left this world, and ascended up on high. It tells us what His disciples experienced after their Master left them, and what all true Christians may expect until He appears again.

Let us mark, in these verses, *the place to which our Lord went when He had finished His work on earth, and*

the place where He is at this present time. We are told
that "He was received up into heaven, and sat on the
right hand of God." He returned to that glory which
He had with the Father before He came into the world.
He received, as our victorious Mediator and Redeemer,
the highest position of dignity and power in heaven
which our minds can conceive. There He sits, not idle,
but carrying on the same blessed work for which He died
on the cross. There He lives, ever making intercession
for all who come unto God by Him, and so able to save
them to the uttermost. (Heb. vii. 25.)

There is strong consolation here for all true Christians.
They live in an evil world. They are often careful and
troubled about many things, and are sorely cast down by
their own weakness and infirmities.—They live in a dying
world. They feel their bodies gradually failing and
giving way. They have before them the awful prospect
of soon launching forth into a world unknown.—What
then shall comfort them? They must lean back on the
thought of their Saviour in heaven, never slumbering,
and never sleeping, and always ready to help. They
must remember that though they sleep, Jesus wakes,—
though they faint, Jesus is never weary,—though they
are weak, Jesus is Almighty,—and though they die,
Jesus lives for evermore. Blessed indeed is this thought!
Our Saviour, though unseen, is an actually living person.
We travel on towards a dwelling where our best Friend
is gone before, to prepare a place for us. (John xiv. 2.)
The Forerunner has entered in and made all things ready.
No wonder that St. Paul exclaims, "Who is He that
condemneth? It is Christ that died; yea, rather that is

risen again,—who is even at the right hand of. God,—
who also maketh intercession for us." (Rom. viii. 34.)

Let us mark, for another thing, in these verses, *the
blessing which our Lord Jesus Christ bestows on all who
work faithfully for Him.* We are told that, when the
disciples went forth and preached, the Lord " worked
with them," and " confirmed the word with signs
following."

We know well from the Acts of the Apostles, and from
the pages of church history, the manner in which these
words have been proved true. We know that bonds
and afflictions, persecution and opposition, were the first
fruits that were reaped by the labourers in Christ's harvest.
But we know also that, in spite of every effort of Satan,
the word of truth was not preached in vain. Believers
from time to time were gathered out of the world.
Churches of saints were founded in city after city, and
country after country. The little seed of Christianity
grew gradually into a great tree. Christ Himself wrought
with His own workmen, and, in spite of every obstacle,
His work went on. The good seed was never entirely
thrown away. Sooner or later there were "signs following."

Let us not doubt that these things were written for
our encouragement, on whom the latter ends of the
world are come. Let us believe that no one shall ever
work faithfully for Christ, and find at last that His work
has been altogether without profit. Let us labour on
patiently, each in our own position. Let us preach, and
teach, and speak, and write, and warn, and testify, and
rest assured that our labour is not in vain. We may die
ourselves, and see no result from our work. But the last

day will assuredly prove that the Lord Jesus always works with those who work for Him, and that there were "signs following," though it was not given to the workmen to see them. Let us then be "stedfast, immovable, always abounding in the work of the Lord." We may go on our way heavily, and sow with many tears; but if we sow Christ's precious seed, we shall "come again with joy and bring our sheaves with us." (1 Cor. xv. 58; Psal. cxxvi. 6.)

And now let us close the pages of St. Mark's Gospel with self-inquiry and self-examination. Let it not content us to have seen with our eyes, and heard with our ears, the things here written for our learning about Jesus Christ. Let us ask ourselves whether we know anything of Christ "dwelling in our hearts by faith?" Does the Spirit "witness with our spirit" that Christ is our's and we are His? Can we really say that we are "living the life of faith in the Son of God," and that we have found by experience that Christ is "precious" to our own souls? These are solemn questions. They demand serious consideration. May we never rest till we can give them satisfactory answers! "He that hath the Son hath life, and he that hath not the Son of God hath not life." (1 John v. 12.)

W. HUNT, STEAM PRESS, TAVERN STREET, IPSWICH.